Social Sustainability in Urban Areas

Social Sustainability in Urban Areas

Communities, Connectivity and the Urban Fabric

Edited by
Tony Manzi, Karen Lucas,
Tony Lloyd-Jones and Judith Allen

publishing for a sustainable future

London • Washington, DC

First published in 2010 by Earthscan

Earthscan Ltd, Dunstan House, 14a St Cross Street, London EC1N 8XA, UK
Earthscan LLC, 1616 P Street, NW, Washington, DC 20036, USA
Earthscan publishes in association with the International Institute for Environment and Development

For more information on Earthscan publications, see www.earthscan.co.uk or write to earthinfo@earthscan.co.uk

ISBN: 978-1-84407-674-1

Typeset by 4word Ltd, Bristol
Cover design by Susanne Harris

A catalogue record for this book is available from the British Library

Library of Congress Cataloging-in-Publication Data

Social sustainability in urban areas : communities, connectivity, and the urban fabric / edited by Tony Manzi ... [et al.]. – 1st ed.
    p. cm.
  Includes bibliographical references and index.
  ISBN 978-1-84407-674-1 (hardback)
  1. Sociology, Urban. 2. Cities and towns – Growth. 3. Sustainable development. I. Manzi, Tony, 1960–
  HT151.S6213 2010
  307.76--dc22
                          2009049682

At Earthscan we strive to minimize our environmental impacts and carbon footprint through reducing waste, recycling and offsetting our CO_2 emissions, including those created through publication of this book. For more details of our environmental policy, see www.earthscan.co.uk.

FSC

Mixed Sources
Product group from well-managed forests and other controlled sources

Cert no. SGS-COC-2482
www.fsc.org
© 1996 Forest Stewardship Council

Printed and bound in the UK by TJ International.
The paper used is FSC certified.

Contents

Section 2: The Role of Place and Connectivity in the Urban Socio-Physical Environment

Section 3: Regeneration and Economic Development

List of Figures, Tables and Box

Figures

Tables

Box

List of Contributors

Judith Allen is Principal Lecturer in Neighbourhood Management. She is a member of the Max Lock Centre and is also the programme leader for undergraduate urban studies and postgraduate neighbourhood studies. She has been the scientific manager for three major cross-European studies in neighbourhoods: focusing on social exclusion, neighbourhood management and governance. Her current research on small areas focuses on migrancy and settlement (British in Bulgaria, Brazilians in Portugal), as well as consultancies for neighbourhood projects in London, for the Housing Observatory in Madrid, and for UN-Habitat.

Nick Bailey is Professor of Urban Regeneration. He originally qualified as a town planner, has worked in a number of planning and housing posts, and has many years of teaching experience at undergraduate and postgraduate levels. He has carried out extensive research on the role of third-sector organizations in urban regeneration in the UK and was the co-author of a study of community development trusts for the Calouste Gulbenkian Foundation. He has also carried out a study of community involvement in local strategic partnerships and led a team investigating mixed tenure housing developments in England and Scotland for the Joseph Rowntree Foundation. He is a board member of a community development trust in central London.

Adam Eldridge is Research Fellow with the Central Cities Institute at the University of Westminster. His recently completed PhD examined the articulation of history, identity and geography within a themed environment. His current research continues to examine the relationship between consumption, community and public space, with a particular emphasis on town and city centres after dark. Dr Eldridge is currently investigating how the Licensing Act (2003) has impacted upon the evening economy in terms of residents and town centre decentralisation. He also teaches in the Department of Urban Planning and Regeneration at the University of Westminster, and is a Visiting Lecturer with the Department of Media and Communications at Goldsmiths College.

Catalina Gandelsonas is Senior Lecturer in Property and Construction at the University of Westminster in London. She originally qualified as an architect and a planner with an emphasis in urban design, and as such she taught in various universities including Berkeley, Princeton, Lefke University in Cyprus and Development Planning Unit, University College London. She carried out research as a senior researcher for the Max Lock Centre doing research on transferring knowledge for development and edited a book on communication in development. She also coordinated and participated in various workshops in India and Kenya in connection with the Research Project Localising Habitat Agenda and published various papers in international magazines on gender, social networks and design management.

Tony Lloyd-Jones is Principal Lecturer in Urban Design, International Planning and Sustainable Development at the University of Westminster. He is Director of Research and Consultancy at the Max Lock Centre and currently coordinator of the Centre for Sustainable Development. He has conducted a number of urban development-related research and consultancy projects, delivered papers and published in journals and books, worldwide. An architect-planner by profession, he has many years' experience in community planning and planning for sustainable urban development. He was lead consultant to the Working Group on Urban Design for Sustainability, reporting to the European Union Expert Group on the Urban Environment, and Urban Policy Adviser to the Department for International Development, advising the UK government on sustainable urban development matters at the United Nations from 1997 to 2005.

Karen Lucas was the research director of SABE's Centre for Sustainable Development from April 1999 to October 2008, when she joined the Transport Studies Unit at Oxford University as a research fellow. Her PhD was in transport and sustainability in the context of the regeneration of the Thames Gateway. Her specialist research interest is in making evident the links between the social and environmental aspects of sustainable development, with a particular focus on meeting the needs of people living in deprived and excluded communities within developed societies. In 2002/03, she was a policy adviser for the UK Social Exclusion Unit's study of transport and social exclusion. Karen's chapter is co-authored by Derek Halden, director of Derek Halden Consultancy based in Scotland, and Dr Sarah Wixey, a principal consultant with JMP Consulting. Both are specialists in using accessibility planning to develop new and improved urban and rural transport systems, and have collaborated extensively with Karen on a number of projects in this respect.

Tony Manzi is Principal Lecturer in Housing and the course leader for the MA in Housing Practice. He is a Fellow of the Chartered Institute of Housing. His doctoral thesis was on housing associations, cultural theory and the management of change. His research interests are in sociology, organizational theory and housing management.

Chris Marsh is Principal Lecturer in Planning and Development (part-time). His practice, Christopher Marsh & Co. Ltd, specializes in advising local planning authorities in negotiating agreements with developers that maximize affordable housing and planning obligations on behalf of local communities.

Suzy Nelson is Senior Lecturer in Urban Studies and Course Leader for MA Urban Regeneration. She is an architect with extensive experience of developing and implementing urban policy. The subject of her doctoral research was the changing relationships involved in urban redevelopment in Paris and London. She is particularly interested in the changing roles of public and private actors in the development process. As well as undertaking research on the process of intensification of development in London, she is currently researching career opportunities and career development in regeneration.

Andrew Smith is Senior Lecturer in Tourism within the School of Architecture and the Built Environment at the University of Westminster. Dr Smith leads MA and BA modules in sustainable tourism, as well as the new MA Events Tourism module. He has published research on the relationship between sport events, tourism and urban regeneration and was involved in evaluating the SRB programme associated with Manchester's 2002 Commonwealth Games. He recently won an award for his paper on the value of 'Sports-City Zones' that compared actual and planned examples in Dubai, Doha, Cardiff and Manchester.

Peter White is Professor of Public Transport Systems in the Department of Transport Studies within the School of Architecture and the Built Environment at the University of Westminster. For many years he has been responsible for postgraduate teaching and research in this field. He is author of a textbook and numerous published papers. He was responsible for managing a study of teleworking impacts described in Chapter 8. This work was undertaken jointly with Georgina Christodoulou of the same department; Professor Roger Mackett, Dr Helena Titheridge and Roselle Thoreau of the Centre for Transport Studies at University College London; and Professor John Polak of the Centre for Transport Studies at Imperial College London.

List of Acronyms and Abbreviations

BCO	British Council for Offices
BSF	Building Schools for the Future
BT	British Telecommunications plc
CAM	community asset management
CFS	Community Finance Solutions
CIC	Community Interest Company
CIL	Community Infrastructure Levy
CLG	Communities and Local Government
CLTs	Community Land Trusts
CLU	Community Land Unit
CRHA	Cornwall Rural Housing Association
Defra	Department of Environment, Food and Rural Affairs
DCSF	Department for Children, Schools and Families
DCLG	Department of Communities and Local Government
DFID	Department for International Development
DfT	Department for Transport
EP	English Partnerships
EU	European Union
GLP	Gloucestershire Land for People
HCA	Homes and Communities Agency
HLCs	Healthy Living Centres
IDeA	Innovation and Development Agency
IPPR	Institute for Public Policy Research
IUCN	International Union for the Conservation of Nature
LDF	local development framework
LPAs	Local Planning Authorities
LSPs	local strategic partnerships
LTPs	Local Transport Plans
MHO	mutual home ownership

MHOS   Mutual Home Ownership Society
MPCs   master planned communities
NGOs   non-governmental organizations
NHF   National Housing Federation
NTS   National Travel Survey
ONS   Office for National Statistics
PATs   policy action teams
PCT   Primary Care Trust/Primary Health Care Trust
PFI   private finance initiative
PPS3   Planning Policy Statement 3
RIBA   Royal Institute of British Architects
RSL   Registered Social Landlord
SEU   Social Exclusion Unit
SRB   Single Regeneration Budget
TfL   Transport for London
TSA   Tenant Services Authority
UKEA   UK Environment Agency
UNDAW   UN Division for the Advancement of Women
UNDP   United Nations Development Programme
WCED   World Commission on Environment and Development

Introduction

This book was born out of the desire of a number of lecturers and researchers within the School of Architecture and the Built Environment at the University of Westminster to offer the students and practitioners we engage a useful background discussion of the theoretical and practical challenges associated with achieving greater social sustainability.

To our knowledge, while several texts have dealt with this to a certain extent within the wider discourse of sustainable development, none have tackled the subject head-on. Our intention is to provide those who are already familiar with broader discussions of sustainable development with a 'hands-on' guide to the key issues associated with the social progress and equity aspects of achieving a more sustainable future in an urban planning context within the developed world.

Given the disciplinary backgrounds of the authors and the school in which we are all based, we focus specifically on urban policy. This is not to suggest that parallel issues and challenges cannot be found within rural communities or to deny the strong interactions that occur between rural and urban living. But given that the overwhelming majority of people now live, work and play within the urban environment, we believe that urban policy faces the greatest challenge in ensuring social sustainability of populations both now and in the future.

The book maintains that the analysis and practice of social sustainability requires a multi-disciplinary approach and hence the authors hail from a wide range of academic disciplines and policy areas, including planning, housing, regeneration, transport, tourism and urban design. The underlying principles within the book are: an interest in the urban arena; attention to theory and practice across a range of academic disciplines; and a concern with questions of governance and social justice. It is clear, however, that there are many aspects of social sustainability that we do not consider; most notably, issues of welfare and employment provision and governance are all missing from this text. This is not because we consider these social policy issues to be of lesser importance or lower in priority, but simply because each deserves a level of detailed consideration in its own right that would not be appropriate in this context. We therefore concentrate only on the aspects of social sustainability that we consider of direct relevance to the urban planning question and would encourage the reader to search elsewhere when considering these other aspects of the debate.

In Chapter 1, we identify some of the key concepts associated with the issue of social sustainability, including how we see this fitting within the broader concept of sustainable development. The remainder of the book is then split into three sections.

We begin in Section 1 by looking at the micro level of social organization outside of the household, namely that of neighbourhoods or communities, and how these can be assisted in becoming more self-supporting and beneficially reinforced through new institutional arrangements and management structures and by building social capital at the community level.

In Chapter 2, Tony Manzi considers the extent to which UK government policy of creating mixed communities can alleviate poverty and stigma or whether the implementation of policy can in some senses reinforce isolation by assisting in the gentrification of neighbourhoods.

Chapter 3 (by Nick Bailey) examines the way in which third-sector organizations, in particular community land trusts (CLTs), help to create sustainable environments. CLTs aim to create a virtuous circle by promoting community engagement, developing democratic systems of governance and by providing affordable housing and related community services. In Chapter 4, Tony Lloyd-Jones and Judith Allen provide a broader comparative focus and consider the way in which community asset management can be an important factor in sustainable development.

In the final chapter of this section, Catalina Gandelsonas offers a gendered analysis of the role of social capital in building the social sustainability of communities.

In Section 2, we move to the next 'layer' of the jigsaw to consider issues of density, place and connectivity in facilitating people's wider activity needs outside their immediate community. The big question here is how much space and movement is needed in order for people to live in quality urban environments and fully realize their life chance opportunities without undermining the well-being of other people and communities both in their immediate area, but also further afield and even globally and into the next generation.

In the light of such considerations, Suzy Nelson (Chapter 6) considers the densification of urban areas that has become such a regular feature of urban regeneration, particularly in the south-east of England, in recent years.

Chapter 7 (by Karen Lucas and colleagues) provides a detailed discussion of the opportunities and constraints offered by transport policies. The issue of connectivity between communities and places is an important but often neglected feature in discussions of social sustainability in urban planning circles.

In contrast, in Chapter 8, Peter White and colleagues consider the impacts of teleworking (and the reduced travel and physical interactions it brings about) on social sustainability. This is a highly significant development in a digital world, where access to electronic communications can facilitate integration but, conversely, lack of access to the 'digital economy' can serve to increase the marginalization and social exclusion of already vulnerable communities.

Section 3 is largely concerned with how local and national governments have sought to stimulate the local economic growth and regeneration of communities, neighbourhoods and larger areas of the UK urban fabric. While economic growth is seen as a public good, the new orthodoxy views this as not an unconstrained good. The sustainability agenda understands that economic development should be constrained by attention to ecological concerns; a concept that can be problematic for developing countries.

Chapters 9–11 provide further case studies and evidence about the effectiveness of economic policies to stimulate sustainable communities for the future. In Chapter 9, Chris Marsh looks at the present and future role of what are broadly referred to as planning gains from private sector developers in financing social infrastructure projects in new developments. In Chapter 10, Adam Eldridge considers the role of the evening economy in helping to stimulate local economic growth in town centres, calling into question the approach of the 'urban renaissance' agenda (Urban Task Force, 2005) to sustainable city centres. Finally, Chapter 11 (by Andrew Smith) examines the use of so-called 'mega-events', in particular whether they can be agents of urban social sustainability rather than merely forms of 'civic boosterism' and place marketing.

What becomes clear from Chapters 9–11, in the final section, is that while we as urban planning academics and practitioners may be able to a lesser or greater extent to identify the core elements of a socially sustainable society, we are a long way from realizing this in practice. Furthermore, the challenge is hard enough in times of plenty but even more difficult in the constrained financial markets that we are now experiencing.

To this end, Chapter 12 brings together the key findings from the case study evidence that has been presented within each chapter of the book, and identifies some core principles for urban planners and other related practitioners to consider in the development of new communities and regeneration of existing ones.

Understanding Social Sustainability: Key Concepts and Developments in Theory and Practice

Tony Manzi, Karen Lucas, Tony Lloyd-Jones and Judith Allen

Introduction

We begin our discussions from a basic premise that:

> Cities need to be emotionally and psychologically sustaining, and issues like the quality and design of the built environment, the quality of connections between people and the organisational capacity of urban stakeholders become crucial, as do issues of spatial segregation in cities and poverty. (Landry, 2007, p11)

From this starting point, the concept of 'social sustainability' can be described as the dominant element in discourses surrounding urban regeneration, both in the UK and elsewhere (Imrie et al, 2009, p10). However, different people mean different things when they discuss social sustainability. The purpose of this book is, therefore, to provide a better understanding of this concept in practical and conceptual terms. It does this by critically analysing how social sustainability has been applied within a variety of urban arenas; questioning how the notion of social sustainability operates in these contexts; and exploring the strengths and weaknesses of a variety of approaches. The main argument is that a 'holistic' approach to urban governance can only be understood by detailed reference to a range of interventions in urban policy.

Consequently, this book aims to:

- Understand the main concepts applied to an analysis of social sustainability.
- Explain how UK discussions about social sustainability can be linked to wider international developments.
- Examine interlinked policy areas of intervention within urban policy.
- Provide a critical account of contemporary interventions in urban regeneration.

This chapter will outline what we mean by social sustainability in the context of urban policy and urban development. The words 'sustainability' and 'social sustainability' have three different and inter-related components. First, they have a strong *normative* component, indicating a broad vision of a desired end state that is both holistic and long term. Second, they have a *strategic* component, indicating the desire to align a wide range of specific actions towards achieving the desired end state. Third, they have a *descriptive* component, which talks about 'what is' in terms of how it can be measured against strategy and vision (Colantonio, 2008a, 2009).

In order to define the meaning of social sustainability, this chapter adopts four approaches. First, we discuss how social sustainability is defined in relationship to economic and environmental sustainability. Second, we note the global nature of discourses of sustainability (international, trans-national, cross-national, intra-national, urban and localized) and outline the key elements of the international debates that are relevant to localized practices in the UK. Third, we discuss three concepts that are closely associated with visions of social sustainability: *social exclusion*, *social capital* and *governance*. Fourth, we consider UK and English policy on social sustainability, emphasizing the inseparability of political and policy thinking and issues about scale. Finally, we note some of the conceptual problems that need to be taken into account in discussing localized practices.

Conceptualizing 'social' sustainability: understanding multi-dimensionality

Despite a wealth of discussion about sustainable development, the concept remains unclear and contested. Most commentators agree that it lies at the intersection and implies policy integration of environmental, social and economic issues and the need to consider long-term change. However, there is no common position on the nature of this change or how it is to be achieved. There are many overlaps in the interactions between economic, social and environmental issues. Typically, in the sustainable development discourse (see, for example, Adams, 2006, p2), this is depicted in the form of overlapping circles (see the Venn diagram interpretation – Figure 1.1) or as concentric circles (see the 'Russian Doll' model – Figure 1.2).

The Venn diagram suggests there are potential positive-sum 'win-win' calculations in the overlaps, but also areas outside that need prioritization. If each of the circles is associated with the interests of particular stakeholders/actors, at whatever level of intervention, then the areas of overlap represent potential spheres of cooperation or partnership (Meadowcroft, 1999). The 1992 Rio Declaration suggests that sustainable development is about 'balancing' these

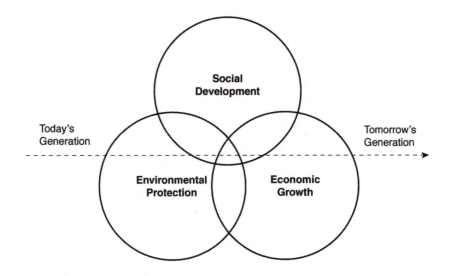

Source: United Nations Non-Government Organization Committee on Sustainable Development website, www.unsystem.org

Figure 1.1 *The dimensions and interactive process in sustainable development*

three dimensions and achieving some kind of trade-off among them in the prioritization process.

In contrast, the Russian Doll explanation (see Figure 1.2) suggests that sustainable development is primarily concerned with economic development, which must benefit society within strictly observed, unchangeable environmental limits.

In other words, the Russian Doll model downplays the importance of governance and negotiation in sustainable development. In contrast, we argue that these areas are of central importance in understanding social sustainability, and that the concept can be understood through a distinction between *eco-centric* and *anthropocentric* approaches to the question (Kearns and Turok, 2004).

Until recently, eco-centric models have dominated UK discussion, reflecting anxieties about environmental collapse, limited natural resources and the natural environment. The models emphasize the need for the efficient use of resources and are heavily influenced by environmental movements. They rest on implicit and explicit assumptions about the negative impact of human interventions on the natural world. In contrast, an anthropocentric approach focuses on human relationships, marking what is commonly referred to as social sustainability. As Kearns and Turok (2004) argue, this approach has become increasingly influential as it considers human needs and quality of life issues, as well as environmental concerns. However, some argue that

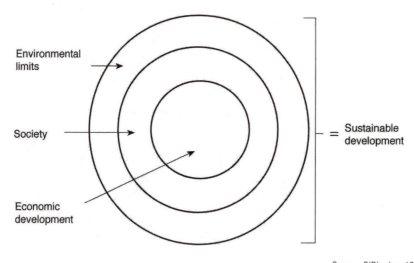

Source: O'Riordan, 1998

Figure 1.2 *The Russian Doll explanation of sustainable development*

anthropocentric approaches that take 'soft issues' into consideration may be more appropriate in the global north than in the global south, which struggles with the 'hard issues' of economic development and deep poverty (Colantonio, 2008b).

It is clear that the nature of sustainable development is both complex and dynamic (Jarvis et al, 2001, p129), incorporating social, cultural, economic and community dimensions, demonstrating a strong interdependence between environment and people. Such interdependence can be interpreted through what Giddens (1986) would term a 'structurationist' framework, wherein the 'environment, development and people should not be seen as discrete entities, as a dualism. Rather, they represent an interdependent whole, a duality of people's livelihoods and their environments' (Jarvis et al, 2001, p130). As the boundaries between natural and built environments become increasingly blurred, issues about sustainability, or the lack of sustainability, are seen as essentially social problems – created by and eventually impacting on people themselves (Beck, 1992, p81); 'nature can no longer be understood outside of society, or society outside of nature' (p80).

Hence:

> Social sustainability... is mainly concerned with the relationships between individual actions and the created environment, or the inter-connections between individual life-chances and institutional structures... This is an issue which has been largely neglected in main-stream sustainability debates. (Jarvis et al, 2001, p127)

Therefore, the interdependent nature of social sustainability should acknowledge a political dimension; in particular by questioning how processes of power and control operate in urban policy contexts. As a consequence, a more useful conceptual framework involves a multi-dimensional understanding of social sustainability, as illustrated in Figure 1.3.

The benefit of such a multi-dimensional understanding is that it can provide a framework indicating how different social, economic, environmental and institutional imperatives influence the delivery of urban policy. These imperatives allow concepts of participation, justice, democracy and social cohesion to be introduced alongside more traditional concerns about the relationship between economic competitiveness and environmental efficiency. The relations involve difficult decisions about problem definition and agenda-setting; decisions that involve significant trade-offs or 'burden-sharing' among community members, dependent on priorities accorded at particular moments in time and upon specific resource constraints. The extent to which these different burdens are shared within communities forms a central part of the debate about what is meant by social sustainability and how it can be applied to different policy contexts.

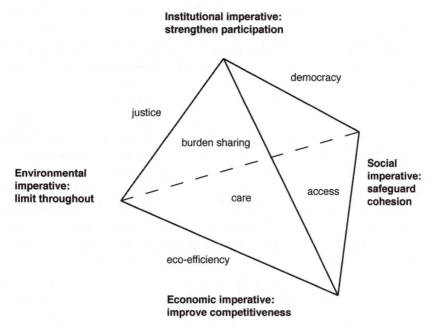

Source: Centre for Sustainable Development, University of Westminster, and the Law School, University of Strathclyde (2006), p30 (adapted from EPA Ireland, 2004)

Figure 1.3 *A multi-dimensional understanding of sustainable development*

In this book, we argue that it is vital to understand the *dynamic relationship* between the different economic, social and environmental processes within the broad policy umbrella of sustainable development. This relationship may be cumulative and virtuous or there may be negative feedback effects. While some synergies do exist between a desire to protect the planet and human economic and social advancement, there are also important tensions between these often divergent policy goals. Throughout the book, this is a commonly recognized and repeated theme, reflecting a broad consensus in policy circles that achieving a balance between economic, social and environmental development is probably the greatest challenge for society today.

Think global: act local

To understand social sustainability we need to consider how it fits within the wider context of the debate surrounding sustainable development and the ways that have been put forward for achieving it. For this, a brief historical overview of the processes and circumstances whereby sustainable development entered the global policy arena is useful. The concept of sustainable development was introduced as a major social goal at the first United Nations (UN) Conference on the Human Environment, held in Stockholm in 1972. The conference was prompted by global concerns about the persistence of poverty and increasing social inequities, combined with growing local and global environmental problems and the realization that aural resources to support economic development were finite.

These concerns about scarcity of resources can be traced much further back. Fears that it may limit the growth of the human population informed Thomas Malthus' classic work, *An Essay on the Principle of Population* (2008 [1798]). Rapid industrial development in the 19th century was accompanied by pollution and the growing concentration of people living and working in poor conditions in towns and cities. An era of social unrest and urban reform included movements concerned with the environmental health and well-being of the urban population. Proto-environmentalist ideas emerged in some strands of 19th-century radical and romantic thought. Meanwhile, strides were made in the scientific and systematic understanding of the inter-relationships among natural species, populations and their environments in Darwin's work on evolutionary theory and the origins of the science of ecology (Goodland, 1975).

However, it was not until the 1960s and growing protests against environmental pollution that these themes came together in focused thinking about the inter-relationship of human activity and the natural environment. Using a 'systems' approach and computer modelling, the 'Limits to Growth' Report to the

Club of Rome (Meadows et al, 1972) explored the interactions between population, industrial growth, food production and the limits in the ecosystems of the Earth. The wave of sustainable-development literature expanded during the 1980s, when the International Union for the Conservation of Nature's influential World Conservation Strategy (1980) put forward the concept of 'sustainable development', meaning development that would allow ecosystem services and biodiversity to be sustained.

However, despite an emerging mass of literature, no broadly accepted definition of sustainable development emerged until that of the now ubiquitously quoted Brundtland Commission Report: 'development that meets the needs of the present without compromising the ability of future generations to meet their own needs' (World Commission on Environment and Development, 1987, para. 2.III.27).

Building on the Brundtland Report, the core principles of sustainable development can be outlined in the following ways (Barton, 2000, p7):

* Public trust: there is a duty on the state to hold resources in trust for the benefit of the public.
* Precautionary principle: measures to prevent serious or irreversible damage should not be postponed due to lack of scientific certainty.
* Inter-generational equity: future generations should not be adversely affected by decisions made in the present.
* Subsidiarity: decisions should be made at the lowest appropriate level.
* The polluter pays: the costs of environmental damage should be borne by those responsible.

In addition to these principles, concerns about persistent poverty and lack of social equity within and between nations, and for present and future generations, lie at the heart of the sustainable development debate. Public trust, participation and local governance are also core central themes within this narrative. It is these core principles to which we refer when we discuss 'social sustainability' in this book.

The international development context

From the start, the concept of sustainable development linked the local to the global and was set in the context of the 'development' agenda, with a focus on social justice and welfare and what is now called 'international development cooperation'. In more developed countries, with increasing general levels of affluence, the policy discourse has shifted through the last century, from a concern with absolute poverty to a focus on relative poverty based on a notion of social inequality, where poverty levels are defined relative to average income levels (Townsend, 1993, p36; Wratten, 1995, p14). This focus was initially addressed through 'welfare state' policies, including progressive taxation, augmented more recently by an area-based approach with urban regeneration policies targeted at pockets of 'social exclusion' (Rogers, 1995).

Internationally, the focus has been more on absolute mass poverty, mainly in rural areas (but increasingly also in cities) in developing countries. The concept of 'vulnerability' and the coping strategies of the poor have become central, arising out of humanitarian concerns, with periodic crises caused by droughts or other natural hazards, conflicts, political or economic shocks affecting the poorest households and communities operating largely at a subsistence level (Sen, 1981; Chambers, 1989). While poverty is primarily a static concept, vulnerability is dynamic, suggesting change over time as 'people move in and out of poverty' (Lipton and Maxwell, 1992, p10).

While overcoming absolute or abject poverty has remained a priority, the human 'capabilities' approach of development economists, in particular Amartya Sen (1985), has exercised an important influence in discussions of sustainability. The 'human development' approach was adopted by the UN Development Programme (UNDP) and other agencies emphasizing human rights, freedom of individual choice and the multi-dimensional nature of welfare. Alongside basic economic development, this approach involves a broad-ranging social development policy response through improving access to basic education and health care, addressing gender equity, building human and social capital, and enabling poor people to have a political 'voice'. Although the context is different, there is an overlap with Western European concerns about addressing social exclusion (Madanipour et al, 1998), which also often involves a wide-ranging public policy response.

International development policy crystallized in a series of major UN conferences concerned with human, social and environmental development that took place in the 1990s. The outcome of these formed the basis for the agreed development agenda for the UN, the eight Millennium Development Goals and the associated targets and indicators that formed part of the Millennium Declaration of 2000 (UN Statistics Division, 2009).

The Brundtland Commission Report of 1987 became the basis of Agenda 21, the UN programme for sustainable development adopted at the UN Conference on Environment and Development in Rio in 1992 (UN Department of Economic and Social Affairs, 2009). The later Johannesburg Earth Summit in 2002 ('Rio+10') set out a Plan of Implementation for Agenda 21 and the achievement of the Millennium Development Goals. Much of the focus of the Rio conference was on national states' 'responsibility to ensure that activities within their jurisdiction or control do not cause damage to the environment of other states or of areas beyond the limits of national jurisdiction' (UN, 1992). This issue has been subsequently brought sharply into focus with climate change concerns, but it encompasses many other environmental issues, including atmospheric pollution, water resources, loss of biodiversity and resource depletion. These cannot be dealt with separately from wider development concerns such as food and energy security at the national level, or international trade and finance, political relations and development assistance.

Developing countries at the 2002 Earth Summit took the view that, since the rich world is primarily responsible for causing environmental problems, it should pay the cost of dealing with them. It was not considered politically feasible, for example, to include developing countries within the framework of limiting carbon emissions in the Kyoto Treaty on Global Climate Change in 1997. Concern with the environment was not regarded as a priority in developing countries, where rapid industrialization is seen as a main route to catching up with the rich world and overcoming poverty. At the heart of the matter, then, is the question of social equity and justice within the framework of international relationships between nation states (a key driver, for example, of the Social Cohesion Agenda within European Union (EU) policy at the regional level). This is not just a question of national pride, but also of political necessity. Governments in most countries, democratically elected or not, stand or fall on whether they deliver development through economic growth. Failure to deliver growth implies social stagnation, a heightened concern with social justice and a heightened possibility of social unrest and instability.

Implementing social sustainability

As noted above, sustainability as a concept includes principles of social equity, access to resources, participation and social capital (Goodland, 2002), as well as a concern with human rights and exclusion. This approach has much in common with the environmental justice agenda, located in the USA (Agyeman, 2005) and based on the idea that marginal and poor groups should not disproportionately bear the costs of public or private activities or policies.

The EU has been a highly influential institution in implementing sustainable development policies. The Treaty of Amsterdam in 1997 (Article 2) and the 1998 Aarhus convention determined sustainable development should comprise an underlying principle of all EU policies. The Lisbon strategy in 2000 (see European Commission, 2004) produced a programme for economic and social renewal, adding an environmental dimension to 'complementary strategies', and the Gothenburg declaration (European Commission, 2001) resulted in the formulation of the first EU sustainable development strategy. This strategy reflected the 2000 Millennium Development Goals (see UN, 2009) and was linked to global pledges to increase official development and to take account of the needs of developing countries in international trade. The strategy included policy measures to tackle 'key unsustainable trends', alongside what was seen as a new approach to policymaking, ensuring that economic, social and environmental policies were mutually reinforcing. In addition, each new policy proposal was to be subject to an impact assessment. In 2005 an amended set of guiding principles was established for sustainable development, and a new EU Sustainable Development Strategy (see European Commission, 2007) was formulated to encompass the core areas of:

- Climate change and clean energy.
- Sustainable transport.
- Sustainable consumption and production.
- Conservation and management of natural resources.
- Public health.
- Social inclusion, demography and migration.
- Global poverty.

Hence, linkages between social and environmental sustainability have formed a strong theme in EU policymaking (see Pye et al, 2008). However, while strong correlations between poverty, poor housing, health, transport and pollution are acknowledged, precise causal relationships are uncertain. Nevertheless, there is a widespread recognition that policies to ameliorate negative environmental and socio-economic externalities are necessary to ensure sustainable communities.

Concerns with social equity and an agenda of social justice imply that the implementation of policy should be based upon three specific visions of how a good society should function, namely that it should be inclusive, caring and well governed. Each of these visions, like the vision of sustainable development, has spawned conceptual, policy and practical debates. The main elements of these debates, which are all also highly relevant for understanding the holistic nature of social sustainability, are briefly outlined below.

An inclusive society: tackling social exclusion

The general idea of social exclusion is that institutionalized social, political and economic processes erect barriers that prevent specific social groups participating fully in the society in which they live. The effects of these barriers can be seen in the conjunction of material poverty and the processes that define particular groups as outsiders. These barriers also prevent people from improving their circumstances through their own efforts. The significance of tackling social exclusion emphasizes the relativity, agency and dynamics of multiple deprivation (Atkinson, 1998). While a traditional emphasis on poverty involved an emphasis on distributional issues (a lack of resources), social exclusion was concerned with inadequate levels of participation, poor social integration and discrepancies in power (Room, 1995). Policy approaches therefore operated at a variety of levels, including addressing individual behaviour, reforming institutions and systems, and challenging discrimination and a lack of rights (Burchardt et al, 2002, p3).

The notion of tackling social exclusion was imported to the UK from the EU at a specific time: the election of the New Labour Government in 1997, which had a political need to establish its social redistribution credentials. The policy to combat social exclusion was announced in the prime minister's first big speech after the election (Blair, 1997), and was followed by a series of policy action team reports to consider cross-cutting departmental and partnership-based strategies (Social Exclusion Unit, 2001).

The Government's initial approach focused strongly on small neighbourhoods of about 10,000 people, which were characterized by high levels of multiple deprivation. Considerable sums of money were committed to these neighbourhoods in the expectation that they could be turned around in ten years and that all the relevant local agencies (health, education, policy, employment services, voluntary groups and residents) would combine to ensure this happened. At the same time, each of the ministries concerned with service delivery to poor groups were expected to develop their own small area-based initiatives, which would involve client groups in improving service delivery.

Underlying the focus on small areas or neighbourhoods was the idea that by tackling social exclusion, and in particular minimizing the adverse consequences of area or 'neighbourhood effects', communities would become more socially sustainable (Atkinson and Kintrea, 2002, 2004). As government statements expressed it, 'nobody should be disadvantaged by the area in which they live' (Social Exclusion Unit, 2001). Locational disadvantage, or socio-spatial segregation, compounded the effects of other forms of social exclusion. Neighbourhood effects were seen as reinforced by the concentration of specific excluded groups within social housing and concentrations of deprivation have a cumulative impact on the quality of life of residents within a particular area. Concentration has significant implications for opportunities to gain employment and access to training and educational attainment; in such areas, local indicators tended to be lower than normal given the socio-economic profile.

Policy approaches were therefore aimed at reducing socio-spatial segregation to ensure that areas do not contain high concentrations of multiply deprived households. This led to two different approaches in practice. The first aimed to help individuals and households climb out of poverty in the areas in which they lived by improving the quality of the services and the environment. The second sought to create mixed communities, either through introducing owner-occupied housing in large-scale renovation schemes or by insisting on a proportion of social housing in newly-built private estates. This second approach has been of great interest to social housing providers and urban planners although it is inherently limited in scale, as only about 1 per cent of the UK housing stock is renewed each year (Francis and Wheeler, 2006, p6).

The main lessons that have been learned from small area-based approaches to preventing social exclusion are that they cannot remove deeply rooted divisions within the society as a whole, such as barriers in the labour market, racism, gender or disability. They can, however, improve the material and social living conditions of the poorest and most stigmatized groups.

The Government's social exclusion policy has now metamorphosed into a social inclusion policy and is strongly aligned with EU programmes to promote social integration. The notion of social exclusion has been replaced by a wider concept of poverty to include low income plus factors leading to alienation and disenfranchisement. Monitoring now emphasizes broad age groups, with a strong focus on achieving the Government's objective to end child poverty by the year 2020.

A caring society: developing social capital

EU and UK urban policy has been strongly influenced by Putnam's concept of social capital, which focuses on individuals and their participation in small groups (Putnam, 2000; Office for National Statistics, 2001; Performance and Innovation Unit, 2002). When relationships within these groups are characterized by high levels of reciprocity and mutual trust, 'bonding' social capital is said to exist. Although most such groups are socially homogeneous, some individuals may have overlapping memberships, thus introducing relationships that bridge socially heterogeneous groupings. Putnam argues that the norms of reciprocity and mutual trust associated with group membership bring tangible benefits to the members of the groups, and so constitute social capital. His research documented the rise and demise of a wide variety of organized and publicly visible groups over the 20th century in the USA, and he drew the normative conclusion that the way to help poorer people is to support them to form active groups. There is now an extensive literature that subjects Putnam's work to critique in a variety of ways (DeFilippis, 2001; Widmalm, 2007; Dawkins, 2008; Radnitz et al, 2009). From the standpoint of this book, it is important to note that the groups Putnam investigated were drawn from the middle strata of American society (Arneil, 2006). In particular, he did not include groups from among the lowest social strata and most marginalized and excluded members of the society, especially black people, although he has attempted to rectify these omissions in his later cross-sectional national survey (Putnam, 2007).

An alternative approach to the concept of social capital can be found in the work of Bourdieu (1989), whose primary concern was to explain how social classes are reproduced over time. His overarching notion is the idea of *habitus*, which roughly means 'habitual', 'usual', 'traditional', 'taken for granted' or, in other words, 'the ways things are done here'. What is important for Bourdieu is that *habitus* is pre-conscious, unremarked and embodied in everyday forms of behaviour. He sometimes uses the concept of social capital in a generalized sense and sometimes distinguishes different forms of capital – social, economic, cultural – that are said to be 'possessed by' specific individuals and are to some extent, but not always, fungible, in that one form of capital can be turned into another. Paralleling Putnam's concept, social capital confers privileges on those who hold it. What distinguishes Bourdieu's concept of social capital from Putnam's is that its existence is a function of *habitus*, that is, it arises out of the ways that social structures are embedded and embodied in everyday behaviour. Bourdieu perhaps underestimates the extent to which there are also everyday forms of resistance (de Certeau, 1984), but he is primarily concerned to show how structures of privilege reproduce themselves and how difficult it may be to challenge them. Indeed, English urban policy and participation literature is full of examples of how easily men in suits dominate ordinary folk in meetings (see Hart et al, 1997, for a particularly useful analysis).

The second alternative to Putnam's concept of social capital derives from Coleman's work on educational attainment (1988). He investigated two groups of socio-economically identical students, one in state schools and one in (private) Roman Catholic schools in the USA, who displayed different levels of educational achievement (Coleman, 1988). His explanation was that the social or organizational infrastructure provided by the church, as a social institution, combined with the network of parents connected with it to create social capital. This social capital, absent in the state school, provided much greater support for the children's achievement. Pennington and Rydin (2000) develop the same point in their investigation of local environmental policies in England. They argue that the type of network identified by Putnam, characterized by reciprocity and high levels of mutual trust, is simply descriptive of human associational activity. Such networks only become significant as a form of social capital when they are set within an appropriate and supportive institutional framework.

A well-governed society: instituting effective governance mechanisms

The word 'governance' describes styles of governing in which boundaries between and within public and private sectors have become blurred, and in which actions do not depend on recourse to the formal authority and sanctions of government. 'The interaction of a multiplicity of governing and each other influencing actors' (Kooiman and van Vliet, 1993, p64) create the conditions for ordered rule and collective action (Stoker, 1998).

Seeking social sustainability promotes new alliances and new ways of mobilizing resources through the new machineries of governance (Allen and Cochrane, 2007). Governance is a core issue within debates about sustainability, partly because existing arrangements are responsible for the problem and partly because creating new ways to do things together is a part of the solution. Partnership arrangements among public, private and voluntary sector agencies, managing through networks and community involvement – the techniques of governance – are all expected in the practices through which urban policies are delivered.

New interdependencies among actors, and the blurring of boundaries between public, private, voluntary and community create new problems associated with the efficient and accountable delivery of services. A lack of clarity about who is in charge, when 'we are all in charge here', means that it is also unclear who is responsible for seeing that things are done, that money is spent well and wisely, and so forth. The complex architecture of governance arrangements spans different types of actors, each with their own internal accountability arrangements and operating across a wide variety of fields of activity and spatial levels of government. Consequently, governance involves complex power interdependencies that require constant attention, either to maintain or to change. At the same time, specific governance arrangements can constitute barriers to social inclusion or they can contribute to building localized social capital.

The most commonly discussed techniques of governance in urban policy are partnerships and networks. In partnerships, organizations negotiate joint projects, blending their capacities in a way that allows each partner to achieve its own objectives. Negotiated partnerships can, in the right circumstances, establish a level of mutual understanding that allows the development of a shared vision and joint-working capacity. In turn, this can lead to the formation of a self-governing network. Within negotiated and mutualized partnerships, there is still accountability within the partner organizations. In self-governing networks, accountability becomes more diffuse, and the social glue that holds them together may preclude challenges from within and exclude external actors. An additional problem is that voluntary and community sector groups may start out as relatively autonomous networks but, as they are drawn into negotiated or mutualized partnerships, the ways they function internally may change. An important consequence is that the outcomes from partnership activity are to some extent unpredictable.

All these processes are normal and all of them raise important questions about the role of government and wider democratic accountability, as well as questions about transparency. The same questions arise at all levels of government: local authorities; central governments; and international organizations such as the International Monetary Fund, the World Bank, the World Trade Organization, the Organization for Economic Co-operation and Development, and the EU.

Governance mechanisms allow flexibility and innovation and, by allowing a wide range of groups and organizations to work together and determine their own objectives and activities, they are a key component of ensuring social sustainability. They overcome problems associated with the vertical hierarchies that characterize formal governmental organizations. But at the same time, the configuration of governance arrangements in any specific time and place may also strengthen entrenched social divisions and exclusions.

Thus, the key question becomes the competence of governments to steer partnerships and networks. This question lies at the heart of the reorganization of UK government over the last 12 years. More substantively, governance mechanisms are increasingly seen as being bound up with concepts of participation, empowerment, efforts to develop social capital and ensure more collaborative working arrangements. Hence, social sustainability is understood not simply as a requirement upon central government to change its mode of operation, but as a general injunction to incorporate a wider range of stakeholders in the delivery of urban processes.

Social sustainability: UK policy and practice

Previous sections have discussed how the idea of local social sustainability emerged alongside global debates, how social sustainability is related to economic and environmental sustainability, and how it overlaps with three other 'grand policy' ideas: social exclusion, social capital and governance. However, the main focus of our book is on the ways in which the idea of social sustainability has been localized in Britain. The remainder of this chapter discusses how central government has framed the idea and changed local governance processes around it. We comment on how the idea creates a complicated rhetoric, mixing political and policy languages, then summarize the questions raised, outlining the contents of the following chapters.

The UK's first Sustainable Development Strategy (HM Government, 1994) emerged from the global action plan outlined at the 1992 UN Earth Summit, including the proposal to establish Local Agenda 21 strategies at local authority levels. By 2000, more than 93 per cent of local authorities in the UK had produced Local Agenda 21 documents in consultation with communities, although with varying levels of success (IDeA, 2000). Nevertheless, the Government's strategy has encouraged participation and partnership working and has promoted sustainable development as a core policy objective. The strategy was updated in 2005 and in 2008 and now includes 68 indicators in the following key areas (HM Government, 2005):

• Sustainable consumption and production.
• Climate change and energy.
• Protecting natural resources and enhancing the environment.
• Creating sustainable communities and a fairer world.

In addition to more traditional environmental indicators (greenhouse gas and carbon dioxide emissions; renewable electricity generation; efficient resource use and reducing waste), the strategy incorporates indicators on: community participation; reducing the fear of crime; creating employment and education opportunities; improving access and mobility; reducing poverty; and ensuring social justice, environmental equality and promoting well-being.

In 2000, the Government set up the Sustainable Development Commission and charged it with an advisory and advocacy role. In 2005, the new Sustainable Development Strategy gave the Commission an additional role as a watchdog for sustainable development. A significant element in its work is capability building within a wide range of governmental organizations in the UK. In 2009, it became an executive non-departmental public body, a legal entity separate from the Government, with more control over its own operations. Its history illustrates the significance of new governance structures and techniques for installing a commitment to sustainable development throughout UK society.

Running in parallel, the Sustainable Communities Plan (ODPM, 2003) emphasized the importance of sustainable long-term housing and community development. It established a vision for new-build settlements in the south-east of England and for regenerating urban centres across the UK, leading to a programme of Housing Market Renewal in areas of low demand, mainly in the north of England, and to creating growth areas in the south-east. Delivery of this programme rests with local authorities and a variety of regionally-based partnerships. Implementation of the Sustainable Communities Plan was reviewed by the Sustainable Development Commission in 2007. Although there is considerable overlap between the Department of Communities and Local Government (CLG), which implements the Sustainable Communities Plan, and the Sustainable Development Commission, the Department tends to take responsibility for aspects of social sustainability, while the Commission is more concerned with environmental sustainability.

In 2004, the OPDM commissioned the Egan Review of Skills for Sustainable Communities (ODPM, 2004), which has provided an influential framework shaping contemporary debates about sustainable communities. Egan defined sustainable communities as those that:

meet the diverse needs of existing and future residents, contribute to a high quality of life and provide opportunity and choice. They achieve this in ways that make effective use of natural resources, enhance the environment, promote social cohesion and inclusion, and strengthen economic prosperity. (ODPM, 2004, p7)

The review also led to the establishment in 2006 of the Academy for Sustainable Communities, designed to disseminate knowledge and provide opportunities for training in key skills to develop sustainable communities. In 2008, the academy was incorporated into the Homes and Communities Agency, set up at the same time as a non-departmental spending body, sponsored by the CLG and charged with delivering the national housing and regeneration programme.

Egan's review of the skills base for developing sustainable communities also produced what is referred to as the 'Egan Wheel', which can be seen as a tool for evaluating socially sustainable communities. Figure 1.4 illustrates the

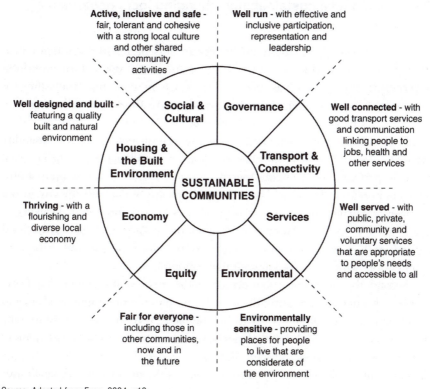

Source: Adapted from Egan, 2004, p19

Figure 1.4 *The Egan Wheel*

way in which the different components and key elements of sustainability are combined.

Combining an analysis of the current UK Strategy for Sustainable Development and the Strategy for Sustainable Communities helps us to construct a set of core concepts and guiding principles for a localized social sustainability agenda within the UK context, namely:

1   Promoting neighbourhood well-being and 'liveability'.
2   Supporting resident participation and empowerment.
3   Encouraging social cohesion and integration.
4   Integrating core services, such as housing, planning, education, transport and health.
5   Facilitating partnership and collaboration in service provision.
6   Ensuring safety, security and protection from environmental hazards.
7   Promoting access to communications and information technology.
8   Providing the conditions for equality of opportunity for all.

Promoting social sustainability: changing local governance structures

If localized social sustainability initiatives can only be realized through extensive governance mechanisms, the reorganization and restructuring of local government since 2000 has been a necessary precondition for achieving this. Since 2000, the Government also turned its attention to strengthening local government's capacity to steer local governance.

Four changes have facilitated the emergence of local social sustainability agendas. First, all local authorities are now responsible for setting up local strategic partnerships, bringing together public, private and voluntary sector actors important in the area. These partnerships are responsible for setting out an overarching vision for the area in what is now known as a Sustainable Community Plan. The Sustainable Communities Act 2007 also gives local authorities the power to propose transfers of function from one public body to another, following consultation with the community.

Second, the Government has promoted the creation of single-tier local government through unitary authorities, replacing the two-tier county and district structure (this programme is yet to be completed). After considerable public debate over requiring local authorities to set up internal, neighbourhood-based administrative structures, the Housing and Regeneration Act 2008 has left the definition of localized areas and their relationship to political administrative structures with the authorities themselves.

Third, in terms of political management, all local councils are now required to set up executive-and-scrutiny procedures with the aim of supporting backbench councillors to provide an active political presence in their wards.

Fourth, responsibility for negotiating local spending plans has been extended across a range of local agencies, and the Sustainable Communities Act gives local councils extended powers to take any actions that will improve the economic, social and environmental well-being of the area (Steuer and Marks, 2007; Hothi et al, 2008). Through these changes, local authorities have been given the tools to steer governance within their boundaries and thus to make localized social sustainability a feasible project rather than simply a normative aspiration.

Shaping social sustainability: politics, policies and criticisms

As noted above, the concept of social sustainability acknowledges a tension between economic activity, social relationships and ecological impact. In particular, understanding social sustainability entails an awareness of different spatial dimensions in shaping the debate. The concept acknowledges that issues of governance, democracy and participation need to be determined at a range of levels. In addition, policies are based on principles of partnership, including all relevant stakeholders, and participation by local communities. The problem lies, partly, in the principle of subsidiarity, the idea that powers should be devolved to the lowest *appropriate* level. In the UK the lowest level is presently local authorities, even though the creation of unitary authorities is expanding the spatial territory of some authorities. The issue of neighbourhood governance or double devolution (Mulgan and Bury, 2006) was quietly buried when the Housing and Regeneration Act 2008 was passed. Thus, a central concept in sustainability, 'think global: act local', raises important issues of precisely how large or small the local is. However, the terms of the debate, the concepts that shape debate at different spatial levels, are significantly different, as shown in Table 1.1.

In the first part of this chapter we defined social sustainability, and in the second part we have outlined the main elements in UK sustainability policy and

Table 1.1 *Dimensions of sustainability*

Scale	Main concern	Desired outcome
Global	Resource depletion	Avoiding environmental damage
City	Efficient interactions	Meet increasing economic/welfare needs within available resources
Neighbourhood	Liveability	Sustained demand to live in area

Source: Kearns and Turok, 2004, p10

how they come together in the Egan Wheel in terms of urban initiatives. However, no matter how organized the discussion of sustainability may be, the policy discussions rarely consider the limitations of the concept. The following section addresses some of the main criticisms.

Criticisms of the 'social sustainability' concept

The extent to which social sustainability forms a dominant discourse in urban policy has tended to obscure the limitations of the concept. In particular, four main criticisms can be identified in contemporary policies:

1   It is too abstract to be practicably implemented.
2   It fails to appreciate the complexity of local political contexts.
3   It does not acknowledge the basic constraints of an empowerment and participation agenda.
4   Only lip service is paid to the international and global dimension.

We will now examine each of these criticisms.

Too abstract to be implemented

Discussions of sustainability have tended to be conducted at a relatively abstract level, where definitions remain highly ambiguous. Environmental sustainability has been criticized as a concept 'more talked about than practised' (Landry, 2007, p278) and 'used with casual abandon as if mere repetition delivers green probity' (Barton, 2000, p6). Gaps in communication result from the different roles played by politicians (politics) and by professionals (policy), and social sustainability can be seen as an elastic and ever-moving concept. This is both its strength and weakness. It can be used as an effective concept to indicate the broad objectives of policy, implicitly referring to 'warm words' such as participation, empowerment, social justice and social capital. It is thus highly attractive to policymakers, indicating broad aims, but not committing agencies to a particular course of action.

Some argue (such as Tuxworth, 2001) that abstract and academic language is used deliberately in order to avoid the hard work of communicating the concept. Thus, writers such as Church and McHarry (March 2006) or Pacione (2007) have noted a deliberate avoidance of clear definitions of social sustainability on the part of delivery agencies. However, they also note a tendency to link back immediately to wider sustainable development issues and from there to stress the social benefits of environmental action. Thus, social sustainability is often more useful as an ambiguous and poorly defined phrase that users can shape to their own circumstances.

Consequently, solutions to social sustainability have tended to be highly generalized, 'motherhood and apple pie' responses, which promise more than they deliver. On the normative side, can we set a level or standard below which a development could be said to be unsustainable, accepting that such standards can change over time? At the local level, there are planning standards for social infrastructure, for example, establishing the number of hospital beds or school spaces to be provided, but these are often related just to the size of the population in an area rather than accessibility, which requires looking at transport links and different types of facility/amenity at different levels. Such responses are likely to raise expectations to unrealistic levels and to result in increased frustration on the part of local residents.

The effect of changing governance mechanisms, joined-up working and community consultation is to introduce a wealth of voices into the conversation, and it is not clear whether all these voices are speaking the same language. For example, a core objective of local social sustainability involves improving public health and educational facilities. Evidence of the negative health impact of poor housing and environment has clearly informed policy debates, and these ideas have played an increasingly important role in discussions of sustainability. Innovative, joined up practices have emerged from early small-area initiatives, but communicating these practices still requires investing considerable energy, using a variety of media, to reach professionals within their often divided organizations and institutions.

Insensitivity to local political complexities

Following on from this point about communication, the second main criticism is that the concept of social sustainability explicitly involves a political dimension, being concerned with questions of democracy, participation, equity and accountability. Hence, discussions of sustainability will commonly consider questions about poverty, inequality and social exclusion, in addition to questions about the use of natural resources and economic efficiency. What is crucial is the way that these social and political issues are played out at local levels in order to determine social justice and the distribution of scarce resources. As Pacione (2007, p249) comments, sustainability is a 'broad-based abstract concept' that should be seen as a process rather than a fixed or predetermined outcome. Moreover, it is dependent on a local context (Pacione, 2007).

In contrast, policies have commonly failed to comprehend the multiplicity of inherent tensions and conflicts at community, neighbourhood, regional and national levels. Most responses assume the desirability and feasibility of 'win–win scenarios' aimed at highly idealized concepts that consensus can be reached. As Marcuse has commented:

> While sustainability may be a useful formulation of goals on environ-
> mental issues, it is a treacherous one for urban policy because it
> suggests the possibility of a conflict-free consensus on policies, whereas
> in fact, vital interests do conflict; it will take more than simply better
> knowledge and a clearer understanding to produce change. (Marcuse,
> 1998, p104)

The sustainability agenda frequently neglects the inherent political dimension. Significantly, it fails to acknowledge the complexity of power relationships and issues of resource redistribution. It therefore needs to engage with directly political questions about inequality, redistribution, citizenship and social jus-tice. Despite a wealth of evidence demonstrating that levels of social sustainability are far higher in more egalitarian societies and that less-equal communities suffer directly in terms of health, education and well-being (e.g., Wilkinson and Pickett, 2009), these questions are regularly ignored in discus-sions of the win–win scenarios associated with the concept of sustainability.

The extent to which social sustainability should be concerned with reduc-ing inequality and aimed at redistribution has proved particularly problematic for politicians and policymakers. Lessons from early neighbourhood initiatives in the UK indicate that the issue is best handled at central government level, raising questions about how local social sustainability policies can contribute to this objective on the one hand, and the efficacy of the tax and benefits systems on the other.

Failure to acknowledge the basic constraints of empowerment and participation

A third criticism is that assumptions about empowerment and participation fail to acknowledge basic constraints. For example, individuals may not have the 'capacities or orientation required by democratic deliberation' and processes often 'reflect existing social conventions and the current distribution of power and interests' (Rosenberg, 2007, p360). The concept of social sustainability has a tendency to be presented in highly simplistic terms and little discussion of the inherent tensions and dilemmas within the broad discourse.

For example:

> There is a real danger... that local participation may dilute rather than
> reinforce the holistic and synergetic type of sustainable development
> that is being aimed for. Translating the sustainable development

concept into a 'quality of life' agenda may increase public participation, but that may be at the cost of the sustainable development policy objective itself. In these circumstances, it may be that transparency and openness about decision-making is more desirable than fully inclusive participation. (Rydin, 2003, p10)

A commitment to participation per se may therefore conflict with other goals such as energy efficiency or providing resources for all groups. Interests can be partial and exclusive, reflecting what some have termed the 'dark side of social capital' (Putzel, 1998, p943), where 'bonding' capital takes precedence over other forms of 'bridging' capital.

Only lip service is paid to the international and global dimension

Finally, despite the considerable attention paid to an international and global dimension in discourses of sustainability, there is a marked lack of comparative analysis and cross-societal comparisons in existing debates. Much discussion of sustainability remains located within specific social environments, so is somewhat parochial in nature. In some ways, this is inevitable given that so much of the discussion takes place at the level of communities and neighbourhoods. However, the principle 'think global, act local' should be taken seriously if sustainability is to form a genuine objective for urban policy. Too often local, short-term economic factors override broader environmental questions.

For example, the economic downturn of 2008 has in large part emasculated debates about energy efficiency in UK policy (despite the provisions of the Climate Change Act 2008). Concern about the impact of carbon emissions appears much more prominent in times of economic growth. As resources become increasingly scarce, it has been tempting for national governments to prioritize immediate and measurable economic policies. Moreover, the broader concept of social sustainability is more easily understood at neighbourhood and community levels, where specific policy initiatives can be effectively implemented and evaluated. Questions of social justice, social cohesion and participation are complex enough at a national level; cross-national implications are much more difficult to comprehend.

Nevertheless, a commitment to social sustainability should acknowledge that the concept involves much more than simply ensuring that short-term national (economic) policy objectives and priorities are met. Consequently, a wider global perspective is needed (even if residents may be uninterested in seemingly abstract questions about social sustainability and more concerned about their immediate priorities for safety, security and effective service provision).

Conclusions

Despite these conceptual flaws and practical difficulties, the fundamental need for a more socially sustainable society and greater social justice in the allocation of the Earth's resources, both within and between nations now and in the future, remains the core social goal of our time. It is thus an important guiding principle for practitioners and academics to understand the direction of policy and ways in which contemporary initiatives can be delivered and evaluated.

This chapter has provided an overview of some of the debates that are pertinent to understanding social sustainability, which are important in order to understand both the strengths and weaknesses of policy responses adopted in the UK and elsewhere. The key insight of this book is that principles of social sustainability are inseparable from environmental and economic factors; however, this is not to say that there are not significant conflicts in terms of approach. The principles need to be clarified and the elasticity of the concept needs to be defined more effectively to produce useful practical strategies; in particular, the concept needs to consider the central question of equity and to 'emphasize the criterion of long-term political and social viability in the assessment of otherwise desirable programmes and not as a goal replacing social justice, which must remain the focal point for our efforts' (Marcuse, 1998, p111).

This edited collection comprises narratives and evaluations of what has happened in the field on projects that have aimed to deliver greater social sustainability, within the UK and elsewhere. It is important to note that the contributions are primarily qualitative in nature, indicating an understanding of social sustainability in broad terms. Hence they do not address statistical indicators of sustainability, but focus on some of the key principles and debates within contemporary discourses. The collection considers policy responses through a practice-based case study approach and examines the limitations and opportunities of a social sustainability agenda in order to promote further debate in this largely overlooked aspect of the wider sustainable development discourse.

References

Adams, W. M. (2006) *The Future of Sustainability: Re-thinking Environment and Development in the Twenty-First Century*, Report of the IUCN Renowned Thinkers Meeting, 29–31 January 2006, The World Conservation Union, www.iucn.org, accessed 12 December 2009

Agyeman, J. (2005) *Sustainable Communities and the Challenge of Environmental Justice*, New York University Press, New York

Allen, J. and Cochrane, A. (2007) 'Beyond the Territorial Fix: Regional Assemblages, Politics and Power', *Regional Studies*, vol 41, pp1161–1175

Arneil, B. (2006) *Diverse Communities: The Problem with Social Capital*, Cambridge University Press, Cambridge

Atkinson, A. (1998) 'Social Exclusion, Poverty and Unemployment', in Atkinson, A. and Hills, J. (eds) *Exclusion, Employment and Opportunity*, CASE paper 4, London School of Economics, London

Atkinson, R. and Kintrea, K. (2002) 'Area Effects: What Do They Mean for British Housing and Regeneration Policy?', *European Journal of Housing Policy*, vol 2, no 2, pp147–166

Atkinson, R. and Kintrea, K. (2004) 'Opportunities and Despair – It's all in There: Practitioner Experiences and Explanations of Area Effects and Life Chances', *Sociology*, vol 38, no 3, pp437–455

Barton, H. (2000) *Sustainable Communities*, Earthscan, London

Beck, U. (1992) *Risk Society: Towards a New Modernity*, Sage, London

Blair, A. (1997) 'The will to win', Speech at the Aylesbury Estate (Southwark, London), 2 June

Bourdieu, P. (1989) 'Social Space and Symbolic Power', *Sociological Theory*, vol 7, no 1, pp14–25

Burchardt, T., Le Grand, J. and Piachaud, D. (2002) 'Introduction', in Hills, J., Le Grand, J. and Piachaud, D. (eds) *Understanding Social Exclusion*, Oxford University Press, Oxford, pp1–12

Centre for Sustainable Development, University of Westminster and the Law School, University of Strathclyde (2006) *Sustainable Development: A Review of International Literature*, Scottish Executive Social Research, www.scotland.gov.uk/Publications/ 2006/05/23091323/0, accessed 1 July 2009

Certeau, M. de (1984) *The Practice of Everyday Life*, University of California Press, Berkeley, CA

Chambers, R. (1989) 'Editorial Introduction: Vulnerability, Coping and Policy', *Institute of Development Studies Bulletin*, vol 20, no 2, pp1–7

Church, C. and McHarry, J. (2006, unpublished report) The Impact of Procurement Policy and Practice: Towards an Operational framework, London, DEFRA

Colantonio, A. (2008a) *Traditional and Emerging Prospects in Social Sustainability*, Oxford Institute for Sustainable Development, EIBURS Working Paper Series, Oxford, www.brookes.ac.uk/schools/be/oisd/sustainable_communities/resources/SocialSusta inabilityProspectspaper.pdf, accessed 1 July 2009

Colantonio, A. (2008b) 'Urban Social Sustainability: North–South Perspectives' presenta- tion to UN-Habitat 4th World Urban Forum, 3–6 November 2008, Nanjing, China, www.brookes.ac.uk/schools/be/oisd/news/resources/UN_Habitat_seminar_2008.pdf, accessed 1 July 2009

Colantonio, A. (2009) 'Social Sustainability Assessment Framework [draft]', Oxford Institute for Sustainable Development, Oxford, www.brookes.ac.uk/schools/ be/oisd/workshops/urss/resources/Colantonio%20Social%20Sustainability%20 Framework.pdf, accessed 1 July 2009

Coleman, J. (1988) 'Social Capital in the Creation of Human Capital', *American Journal of Sociology*, vol 94, Supplement, ppS95–S120

Dawkins, C. (2008) 'Reflections on Diversity and Social Capital: A Critique of Robert D. Putnam's "*E Pluribus Unum*: Diversity and Community in the Twenty-First Century – The 2006 Johan Skytte prize lecture"', *Housing Policy Debate*, vol 19, issue 1, pp208–217

DeFilippis, J. (2001) 'The Myth of Social Capital in Community Development', *Housing Policy Debate*, vol 12, no 4, pp781–806

Egan, J. (2004) *Skills for Sustainable Communities: The Egan Review*, ODPM, London

Environmental Protection Agency Ireland (2004) *ERTI – Sustainable Development*, Technical Document, EPA, Wexford

European Commission (2001) *A Sustainable Europe for a Better World: A European Union Strategy for Sustainable Development: Commissions Proposal to the Gothenburg European Council*, COM2001, 264, European Commission, Brussels, http://ec.europa.eu/environment/eussd/, accessed 30 July 2009

European Commission (2004) *Facing the Challenge: The Lisbon Strategy for Growth and Employment*, Office for Official Publication of the European Communities, Luxembourg, http://ec.europa.eu/environment/eussd/, accessed 30 July 2009

European Commission (2007) *The 2005 Review of the EU Sustainable Development Strategy: Initial Stocktaking and Future Orientations*, SEC2005, 225, European Commission, Brussels, http://ec.europa.eu/environment/eussd/, accessed 30 July 2009

Francis, A. and Wheeler, J. (2006) *One Planet Living in the Suburbs,* WWF/Bioregional, London

Giddens, A. (1986) *The Constitution of Society: Outline of the Theory of Structuration*, Polity Press, Cambridge

Goodland, R. (1975) 'The Tropical Origin of Ecology: Eugen Warming's Jubilee', *Oikos*, vol 26, pp240–245

Goodland, R. (2002) 'Sustainability: Human, Social, Economic and Environmental', in Munn, R. (ed.) *Encyclopaedia of Global Environmental Change,* John Wiley & Sons Ltd, London, pp1–3

Hart, C., Jones, K. and Bains, M. (1997) 'Do the People Want Power? The Social Responsibilities of Empowering Communities', in Hoggett, P. (ed) *Contested Communities: Experiences, Struggles, Policies*, pp180–200, The Policy Press, Bristol

HM Government (1994) *Sustainable Development: The UK Strategy*, CM2426, HMSO, London

HM Government (2005) *Securing the Future: Delivering the UK Government Sustainable Development Strategy*, Cmnd 6467, TSO, London

Hothi, M., Bacon, N., Brophy, M. and Mulgan, G. (2008) *Neighbourliness + Empowerment = Wellbeing – Is there a Formula for Happy Communities?*, The Young Foundation, London

Imrie, R., Lees, L. and Raco, M. (2009) 'London's regeneration', in Imrie, R. , Lees, L. and Raco, M. (eds) *Regenerating London*, Routledge, London, pp3–23

Innovation and Development Agency (2000) *Progress with Local Agenda 21 in England and Wales*, IDeA, London

International Union for the Conservation of Nature (1980) *World Conservation Strategy*, Gland, Switzerland, ICUN, http://data.iucn.org/dbtw-wpd/edocs/WCS-004.pdf, accessed 30 July 2009

Jarvis, H., Pratt, A. and Cheng-Chong Wu, P. (2001) *The Secret Life of Cities: The Social Reproduction of Everyday Life*, Pearson Education, Harlow

Kearns, A. and Turok, I. (2004) *Sustainable Communities: Dimensions and Challenges*, ESRC/ODPM Postgraduate Research Programme, Working Paper 1, ODPM, London

Kooiman, J. and Vliet, M. van (1993) 'Governance and Public Management', in Eliassen, K. and Kooiman, J. (eds) *Managing Public Organizations* (2nd edn), pp58–72, Sage, London

Landry, C. (2007) *The Art of City Making*, Earthscan, London

Lipton, M. and Maxwell, S. (1992) *The New Poverty Agenda: An Overview*, Discussion Paper 306, Institute of Development Studies, Brighton

Madanipour, A., Cars, G. and Allen, J. (eds) (1998) *Social Exclusion in European Cities: Processes, Experiences and Responses*, Routledge, London

Malthus, T. ([1798] 2008) *An Essay on the Principle of Population*, Oxford University Press, Oxford

Marcuse, P. (1998) 'Sustainability is not enough', *Environment and Urbanization*, vol 10, no 2, pp103–111

Meadowcroft, J. (1999) 'The Politics of Sustainable Development: Emergent Arenas and Challenges for Political Science', *International Political Science Review*, vol 20, no 2, pp219–237

Meadows, D., Meadows, D., Randers, J. and Behrens III, W. (1972) *The Limits to Growth. A Report for the Club of Rome's Project on the Predicament of Mankind*, Potomac Associates, Washington, DC

Mulgan, G. and Bury, F. (eds) (2006) *Double Devolution: The Renewal of Local Government*, The Young Foundation, London

Office for National Statistics (2001) *Social Capital: A Review of the Literature*, ONS, London

Office of the Deputy Prime Minister (2003) *Sustainable Communities: Building for the Future*, ODPM, London

Office of the Deputy Prime Minister (2004) *Skills for Sustainable Communities: The Egan Review*, www.communities.gov.uk/publications/communities/eganreview, accessed 9 May 2009

O'Riordan (1998) 'Indicators for Sustainable Development', *Proceedings of the European Commission (Environment and Climate Programme) Advanced Study Course 5th–12th July 1997*, Delft, The Netherlands

Pacione, M. (2007) 'Sustainable Urban Development in the UK: Rhetoric or Reality?', *Geography*, vol 92, no 3, pp248–265

Pennington, M. and Rydin, Y. (2000) 'Researching Social Capital in Local Environmental Policy Contexts', *Policy and Politics*, vol 28, no 2, pp233–249

Performance and Innovation Unit (2002) *Social Capital: A Discussion Paper*, Cabinet Office, London

Putnam, R. (2000) *Bowling Alone: The Collapse and Revival of American Community*, Simon and Schuster, London

Putnam, R. (2007) '*E Pluribus Unum:* Diversity and Community in the Twenty-First Century – The 2006 Johan Skytte Prize Lecture', *Scandinavian Political Studies*, vol 30 no 2, pp137–174

Putzel, J. (1998) 'Accounting for the Dark Side of Social Capital: Reading Robert Putnam on Democracy', *Journal of International Development*, vol 9, no 7, pp939–949

Pye, S., Skinner, I., Meyer-Ohlendorf, Leipprand, A., Lucas, K. and Salmons, R. (2008) *Addressing the Social Dimensions of Environmental Policy: A Study on the Linkages Between Environmental and Social Sustainability in Europe*, European Commission, Brussels

Radnitz, S., Wheatley, J. and Zürcher, C. (2009) 'The Origins of Social Capital', *Comparative Political Studies*, vol 42, no 6, pp707–727

Rogers, G. (ed.) (1995) *Social Exclusion: Rhetoric, Reality and Responses*, International Labour Office, Washington, DC

Room, G. (1995) *Beyond the Threshold: The Measurement and Analysis of Social Exclusion*, Policy Press, Bristol

Rosenberg, S. (2007) 'Rethinking Democratic Deliberation', *Polity*, vol 39, no 3, pp335–360

Rydin, Y. (2003) *In Pursuit of Sustainable Development: Rethinking the Planning System*, RICS Foundation, London

Sen, A. (1981) *Poverty and Famines: An Essay on Entitlement and Deprivation*, Clarendon Press, Oxford

Sen, A. (1985) *Commodities and Capabilities*, North-Holland, Amsterdam

Social Exclusion Unit (2001) *National Strategy for Neighbourhood Renewal: Policy Action Team Audit*, Cabinet Office, London

Steuer, N. and Marks, N. (2007) *Local Wellbeing: Can we Measure it?*, Young Foundation, London

Stoker, G. (1998) 'Governance as Theory: Five Propositions', *International Social Science Journal*, vol 50, no 1, pp17–28

Townsend, P. (1993) *The International Analysis of Poverty*, Harvester Wheatsheaf, Hemel Hempstead

Tuxworth, B. (2001) *Local Agenda 21: From the Margins to the Mainstream and out to Sea?*, ENTEC Tomorrow Paper, Town and Country Planning Association, London

United Nations (1992) 'Report of the United Nations Conference on Environment and Development' (Rio Declaration on Environment and Development), 3–14 June 1992, www.un.org/documents/ga/conf151/aconf15126-1annex1.htm, accessed 12 December 2009

United Nations (2009) End Poverty 2015, Millennium Development Goals, 'The Millennium Development Goals Report, 2009', UN, New York, www.un.org/millenniumgoals, accessed 21 December 2009

UN Department of Economic and Social Affairs (2009) Core Publications, Agenda 21 http://www.un.org/esa/dsd/agenda21/, accessed 21 December 2009

UN Statistics Division (2009) *Millennium Development Goals Indicators, Official List of MDG Indicators*, http://mdgs.un.org/unsd/mdg/Host.aspx?Content=Indicators/OfficialList.htm, accessed 21 December 2009

Widmalm, S. (2007) 'The Utility of Bonding Social Capital', *Journal of Civil Society*, vol 1, no 1, pp75–95

Wilkinson, R. and Pickett, K. (2009) *The Spirit Level: Why more Equal Societies Almost Always do Better*, Allen Lane, London

World Commission on Environment and Development (1987) *Our Common Future*, Oxford University Press, Oxford

Wratten, E. (1995) 'Conceptualizing Urban Poverty', *Environment and Urbanization*, vol 7, no 1, pp11–38

Section 1

Communities, Neighbourhoods and the Creation of Locality-based Social Capital

Introduction to the section

In this first section, our chapter authors focus on the micro-spatial scale of urban planning, namely neighbourhoods or communities. The concept of social capital has assumed considerable importance in discussions about social sustainability and Section 1 deals with this in a number of respects.

The first chapter in this section, by Tony Manzi, considers the extent to which the recent UK government policy of creating *mixed communities* can alleviate poverty and stigma, or whether the implementation of policy can in some senses reinforce isolation and undermine the existing social capital of the local community by assisting in the gentrification of neighbourhoods.

In Chapter 3, Nick Bailey examines the way in which third-sector organizations, in particular Community Land Trusts, can help to create more socially sustainable environments and build social capital within communities through *local community asset-building*.

Chapter 4, by Tony Lloyd-Jones and Judith Allen, then considers how such assets might be more effectively managed and retained by communities, presenting both a conceptual and empirical framework for building a neighbourhood-based social capability for *community asset management*. They argue that there needs to be a systematic analysis for conceptualizing capability building in terms of a set of intermittent practical interventions.

In the final chapter of this section, Catalina Gandelsonas offers a critique of the often 'gender- blind' ways in which sustainability policies are developed by policymakers, despite the pivotal role of women in maintaining the local social capital of many communities. In drawing a distinction between social networks and partnerships, she contends that while *women's social networks* tend to disappear when their purpose is achieved, women's partnerships supported by effective frameworks for urban governance frameworks can provide an important model both for transferring social capital and generating more sustainable communities.

Local social capital is a common theme across all four chapters. We present the argument that this is largely based on the value of the social networks that are present within local communities. This stresses the importance of interdependencies and inter-relationships to the effective functioning of communities, because socially sustainable communities rely on informal networks in order to develop a sense of social cohesion. Popularized by the work of Putnam (2000) in the USA, the idea of local social capital emphasizes how social networks can assist in preventing isolation and social marginalisation.

We also suggest that in order to be socially sustainable, the institutional structures and governance arrangements that oversee local communities need to offer the opportunity to increase the local social capital of residents and facilitate wider social networks to create both 'bridging' (within community) and 'bonding' (across community) networks of support. Thus an important dimension to the concept of locality-based social capital is that communities should aim to minimize the adverse consequences of area or 'neighbourhood effects' (Atkinson and Kintrea, 2002, 2004).

These neighbourhood effects are argued to be compounded by the concentration of particular groups within social housing and the policy solution is therefore to achieve a de-concentration of specific households (such as those affected by low income, unemployment, economic inactivity and vulnerability).

Additionally, social sustainability can be measured at the community level by the provision and quality of local infrastructure such as shops, health facilities, parks and meeting places (both indoor and outdoor), pedestrian footways, primary schools, and other community facilities. Consequently, we advocate that policy should be aimed at reducing spatial segregation and providing more socially mixed and 'connected' communities.

The theme of providing adequate social infrastructure and wider access to services and activities is picked up by our authors in the second section of the book. In this section, we focus on what can reasonably be provided and accessed at the very local level of neighbourhoods. In doing so, we recognize that in practice these various layers of spatial geography are intricately interwoven and cannot so easily be divided up in this way. We also note the wide-ranging debates surrounding what precisely constitutes the 'local', 'neighbourhood' or 'community', and also that for some social groups communities of interest are of far greater importance to their social sustainability than geographically-based communities.

References

Atkinson, R. and Kintrea, K. (2002) 'Area Effects: What Do They Mean for British Housing and Regeneration Policy?', *European Journal of Housing Policy*, vol 2, no 2, pp147–166

Atkinson, R. and Kintrea, K. (2004) 'Opportunities and Despair – It's all in There: Practitioner Experiences and Explanations of Area Effects and Life Chances', *Sociology*, vol 38, no 3, pp437–455

Putnam, R. (2000) *Bowling Alone: The Collapse and Revival of American Community*, Simon and Schuster, London

Social Exclusion Unit (2001) *National Strategy for Neighbourhood Renewal: Policy Action Team Audit*, Cabinet Office, London

2

Creating Sustainable Neighbourhoods? The Development and Management of Mixed-Income Communities

Tony Manzi

The key point is that neighbourhoods need ongoing social maintenance as well as physical maintenance. (Camina and Wood, 2009, p478)

Introduction: housing policy and the concept of mixed communities

The concept of social sustainability has been highly influential in the development of contemporary UK housing policy, the objective being most evident through the policy of creating mixed-income communities, involving a combination of 'affordable' properties and market housing. This agenda aims to confront the problem of social exclusion, identified in the reports of policy action teams (PATs) and through initiatives such as the National Strategy for Neighbourhood Renewal (Social Exclusion Unit, 1998, 2001). There have been two main policy strands: first, to deconcentrate poverty; and second, to provide more effective shaping of personal behaviour (including intensive housing management and the policing of housing estates). Within this framework, development and housing management play a central role in shaping new approaches to urban governance.

This chapter develops three main themes that have emerged from research into the practice of creating and sustaining mixed-income communities: managing the allocation process; confronting fears of antisocial behaviour; and facilitating gentrification. Based on three case studies, the research illustrates different aspects of the development process and management task. While each study possesses unique features relating to design, the stage of development, size of development and socio-economic profiles, there are a number of common factors with relevance to contemporary development and housing management practice. These are categorized as: *limiting neighbourhood effects*, *developing social capital* and *engendering respect*. The focus is both on the initial development process and longer-term management implications.

Limiting neighbourhood effects

As noted above (see Introduction, p17) the first main argument for the development of mixed-income communities is to prevent the adverse consequences of area or 'neighbourhood effects' (Atkinson and Kintrea, 2002). This concept is implicit in government statements that 'nobody should be disadvantaged by the area in which they live' (Social Exclusion Unit, 2001), ensuring that residents should not suffer locational disadvantages in addition to other material forms of social deprivation. These neighbourhood effects are related to the concentration of particular groups within social housing and consequently, policy has been aimed at minimizing spatial segregation and ensuring the prevention of high concentrations of multiply deprived households. However, Atkinson and Kintrea (2002) have argued that the evidence of these neighbourhood effects is at best mixed and relies on an intuitive rather than explicit evidence base (Atkinson, 2006), whilst others (e.g. Cheshire, 2007) have been still more critical, describing the policy as 'essentially belief-based', mainly treating symptoms (tenure mix) rather than addressing the root causes of poverty and marginalization.

Developing social capital

A second approach argues that mixed-income communities offer the opportunity to increase the *social capital* of residents within disadvantaged areas. This is closely related to the neighbourhood effects thesis, but is linked to facilitating wider social networks, creating both 'bridging' (within community) and 'bonding' (across community) networks of support. Hence, government-funded research studies (e.g. Chanan, 2003) have strongly emphasized the importance of the collectivist benefits of participation and their potential for capacity building of residents. According to this argument, social mixing provides appropriate role models and opportunities for community leadership, as well as informal contacts, which can produce significant community benefits.

Related to the notion of social capital is the assumption that social policy should be aimed at achieving social cohesion, particularly in relation to reducing concentrations of minority ethnic groups in specific locations. The 'Cantle Report' (Home Office, 2001), following urban disturbances in Oldham and Bradford, identified problems within specific urban communities, where people led 'parallel lives', containing highly segregated neighbourhoods; residents rarely encountered different ethnic groups either during their day (e.g. at school and at work) or amongst a wider social circle.

The above are primarily collectivist arguments, focusing on the importance of social networks, the linkages between and among communities and groups, and how improvement can be made by mixing different incomes, cultures and interests. They are concerned with reducing social exclusion (whether voluntary or otherwise), understood as social isolation.

Engendering respect

A third and more individualistic explanation is related to the role of housing management, individual responsibility, attitudes and behaviour. This approach has been most evident in policies under the heading of what was termed the Government's 'respect' agenda, which has been an important influence in shaping community and neighbourhood management (CLG, 2007). This strand of thinking has two parts. One is a resident-involvement strategy, to empower neighbourhoods (based on social capital arguments), and the second is a more authoritarian social control function. The approach reflects a 'communitarian' emphasis on rights and responsibilities (Etzioni, 2004) emphasizing social obligations and with neighbourhood management used as an important tool in achieving this goal. Statements from the former prime minister (Tony Blair) about a 'society of responsibility', wherein 'the decent law-abiding majority are in charge; where those that play by the rules do well; and those that don't, get punished' (Blair, 2004), illustrated this theme in neighbourhood management.

Social landlords have embraced this communitarian approach to housing policy, evident in the application of both sanctions and rewards to encourage improvements in resident behaviour. Examples include the Irwell Valley Gold Standard scheme, which offered incentives (such as rent reductions, improved repair services, vouchers, priority transfers and 'goodbye payments'), as well as more punitive measures (such as introductory, demoted tenancies and loss of tenancy rights) for poor behaviour (see Lupton et al, 2003; Foster, 2007).

Mixed-community policies

The policy of mixed communities draws heavily on lessons learned from abroad, in particular the USA, notably the Hope VI initiative of the early 1990s (Cisneros and Engdahl, 2009). Central government in the UK has applied a variety of policy mechanisms to meet this objective and the Local Government White Paper (2006) recommends that local authorities act as strategic enablers and 'place-shapers', applying land-use planning mechanisms to achieve 'sustainable' outcomes, understood as achieving socially, economically and culturally mixed communities.

The Government's Planning Policy Statement 3 (PPS3), issued in 2006, advocated mixed-income sustainable communities, with the specific objective that the planning system should deliver 'a mix of housing, both market and affordable, particularly in terms of tenure and price, to support a wide variety of households in all areas, both urban and rural' (CLG, 2006, p6). However, the agenda of mixed communities includes a diverse set of ambitions:

> Mixed communities contribute to the promotion of choice and equality, avoiding concentrations of deprivation and help address social exclusion and community cohesion. (Housing Corporation, 2006, p9)

The policy therefore contained a variety of aspirations, and government has mainly relied on a private sector-driven approach, with less reliance on public agencies to develop new housing estates; instead, private developers were required to include a proportion of affordable housing on new schemes (under section 106 of the Town and Country Planning Act 1990). These schemes were developed within wider strategies to encourage resident involvement, to promote partnership working and ultimately improve the quality of life or 'liveability' of neighbourhoods. This approach was supported by a comprehensive review into the objectives and goals of housing policy (Hills, 2007), which advocated a strong commitment to mixed-income neighbourhoods.

The range of policy objectives contained within the mixed-communities agenda rests on four different although related assumptions about the benefits that mixed communities can offer. According to Joseph et al (2007), these assumptions can be categorized on the basis of: *social network theory*, which contends that (formal and informal) contact reduces social isolation and provides access to resources; ideas about *social control*, which argue that peer-group pressure will lead to conformity to social norms; concepts of *culture*, which promote behavioural change and increase self-worth; and the *political economy of place*, which contends that higher-income residents will generate improved market demand and political pressure.

However, despite a strong commitment to 'evidence-based' policy, as noted above there has been little clear evidence that mixed communities result in such a positive contribution to social sustainability. This chapter therefore considers how this understanding of social sustainability has been implemented through practices aimed at developing and managing mixed communities in the case study neighbourhoods.

The case studies and mixed-income communities

This study was based on research initially undertaken for the Joseph Rowntree Foundation and published as two good practice guides (Bailey et al, 2006,

2007). The research involved a number of case studies in England and Scotland, and this chapter draws in particular upon three of these: situated in London, the south-east of England and Edinburgh, Scotland.

The first case study (in inner London) involved a former local authority estate, notorious for a multiplicity of problems; the neighbourhood has undergone extensive regeneration to incorporate a housing association consortium arrangement, including about 30 per cent owner occupation. The scheme is widely regarded as having been successful in countering the negative reputation of the area.

The second study (in the south-east of England) involved a new-build programme, wherein a former Ministry of Defence site has been transformed into an attractive 'urban village', with high-quality landscaping. The scheme was developed and managed by a private developer with a 27.5 per cent affordable-housing component.

The third study involved a regeneration programme on the outskirts of Edinburgh. This neighbourhood is primarily local authority-owned (with 25 per cent owner occupation) and is about to undergo an extensive regeneration programme managed by a private development company. The scheme is at an initial planning stage and the intention is to reverse the tenure profile to ensure about 25 per cent affordable housing and 75 per cent owner occupation.

The regeneration initiatives have all been aimed at countering locational disadvantages associated with neighbourhoods containing high levels of multiple deprivation. Policy is aimed at facilitating low-income residents to mix effectively with more affluent groups to 'deconcentrate' pockets of poverty and the assumption is that this social mix will enable local economies to become more sustainable; local facilities, services and businesses should be of a higher quality and neighbourhoods will become less isolated and more permeable. The following sections consider how these strategies have taken three main forms: first, through promoting policies to allocate social housing; second, in implementing initiatives to prevent antisocial behaviour; and, finally using processes to facilitate neighbourhood gentrification.

Methodology

Using mainly qualitative data, the research incorporated a range of detailed interviews with key stakeholders, including local politicians, local government officers, staff working for registered social landlords (RSLs), architects, private developers and residents. Additional stakeholder interviews were conducted with representatives from the Housing Corporation and the Office of the Deputy Prime Minister (as they were then called), as well as the National Housing Federation (NHF). A total of 20 interviews were conducted. While the initial purpose of the research was to discover good practice, later interviews were designed to provide a detailed explanation of the justifications for developing mixed-income communities and gain an awareness of the key constraints and specific development and management issues facing stakeholders. The research interviews and case study analysis were mainly conducted between 2005 and 2007.

Managing the allocation process

The issue of lettings, local authority nominations and allocations policy was seen as central to the success of mixed-income neighbourhoods in avoiding concentrations of deprivation. As one respondent commented:

> We need to find in any new development a better balance between meeting the needs of the most vulnerable with meeting a wider spectrum of need... we are looking at local lettings approaches so you don't over-concentrate a huge number of children in developments or a huge number of people who have care and support needs when there might not be resources to meet that need. (Interview, RSL manager)

This social balance was in part interpreted as an attempt to maximize the number of economically active households on new developments. For one RSL, this meant a restrictive approach about who they chose to house:

> We still have an incomes policy... Normally it is an upper level to see if people are earning too much, but at the other end we can use the information to offer properties to people who are working. ...Our aim will be to have 50 per cent of people who are working. (Interview, RSL manager)

This objective seemed to apply most strongly to what were considered to be 'flagship' new developments, where design innovations could be presented alongside management initiatives; these schemes were demonstrated to visitors as examples of organizational success. For example:

> We have nomination agreements ... that set out why we can refuse applicants (e.g. rent arrears or previous antisocial behaviour). That applies particularly to our high-profile schemes. (Interview, RSL manager)

Such a system contradicted basic principles of allocation on the basis of need and discriminated against lower income groups. These policies were justified on the basis that previous approaches, which relied solely on accepting local authority 'nominations', had produced unbalanced and marginalized communities. In addition, discrimination was not limited to income levels, with applicants' criminal records taken into account in making allocation decisions:

> I think during the redevelopment process some canny decisions were taken, about who might live there. There was quite a bit of exporting people who might be problematic. (Interview, RSL manager)

Hence, one manager commented: 'Housing need is our main criteria, but we do ask for background and we will take that into account.'

RSLs were also keen to establish their autonomy, despite a rhetoric of partnership; thus one manager commented on nomination agreements between the local authority and the RSL:

> If we have got concerns we will go back to the council and say this person is not suitable. We will either reject them or give them an opportunity to withdraw and then nominate somebody else... We prefer [the local authority] to withdraw the nominations. (Interview, RSL manager)

This comment illustrated how certain RSLs were able to dictate the terms of the nomination agreement that thereby marginalize local authorities. These kinds of local lettings policies encapsulated the conflicts between the local authority objective of reducing their waiting lists and the RSL priority of developing sustainable communities. As the RSLs saw it:

> We have taken a long-term approach; these people have got to live on our estates for the next 10 or 20 years. So we will fight our corner and ultimately the decision is with us. We are an independent organization (independent of the council) and we will make that decision for the best of the community. (Interview, RSL manager)

This comment illustrated how the commitment to social sustainability carried the implicit commitment to the social control of neighbourhoods. This latter objective was treated as the main priority for social landlords, taking precedence over the requirement to provide accommodation for those in housing need. These practices reflected policies in other countries; evidence from the USA had indicated that mixed-income developments are in practice available to very few low-income households and almost certainly exclude the most vulnerable and difficult to house (Popkin et al, 2000). Initial findings appear to indicate that this also may apply to the British context; applying a strategy of 'balance through exclusion' (Cole and Goodchild, 2000, p357) and raising questions about the future role of social housing in meeting need.

Preventing antisocial behaviour

The attention devoted to housing management is an indication of the way in which policy has shifted towards a greater focus on individual behaviour and how to control attitudes, values and a 'responsibilisation' of resident groups (Flint, J., 2006). This government strategy has been enthusiastically advanced at a central government level, through the commissioning of a range of legislation to prevent antisocial behaviour and codes of conduct, such as the 'respect' agenda (Home Office, 2006). The implementation of management standards through Local Area Agreements (Home Office, 2007) also reflects the priority given to preventing and tackling neighbourhood 'low-level' crime and antisocial behaviour.

The management of antisocial behaviour is of particular pertinence within mixed-income communities, where intensive management strategies have been adopted, in large part to reassure private developers and purchasers that social rented tenancies would be effectively controlled: 'Developers will always take the view that [building defects] are down to tenant abuse' (interview, RSL manager). Assumptions made by private sector stakeholders about social rented-sector tenants tended to be both negative and stereotyped:

> They [private developers] want to know how quickly we are going to evict people... They want to be assured that our residents will not run riot. (Interview, RSL manager)

Exclusionary allocation policies were therefore welcomed by private developers as 'I am thinking of my sales values.' (interview, private developer). Private developers therefore exerted considerable pressure on social landlords to take tough measures to limit antisocial behaviour:

> The last thing I can afford is potential purchasers coming up when I have 200 homes for sale, and first thing they see is a lot of kids getting up to no good, cars on bricks and all the rest of it really. They are just going to turn around and go away. (Interview, private developer)

Effective policies and procedures to manage antisocial behaviour were seen as a priority in all the case study neighbourhoods (although the actual scale of the problem varied widely). Therefore, the need to demonstrate landlords could effectively control their residents was regarded as being of paramount importance.

This agenda of social control was often couched within a language of developing trust, which entailed a combination of strong reactive measures and longer-term proactive approaches. Such measures were taken to reassure both private and public sector residents that action against perpetrators would be taken promptly and appropriately. However, within one of the case study areas, the problem was within the community itself:

> I can't continue to come to meetings and say the same things without them making that step to try and assist us. We send dozens of hand-delivered letters with stamped addressed envelopes, we explain that we will appear in court on their behalf but we need them to make the first step. (Interview, local authority officer)

This comment revealed how landlords and statutory agencies lacked trust within the community; residents were seen as reluctant to give evidence due to what was described as a 'no-grass policy' in the neighbourhood. Officers expressed exasperation at the lack of cooperation from the community, to take responsibility for reporting crimes, for giving evidence and for acting as responsible role models for younger members. This lack of responsibility was largely seen as applicable to local authority tenants and the regeneration programme was therefore designed to disperse tenants and incorporate them amongst more 'responsible' owner-occupier groups.

The emphasis of traditional housing management on rights had by the 21st century changed to one of duties and responsibilities. It is this notion of the active citizen that is playing a central role in contemporary political discourse (shared by politicians on all sides of the political spectrum). Whilst there had been uncertainty about the future of the respect agenda (as it became incorporated within the Youth Task Force in the Department for Children and Families), the drive to tackle antisocial behaviour has remained a priority for social landlords within a wider 'neighbourhood management' (Taylor, 2000) agenda. Landlords were encouraged to anticipate problems before they appeared and this represented a further constraint on integrating groups seen as 'problematic', with the potential for committing antisocial behaviour (such as 'vulnerable' residents and 'chaotic' households). This process also assisted in a wider process of ensuring neighbourhood gentrification.

Facilitating the gentrification of neighbourhoods

As Lees (2003) has argued, there has been little interaction between geographers' concerns with gentrification and the implications of a mixed-income agenda. Gentrification is understood to involve a combination of middle-class colonization and working-class displacement. It is difficult to provide firm evidence that working-class communities are being deliberately excluded from new mixed-income community developments. However, there are indications that the focus for policymakers is to provide opportunities for new middle-class gentrifiers at the expense of existing communities (e.g. through the allocation process and providing tougher conditions for social housing residence). At the same time, the mixed-income agenda stresses the importance awarded to providing accommodation to those already in work. As a senior member of staff at the Housing Corporation commented:

> It is by no means automatic that a high proportion of economically inactive tenants will result in tension but it is more likely that you will have increased incidents of antisocial behaviour. It becomes in a sense a self-fulfilling prophecy. It doesn't become a destination of choice so you don't get wealth creation and you don't get the same level of social responsibility. (Interview, Housing Corporation)

An explicit linkage between economic activity and social responsibility was echoed in the suggestion from a former housing minister that tenancies could be withdrawn from those unwilling to take up employment opportunities: 'Social housing should be based around the principle of something for something' (Flint, C., 2008).

A crucial aspect of the mixed communities' agenda is the need to generate economic activity, in order that localities can become 'neighbourhoods of choice rather than neighbourhoods of last resort' (interview, Housing Corporation). These should be areas where private sector businesses would be encouraged to invest and therefore other benefits of economic sustainability could follow. Masterplans were therefore aimed at providing a range of services, including improvements to schooling, health and retail activities.

However, while clear benefits were evident from the opportunities offered by middle-class investment, there were also costs for neighbourhoods. One former Labour councillor, who had been instrumental in establishing one of the schemes, explained that he had ambivalent feelings towards changes within the neighbourhood. On the one hand regeneration had enabled investment, employment opportunities and the introduction of more affluent households. On the other hand:

> I wrote my own political demise because I changed the characteristics of the area to the point where I could never get elected again. (Interview, chair of Community Development Trust)

This quote illustrated the more complex neighbourhood dynamics and community relations resulting from the regeneration process. Many older and longer-term residents perceived a loss of community life: 'Previously they were all in it together' (interview, architect). As residents perceived it:

> There are changes here, there is gentrification ... [the area] has changed quite dramatically by the number of people that have been brought in... you're bringing wealth into an area that didn't have wealth. (Interview, resident)

This injection of wealth provided both opportunities and costs; gentrification attracts higher-income residents, but also leads to higher house prices and the exclusion of lower-income home buyers. As Meen et al (2005) have shown, the attention to economic segregation represents the most fundamental determinant of whether mixed communities can work. Without an underlying commitment to economic regeneration in order to support infrastructure and core services, it is highly unlikely such communities will be sustainable.

Conclusion

This chapter has demonstrated how the key justifications for social sustainability through income mix have been applied and their relevance for housing practice. Both new and existing developments have attempted to secure a sense of anonymity through imposing neighbourhood benefits at the same time as minimizing the segregation associated with mono-tenure developments, where tenure is normally used as a proxy for income in the absence of other indicators. However, for most residents the key determining factor is the level of economic activity in contrast to other social factors and the ability to support infrastructure and core services; the key problems arise from a lack of skills and position within an increasingly competitive global labour market rather than in a local area per se (Kleinman, 2000; Meen et al, 2005). The central issue is whether economic activity is to be improved by simply moving higher-income residents into existing areas rather than devoting resources to existing residents to develop their skills and abilities and gain employment opportunities.

The development of social capital has been strongly advocated by policymakers and is evident in initiatives to encourage participation and partnership. While landlords may strongly advocate the notion of resident empowerment, evidence at ground level from practitioners is that other priorities are likely to take precedence. There may be rhetorical commitment, but there remain considerable barriers to devolving power and autonomy and encouraging truly collaborative working practices. The commitment to longer-term social sustainability is therefore often lost in the prioritization of effective management.

The result has been the application of allocation policies premised not on housing need, but on the requirement to minimize management difficulties, in particular antisocial behaviour.

The concept of engendering 'respect' appears to echo resident (and developer) concerns about low-level antisocial behaviour. However, a neo-liberal, individualistic and moralistic rhetoric contrasts with much of the rhetoric of participation and empowerment. Nevertheless, this agenda illustrates the challenges of managing and developing mixed-income communities, and how this is shaping the nature of housing management influenced by a communitarian emphasis on individual duty and responsibility. These processes reflect the development of a more exclusionary approach to social policy, reflected in allocation processes; what Cochrane (2007) terms an 'active social policy' that constructs new forms of citizenship (Raco, 2007, p16).

The case studies indicate how contemporary housing management and development has adopted exclusionary and individualistic policies to address the challenges of mixed-income communities. It is clear that while new approaches to managing mixed-income communities have attempted to minimize the path dependencies associated with poor design, lack of planning and an absence of resident voices, the way that this issue is being addressed takes very different forms. Mixed communities are not a panacea; the policy may simply contribute to a form of state-sponsored gentrification rather than a longer-term commitment to improving the economic infrastructure and providing effective resources to develop services and facilities within low-income neighbourhoods.

The response to the problems associated with the social rented sector has been to move towards the creation of mixed communities, where concentrations of deprivation are more dispersed. However, as this chapter has shown, the commitment to social sustainability has been concerned not so much with tackling poverty as with making it less noticeable. In this way social sustainability has been defined by the term 'liveability', understood mainly as increasing prosperity and dispersing poverty. Rather than a policy designed to tackle marginalization and social exclusion, the mixed income agenda constitutes a somewhat static contribution to social sustainability within a dynamic environment of neighbourhood change.

References

Atkinson, R. (2006) *Neighbourhoods and the Impacts of Social Mix: Crime, Tenure Diversification and Assisted Mobility*, Housing and Community Research Unit, paper 1, University of Tasmania, Tasmania

Atkinson, R. and Kintrea, K. (2002) 'Area effects: What do they mean for British housing and regeneration policy?', *European Journal of Housing Policy*, vol 2, no 2, pp147–166

Bailey, N., Haworth, A., Manzi, T., Roberts, M. and Paranagamage, P. (2006) *Creating and Sustaining Mixed Income Communities: A Good Practice Guide*, Joseph Rowntree Foundation, York

Bailey, N., Haworth, A., Manzi, T. and Roberts, M. (2007) *Creating and Sustaining Mixed Income Communities in Scotland: A Good Practice Guide*, Joseph Rowntree Foundation, York

Blair, T. (2004) 'Speech on the launch of the five-year strategy on crime', 19 July, www.number10.gov.uk/output/Page6129.asp, accessed 11 May 2007

Camina, M. and Wood, M. (2009) 'Parallel lives: Towards a greater understanding of what mixed communities can offer', *Urban Studies*, vol 46, no 2, pp459–480

Chanan, G. (2003) *Searching for Solid Foundations: Community Involvement and Urban Policy*, ODPM, London

Cheshire, P. (2007) *Segregated Neighbourhoods and Mixed Communities: A Critical Analysis*, Joseph Rowntree Foundation, York

Cisneros, H. and Engdahl, L. (2009) *From Despair to Hope: Hope VI and the Transformation of America's Public Housing*, Brookings Institute, Washington, DC

Cochrane, A. (2007) *Understanding Urban Policy: A Critical Approach*, Blackwell Publishing, Oxford

Cole, I. and Goodchild, B. (2001) 'Social mix and the balanced community in British housing policy – a tale of two epochs', *GeoJournal*, 51, pp351–360

Communities and Local Government (2006) *Planning Policy Statement 3 (PPS3): Housing*, The Stationery Office, London

Communities and Local Government (2007) *The Respect Standard for Housing Management: A Guide for Landlords*, CLG Publications, London

Etzioni, A. (2004) *The Common Good*, Polity Press, Cambridge

Flint, C. (2008) 'Address to the Fabian society conference', 5 February, www.communities.gov.uk/speeches/corporate/fabiansocietyaddress, accessed 11 July 2008

Flint, J. (2006) 'Housing and the new governance of conduct', in Flint, J. (ed.) *Housing, Urban Governance and Anti-Social Behaviour*, Policy Press, Bristol, pp19–37

Foster, A. (ed.) (2007) *Social Housing: Breaking New Ground*, Smith Institute, London

Hills, J. (2007) *Ends and Means: The Future Roles of Social Housing*, CASE Report 34, London School of Economics and Political Science, London

Home Office (2001) *Community Cohesion: A Report of the Independent Review Team, Chaired by Ted Cantle*, Home Office, London

Home Office (2006) 'Tackling Antisocial Behaviour and Its Causes', www.respect.gov.uk, accessed 12 July 2007

Home Office (2007) *The Respect Handbook: A Guide for Local Services*, Home Office, London

Housing Corporation (2006) *Neighbourhood and Communities*, Housing Corporation, London

Joseph, M., Chaskin, R. and Webber, H. (2007) 'The theoretical basis for addressing poverty through mixed-income development', *Urban Affairs Review*, vol 42, no 3, pp1–41

Kleinman, M. (2000) 'Include me out? The new politics of place and poverty', *Policy Studies*, vol 21, no 1, pp 49–61

Lees, L. (2003) 'Visions of "urban renaissance": The Urban Task Force Report and the Urban White Paper', in Imrie, R. and Raco, M. (eds) *Urban Renaissance? New Labour, Community and Urban Policy*, The Policy Press, Bristol

Lupton, M., Hale, J. and Springings, N. (2003) *Incentives and Beyond? The Transferability of the Irwell Valley Gold Service to Other Social Landlords*, ODPM, London

Meen, G., Gibb, K., Goody, J., McGrath, T. and McKinnon, J. (2005) *Economic Segregation in England: Causes, Consequences and Policy*, The Policy Press/JRF, London

Popkin, S., Burron, L., Levy, D. and Cunningham, M. (2000) 'The Gautreaux legacy: What might mixed-income and dispersal strategies mean for the poorest public housing tenants?', *Housing Policy Debate,* vol 11, no 4, pp 911–942

Raco, M. (2007) *Building Sustainable Communities: Spatial Policy and Labour Mobility in Post-War Britain*, Policy Press, Bristol

Social Exclusion Unit (1998) *Bringing Britain Together: A National Strategy for Neighbourhood Renewal, Cm4045*, The Stationery Office, London

Social Exclusion Unit (2001) *A New Commitment to Neighbourhood Renewal: National Strategy Action Plan*, Cabinet Office, London

Taylor, M. (2000) *Top Down Meets Bottom Up: Neighbourhood Management*, Joseph Rowntree Foundation, York

3

Building Sustainable Communities from the Grassroots: How Community Land Trusts Can Create Social Sustainability

Nick Bailey

Introduction

The intention to build 'sustainable communities' has been on the political agenda at least since 2003 (ODPM, 2003), but there is a continuing debate about how this strategy can best be achieved. For at least a decade, the rate of construction of new homes has been insufficient to meet the level of need, particularly of affordable housing, in both urban and rural areas. In response, central government is determined to increase the rate of construction of all forms of tenure and explore new forms of delivery through the formation of collaborative arrangements and by creating a larger role for community-based approaches, including development trusts, housing associations and, in particular, Community Land Trusts (CLTs). CLTs engage local communities in the production of housing to meet local needs and include a number of organizational and financial features to ensure 'sustainability' in perpetuity. A recent definition of CLTs is that they are:

> Not for profit organizations which allow the community and other stakeholders to take control of and manage assets. They are a flexible concept taking many different legal structures and forms, but they generally have a number of key principles in common. They are a way of acquiring land and property and holding them for the benefit of the community usually for the provision of affordable housing but also affordable workspace and the provision of community facilities and green spaces. (Northern Housing Consortium, 2007, p17)

The Housing White Paper (Department of Communities and Local Government, 2007) set an ambitious target of an additional 240,000 homes per year and three million new homes to be constructed by 2020. The scale of the challenge is substantial because not only must the production of new housing

be increased, but there is also a requirement to create well-designed developments with the full range of services and infrastructure where people want to
live. In addition, new environmental standards are being introduced to reduce
energy consumption, increase water conservation and achieve zero carbon emissions by 2016 (CLG, 2006).

The strategy involves the creation of a range of local delivery vehicles, such
as urban development corporations, local housing companies and the agencies
formed after the merger in 2008 of the Housing Corporation and English
Partnerships – the Homes and Communities Agency (HCA) and Tenant Services
Authority (TSA) for England. Part of the remit of these organizations will be to
deliver integrated communities that are attractive places to live, meet the requirements of all sections of the community according to age, income, household size
and ethnic composition, and achieve high environmental standards.

Affordability is a particularly serious issue, because the average house price is
now more than £210,000, which is over eight times the average salary (CLG, 2007,
p10). Thus, the Government plans to spend £8 billion on at least 70,000 additional
affordable homes a year by 2010–11. Of these, at least 45,000 will be for social
renting and the remainder for shared ownership and shared equity schemes.
A variety of innovative schemes involving local authorities, the private sector,
housing associations and community-based initiatives are being evaluated as
mechanisms to deliver more affordable housing as part of mixed-community
developments. Thus, there is an implicit recognition that a series of top-down policies to address disadvantaged neighbourhoods has not worked (Kintrea, 2007).

One such initiative discussed in the Green Paper is the CLT, which is the
subject of this chapter. CLTs have a long antecedence stretching back to the
early New Town movement, but it is only recently that new models have begun
to emerge. They provide opportunities for local communities to acquire land
and other assets, often at below-market value, in order to provide new forms of
affordable housing and community facilities to meet local needs. They also
ensure that the element of affordability is retained for the long term, that local
communities create social capital and that environmental quality is maintained.

In essence, CLTs provide an opportunity to regenerate urban and rural communities from the bottom up. They build on local tacit knowledge of local
community needs, engage local communities in developing innovative approaches
and experiment with new forms of community governance in order to create genuinely sustainable solutions – in social, financial and environmental terms.

This chapter will examine the potential contribution of CLTs in bridging
the 'affordability gap' and creating sustainable mixed communities. Section 79
of the Housing and Regeneration Act of 2008 created a new definition of CLTs,
and a consultation paper (CLG, 2008) sought advice from interested parties
about how they might be further developed and supported. To date, despite
increased political support, they have faced serious challenges in getting started.

The next section will provide a brief discussion of the historical origins of CLTs. The third section will explore the organizational, financial and legal dimensions of CLTs as a vehicle for achieving sustainability. This will be followed by a review of the progress achieved in some recent examples in England and an examination of some of the challenges they face. Finally, the conclusions will discuss the potential contribution of CLTs to the broader policy context and identify how far they add to our understanding of sustainability.

Early forms of CLT

The origins of CLTs emerged over several centuries in a variety of protest movements against the capitalist exploitation of land for private gain. They can be traced back to the founding of the cooperative movement in the 18th century, the Chartist land reform movement, the establishment of the early New Towns and developments by industrialists such as Richard Cadbury and Joseph Rowntree.

Robert Owen became the manager of a large cotton mill in Manchester in 1790. After repeated attempts to persuade Parliament to pass Factory Acts to cut working hours and reduce child labour, he planned a series of villages based on mutual cooperation. In developing these ideas, he produced a plan for cooperative villages in the county of Lanark and persuaded philanthropists such as Archibald Hamilton to underwrite these. The first of these was at Orbiston near Glasgow and perhaps the best known is New Lanark, which was run on a cooperative basis. These ideas were taken up in the mid-19th century by the Chartist land reform movement, which developed estates of smallholdings in several counties.

As the problems of industrialization and urban growth became more apparent in the 19th century, new solutions were advocated to improve living conditions and protect the environment. In 1865 the Commons Preservation Society was formed to protect common land under threat from urban development, and one of the protagonists, Octavia Hill, went on to form the National Trust. John Ruskin also advocated the 'trusteeship company' – 'a distinctive form of social enterprise whose purpose as a business was not profit but to secure "enduring community benefit" for local people' (Conaty, 2007). These ideas were later taken up by industrialists such as William Lever in Port Sunlight, Cadbury in Birmingham and Rowntree in York. Many of these initiatives are still in place today and are frequently referred to as models for the management of sustainable, mixed communities. The extent to which the New Towns movement drew on previous urban experiments has been discussed in detail elsewhere (MacFayden, 1970; Hall, 1994). Early examples, such as Letchworth, were planned along cooperative lines, although from the 1940s onwards the state gained powers to acquire and develop land for itself and alternative approaches largely receded into the background.

In the last decade there has been a resurgence of community-based initiatives, many of which are achieving legal status and entering into the realm of public policy. In Scotland, land reform was a major plank of the newly established Scottish Parliament. The Community Land Unit (CLU) was set up in 1997 within the Highlands and Islands Enterprise Board to provide technical assistance, and in 2003 the Land Reform (Scotland) Act provided a legal framework for community acquisitions and buy-outs. A Scottish Land Fund of about £6 million is administered by the CLU and is available to all rural communities in Scotland of less than 10,000 members. Non-profit organizations can register an interest in land and, when it comes up for sale, they have six months to consult, arrange an independent valuation, conduct a community ballot, prepare a business case and raise the purchase money (Conaty, 2007). Notable examples include the Isle of Eigg Trust, the Abriachan Forest Trust and the Knoydart Foundation.

In the USA, CLTs have expanded rapidly since the 1960s. In 2005 about 200 CLTs managed 8000 affordable homes, although numbers have increased significantly since then. They are recognized for funding purposes by the federal government and are also eligible for tax-exempt, charitable status. The Institute for Community Economics provides technical support and operates a revolving fund. The principle underlying the US model is that the land is held in trust by the CLT for present and future generations, while the homeowner would have possession of the building.

An amendment to the National Affordable Housing Act (42USC 12773) sets out a legal definition of CLTs. Essentially, they should have a corporate membership open to all residents of a defined area and have a board with a majority of elected members and equal proportions of lessees, corporate members who are not lessees, and others as defined by the organization's by-laws (Conaty, 2007). By separating ownership of the land from that of the structures on it and by retaining first option to repurchase, the affordability of the housing can be secured forever.

A good example of CLTs in the USA is the Champlain Housing Trust. This was formed in 1984 by the City of Burlington in Vermont to provide low-cost housing in three counties. It has a portfolio of 1400 rental apartments, 400 single-family residences and six cooperatives with 115 homes (see Champlain Housing Trust, 2006).

The organizational, legal and financial considerations

In England the Housing and Regeneration Act 2008 created a legal definition of a CLT so that they can now register with the social housing regulator, the

Tenant Services Authority (TSA). In particular, they need to ensure that any increase in land values over time is 'locked' into the trust, while ensuring that the housing provided continues to be available to those who qualify for afford-able housing. Trusts also need to be able to acquire the resources necessary on advantageous terms in order to become operational. This section begins by con-sidering how CLTs can acquire the assets and then explores the legal and operational models available for them to pursue their objectives.

Government policy has attempted to meet the need for affordable housing by providing social-housing grants to housing associations to build social hous-ing for rent. Acute shortages have been experienced, particularly in London and the south-east of England, and more recently additional assistance has been pro-vided through HomeBuy and related schemes to bridge the 'affordability gap'. In 2005 a new shared-equity scheme was introduced, but this will only fund an estimated 4000 households a year.

Although in theory it is possible for housing associations to set up CLTs, in practice there are few incentives for them to do so. For a variety of financial reasons, they tend to favour the development of sites for their own programmes, which can then be used to borrow further funding on commercial terms. CLTs usually rely on acquisition through the planning system, such as through Section 106 agreements or as 'exception' sites in rural areas. However, negotiating land acquisition and ensuring that subsequent planning permission will be forth-coming require a detailed understanding of the planning process. In urban areas, it may be possible to transfer social housing to CLTs within New Deal for Communities areas or under other asset-transfer arrangements. In two of the examples discussed later, CLTs have been able to negotiate transfers of the site of a former hospital in the ownership of English Partnerships and of a small farm from a county council.

As community-based and often charitable organizations, CLTs will also be able to access additional sources of public sector funding to facilitate the devel-opment process. Much depends on the location of the CLT as to the range of European Union (EU), national, regional and local funding that may be on offer. Those CLTs in areas undergoing regeneration and with high levels of unemployment and poor housing will be in the best position to access these funds.

CLTs have a number of options as far as their constitution is concerned. Most will want to register as charities with the Charity Commission as this con-fers a number of financial and tax benefits, particularly in receiving grants from charitable foundations. In addition to charitable status, most CLTs will choose one of three forms of incorporation:

- A company limited by guarantee: The company is registered and a number of elected or selected directors form a management committee that meets and controls the company through general meetings. There are no share-holders and members are protected to any liability by the guarantee usually to the value of £1. Annual accounts have to be submitted and are publicly available at Companies House.

- An Industrial and Provident Society: Under a variety of legislation, organizations can register with the Financial Services Authority as a community benefit society or a cooperative. The former is set up to benefit the wider community in accordance with the objectives in its rules, while the latter trades or provides services for the benefit of its members. They are similar to companies limited by guarantee in that they do not distribute profits, the liability of members is limited and they have corporate status. A model promoted by CDS Co-operatives is to register the CLT, which owns the land, as a community benefit society separate from the cooperative, which owns the homes on the land: 'The land is held by the CLT for the benefit of the community, while the homes built on it are managed by the cooperative for the benefit of members' (CFS, 2007a, p29).

- A Community Interest Company: CICs were devised to provide a legal structure for social enterprises and are registered by the CIC regulator. Their structure is similar to that of a limited liability company and board members can be paid, but are subject to narrower criteria of working in the interest of the community. CICs can engage in competitive trading, but must be able to convince the regulator that they are operating in the 'interests of the community'. Their administrative and accounting arrangements are similar to those of a conventional limited company.

The various options outlined above confer different advantages and opportunities for emergent CLTs and each needs to be carefully evaluated. Detailed guidance from Community Finance Solutions (CFS, 2007a) recommends that legal advice is sought in deciding which option to choose.

At the heart of the CLT model is the financial mechanism by which ownership of the land is separated from the ownership and management of the property on it. Integral to this is the ability to ensure that any benefits of 'affordability' are passed on to successive occupants of the property. The question of what qualifies as 'affordable' housing depends very much on its location and levels of wages and salaries in the area. The normal assumption is that housing costs should not exceed a third of household income. In many areas, intermediate market housing, where residents are able to buy a proportion of the value of their home and pay rent on the remainder through a variety of HomeBuy schemes, has become popular. This is particularly relevant to 'key workers' (often young professionals in public sector employment) on relatively low salaries in high-value areas.

To achieve these objectives, there are a number of options open to the CLT:

1 'Tenancy-plus' model.
2 Rent-to-purchase model.
3 Equity-purchase model.

In the tenancy-plus model, the CLT builds and finances the homes and keeps the freehold ownership of the property. Residents are offered assured shorthold tenancies. When the tenant wishes to move, the CLT 'can make a small payment to reflect the amount of rent paid less the CLT's costs in servicing the mortgage and in managing and maintaining the home' (CFS, 2006). This payment can be put towards a deposit or for entering into one of the other models discussed here.

This model has limitations because the resident remains a tenant and does not share in any increase in the equity value of their home. It is most likely to be offered by a housing association, although the additional management costs in setting it up and the financial implications in repaying tenants when they move may make it a relatively unattractive option.

Under the rent-to-purchase model, the CLT holds equity in perpetuity for the provision of affordable housing, while the resident takes out an assured rental tenancy with full repairing responsibilities (CFS, 2006). Rents are normally set at 35 per cent of net household income. When residents move they can receive an equity stake of 50–90 per cent of the increased value of that part of the property value their rent has serviced and the debt redeemed on it during their tenancy. Additional charges will be made for insurance, the CLT's management costs, service charges and to fund long-term renewals (CFS, 2006). Residents can change to the equity purchase tenure after two years.

This approach has a number of advantages of flexibility in that the higher the rent, the more residents gain from the share of the enhanced value their rent has serviced. This may be substantial in areas of high demand. However, if the rent level is set at 35 per cent of net household income, this is relatively high in relation to normal levels for social housing or for calculating mortgages for open-market purchase.

Under the equity-purchase model, the incoming household buys a share of the freehold of the property with cash and a mortgage up to the amount they can afford. The remaining equity is retained by the CLT to create long-term affordability for successive generations in housing need. In the case of a flat the CLT retains the freehold, but grants a long lease at a nominal rent for 99–125 years and the residents pay an annual service charge.

With houses, the CLT transfers the freehold to the purchaser, who then secures a mortgage with a bank or building society for between 40 and 80 per cent of the full market value of the property. The CLT takes an equity mortgage for the remaining percentage of the value to secure its long-term interest and enable the purchaser to own the freehold (CFS, 2006). When the purchaser decides to move, the value of their share of the equity is likely to have increased and they will have paid off part of their mortgage, thus creating a sum that can be put towards their next purchase. The purchaser is subject to a covenant, giving the CLT first option to repurchase the property in order to offer it to other priority households. By varying the terms of the equity mortgage, the CLT can influence the proportions of any rise in value that is available to the resident and which is retained by the CLT. This ensures that the property remains 'affordable' indefinitely for incoming occupants. The CLT may also wish to charge an annual ground rent to cover administrative costs.

Leasehold enfranchisement can be an issue for some CLTs, but does not affect those operating under the tenancy-plus model because no leases are granted. In some cases, flat-owners in a block can acquire the freehold, but shared-ownership leases (as discussed above) are excluded by the legislation provided the equity is fixed and 'staircasing' is not permitted. Leaseholders of a charitable housing trust are also excluded from enfranchisement, provided the homes were developed as part of the trust's charitable objectives and the beneficiaries are those with average or below-average household incomes (CFS, 2007a, p40).

A variant of the equity purchase model is mutual home ownership (MHO), developed by CDS Co-operatives. Under this approach, residents in need of housing form a Mutual Home Ownership Society (MHOS), which is registered as an Industrial and Provident Society. A CLT acquires land, preferably at nil cost through a Section 106 agreement, or as a transfer from a public agency such as English Partnerships or the NHS, then grants the MHOS a lease at a peppercorn rent. The MHOS then contracts with an RSL to carry out the development at an agreed price, which includes development profit. When the development is complete, the MHOS takes out a long-term, 30-year corporate mortgage that finances the project construction and development costs. It is a corporate loan rather than a series of individual mortgages, because this can be secured on more advantageous terms.

The value of the portfolio of property owned by the MHO is divided into equal units of, say, £1000, which residents fund through monthly mortgage payments under the terms of a long lease. Residents will take up units of equity according to their income and more can be acquired as their income increases or when they become available. All units of equity must be allocated to and funded by payments from members of the MHOS. When residents decide to move, they assign the lease to another who meets the eligibility criteria and is a member of the MHOS. The outgoing member's share of equity is sold to other members and the incoming member at a lower affordable net cost. The value of the equity assigned is determined by a reference to an index that is incorporated into the lease. This is based on a combination of a local housing market index and average earnings: 'This trading of equity shares ensures that the benefit of the land held outside the market by the CLT and the affordability it creates is recycled from one generation of occupant members to the next' (CDS Co-operatives, 2005, p2). The outgoing member takes 90 per cent of any increase in the index-linked value of units of equity they financed, while 10 per cent remains with the MHOS.

The CDS Co-operative mutual approach and the equity share model are similar in many respects in that ownership of the land and properties on it are separated. Under the former, the CLT acts as freehold owner of the land, then leases it at a peppercorn rent to the mutual organization. Under the latter approach, the CLT owns the land, but also shares with the residents the equity created by the uplift of values in the housing created on it. The CLT can also use any surpluses generated to increase the amount of land in its own-ership or to cross-subsidize the housing in order to cater for special needs. In addition, the equity share model could enable the CLT to provide commer-cial buildings and community facilities with varying degrees of cross-subsidy. An MHO can only provide housing. However, both models depend on the land being acquired at nil value through planning agreements or a transfer from the public sector.

Having reviewed the organizational and financial arrangements underpin-ning CLTs, in the next section we will discuss some case studies that demonstrate the different approaches and identify the key challenges facing CLTs in getting started.

Launching CLTs in town and country: some examples

The debate about how to achieve sustainable communities has initiated the search for new and innovative approaches to delivery. The development of CLTs was endorsed in the housing Green Paper (CLG, 2007), and seven urban and seven rural CLTs have been identified to form a National Demonstration Programme funded by the HCA, Carnegie UK Trust and the Higher Education Funding Council. Community Finance Solutions (CFS) at the University of Salford is providing technical advice and an interactive website. The 14 CLTs will also have access to the HCA's 2008–11 national investment programme.

CLTs encapsulate many of the broader policy objectives espoused by cen-tral government in recent years. They are motivated by community organizations, harness good-will and the resources of a variety of stakeholders, engage local communities in delivering social and environmental improvements, and aim to become self-sustaining in, for example, delivering affordable hous-ing in perpetuity. Yet they also challenge long-standing assumptions about value for money, the ownership and management of resources and competing perceptions of 'sustainability'. To be successful, they must be embedded in the complex web of overlapping policies and priorities, and demonstrate efficiency and the ability to deliver. Not least, they must be able to work closely with existing housing providers such as housing associations and integrate their strategies with planning and housing frameworks produced by local authorities. The following examples demonstrate the enormous opportunities that exist and some of the pitfalls and barriers to be overcome. To date, the rural examples are further advanced than those in urban areas.

Stonesfield Community Trust

Stonesfield Community Trust, which was set up in 1983 in an Oxfordshire village of about 1900 residents, claims to be the first CLT. In the 1980s, local residents became concerned about the falling roll in the local primary school and the lack of affordable housing. With two friends, Tony Crofts set up the trust and donated a quarter-acre site in the village for the first scheme. A donation of £3000 from a local company funded the setting up costs, legal fees and planning permission for the development of four houses. The increase in value of the site after planning permission secured a bank loan to build the first four houses. One was later converted into two flats, and a granny flat was added to another to create six units in all. A second quarter-acre site in the village was bought with a loan from West Oxfordshire District Council, and five houses were completed in 1993 with a variety of loans and donations. The 15 homes owned by the trust are now let to people with local connections and managed by a professional letting agent at minimal cost. A former silk-screen factory has also been acquired with a grant from the Rural Development Commission for conversion to workspaces. The village post office with a flat above has also been purchased by the Crofts and transferred to the trust. Any surpluses generated by the trust are to be used to provide home help for the elderly and to employ a youth worker (CFS, 2007b).

Cornwall CLT project

One of the seven rural CLTs identified in the National Demonstration Project covers the whole county of Cornwall. A project manager has been appointed by the Cornwall Rural Housing Association (CRHA) to work on a two-year project to promote CLTs across the county. Funding has been provided by the County Council, the Tudor Trust and the Department of Environment, Food and Rural Affairs (Defra). Cornwall CLT Ltd was registered as an Industrial and Provident Society in March 2007. A five-year business plan has been adopted, which aims to deliver more than 180 new homes on a number of sites by 2012. So far, two CLTs have been registered. St Minver CLT is a company limited by guarantee, which is developing 12 self-build bungalows at Rock, with an interest-free loan provided by North Cornwall District Council. The St Just in Roseland CLT is also a company limited by guarantee, which intends to build eight affordable homes with assistance from Carrick District Council. Cornwall CLT intends to work closely with local people in setting up new CLTs and acquiring land and existing housing.

High Bickington Community Property Trust

Proposals for a CLT in this small Devon village of 700 people, nine miles from Barnstaple, emerged from a very active parish council, which carried out an appraisal of local needs. On the basis of extensive community involvement, an outline planning application was submitted in 2003 to develop an eight-hectare farm, owned by Devon County Council, south of the village. The application sought permission for 52 affordable, open-market and self-build homes, health, community and retail uses, open space and community woodland. The scheme was approved by Torridge District Council, but was subsequently called in by the Government Office for the South West because it represented a 'departure' from national and local planning policies. In 2006 a planning inquiry was held and the inspector recommended refusal on the grounds that it did not accord with national policy and the local development plan. In addition, he noted that 'the number of proposed affordable units would be in excess of the figures revealed in the most recent housing needs survey... The proposal would also fail to make the best use of land' (Planning Inspectorate, 2006, p28), because the density would only be 22 dwellings per hectare, rather than at least 30 prescribed by national policy (Planning Inspectorate, 2006). Paradoxically, the density had been deliberately kept low in order to integrate the development in its rural setting. The inspector's decision was upheld by the Secretary of State for Communities and Local Government in May 2006.

The CLT was devastated by the decision, especially after receiving support and funding from a former secretary of state for Defra. The refusal drew the attention of the national press (*SocietyGuardian*, 31 October 2007), which contrasted the political rhetoric extolling local community initiatives with the realities of actual delivery. The CLT now proposes to reduce the amount of housing to 16 affordable homes and 14 private houses and engage with the planning system a second time. In January 2009 a revised planning application was approved by Torridge District Council and the Government Office confirmed by letter that all planning policy issues had been resolved.

Gloucestershire Land for People

A similar story comes from the town of Stroud in Gloucestershire, where a group of residents formed a CLT to provide much-needed affordable housing for residents who are increasingly being displaced by second-home owners. They identified a former hospital site at Cashes Green as suitable for a development of 77 homes, of which 50 would be affordable and 27 for sale. The CLT intended to use the mutual housing model and engaged CDS Co-operatives as the development partner. The 4.5-hectare site had been acquired by English Partnerships (EP), which is charged with purchasing brownfield, publicly-owned land in order to increase the housing supply. EP strongly supports local housing initiatives and agreed to hand over the site to the CLT, subject to the approval of its sponsoring department, the CLG.

In November 2007, EP wrote to CDS Co-operatives to say it now intended to develop alternative proposals for the Cashes Green site due to financial constraints. It proposed to offer Gloucestershire Land for People (GLP) a much smaller part of the site and to use the remainder for conventional affordable homes and houses for sale. A press release from GLP suggests that EP would need to pay NHS Estates a much larger sum for the site (overage) because of the increased site value. EP also suggests that the local authority was concerned that GLP might not be able to deliver the agreed plan. The press release states that GLP is seeking an urgent meeting with CLG ministers (GLP, 2007).

In response, a press release from EP states that 'the current proposal would take more than double the amount of public money that would go into providing similar homes in other affordable housing projects in the south-west and that is why we are meeting with GLP and other partners to find a way to address this' (EP, 2007). In December 2007, CFS was invited to review the robustness of the original GLP proposals and to explore the issues raised by the appraisal with a view to seeking agreement on the way ahead between all parties involved. By 2008 a new business plan had been developed that allocated GLP up to 50 per cent of the site, with the remainder being for open market housing. A new masterplan was put out for consultation in early 2009.

Shoreditch Community Equity Trust

This example is in an inner-city location with high levels of deprivation and a large proportion of local authority housing, much of which is in poor condition. The area is undergoing regeneration as part of the New Deal for Communities programme. Plans are at an early stage of development, but a briefing paper ('The community equity trust: A model for urban renewal', Shoreditch Trust, unpublished) sets out the broad strategy. It is also one of the seven urban CLTs included in the National Demonstration Programme.

The intention is that the local authority housing will be transferred in blocks to the equity trust so that it can be redeveloped for a variety of tenures and commercial and community uses, in a phased programme. The CLT will adopt the equity purchase model to ensure affordability is sustained and the board would be made up of one-third elected residents, one-third local authority and public-sector stakeholders, and one-third business and other stakeholder groups.

In a case study of how the CLT might operate, a site of about 4.7 hectares now housing 450 households is examined. It is assumed that the site is transferred at nil capital cost and that the site is cleared and rebuilt. Redevelopment for mixed housing and other uses is then carried out in phases. This would create 1150 homes and 25,555 square metres of commercial space; 24 per cent of the homes would be for social renting and 76 per cent for shared equity sale at 50 per cent to 90 per cent of their open-market value for sale. The remaining equity value would be paid off by a commercial mortgage to be serviced largely from the income stream created by the leases of the commercial property, which on completion would generate about £4.5 million a year. A further £1 million annually would be created from the social rented housing. Unfortunately, this plan did not receive the support of the London Borough of Hackney and it has not been taken further.

Key issues arising from the case studies

As can be seen from this brief review of six examples, most CLTs are in the early stages of organizational development and few have reached the stage of carrying out detailed feasibility studies, preparing business plans and submitting planning applications. They do, however, demonstrate a concerted effort in identifying local need and thinking creatively about how different financial packages might be assembled that are sufficiently viable to be implemented, and stand a good chance of sustaining their key objective – creating a variety of forms of housing that are sustainable in the long term, with appropriate services and facilities. A number of key issues emerge from these examples.

All the cases examined demonstrate considerable ingenuity in building on strong community support and new forms of governance at the local level. However, these are only as good as the ability to acquire land on which to provide appropriate forms of housing and other services. In addition, CLTs need to be able to acquire appropriate sites for development on advantageous terms and negotiate financial arrangements with landowners and funding bodies. Those that have the strong support of their local authorities and national bodies such as the HCA are most likely to be successful. Considerable financial expertise is needed to draw on national funding mechanisms that generally operate in terms of well-established tenures such as social-rented, intermediate and open-market owner-occupied housing. A further important factor is the need to meet the requirements of strict planning policies, as was noted in the case of High Bickington. The long-term viability of the CLT model remains largely untested. Evidence from other similar initiatives, such as community development trusts, suggests that a long period of experimentation and adjustment will be needed before the approach is fully established. Mechanisms for sharing best practice and providing technical advice, for example through organizations such as Community Finance Solutions, must also be sustained.

Conclusions

Many different kinds of organizations have grappled with the two most pressing issues in housing policy: how to increase the supply of housing and how to make it affordable to all income groups. Housing associations, tenants' cooperatives and community development trusts have experimented with a variety of organizational and financial models. It is only since the Housing and Regeneration Act 2008 was passed that CLTs have been absorbed into central government policy, and much depends on the outcome of the consultation period that ended on 31 December 2008. This chapter has examined the role of community land trusts in addressing supply and affordability to meet local needs, as well as confronting the long-term question of achieving affordability in perpetuity.

CLTs are in the early stages of experimentation and have only recently been acknowledged in government policy and in being offered access to the HCA investment programme. All the examples discussed demonstrate considerable innovation and many have received financial and other support from local authorities, universities, parts of the legal profession and agencies such as the HCA. It is likely that in the next five years this business model will be fully tested and applied successfully in both urban and rural areas. But this is not to underestimate the challenges. They have emerged out of a long history of experimentation and protest. As the CFS Practitioner's Guide notes:

> The concept of a Community Land Trust is a curious synthesis of political stances, combining elements of socialist libertarianism, co-operativism, One Nation Toryism, neo-liberal social policy, and Schumacher-inspired Green politics and localism. What they share, to a greater or lesser extent, is an acceptance that humans are social and responsible beings and they are the best agents to make decisions about their future. Moreover, they imply that we are part of communities so that informal social mechanisms are the best means to maintain order. This relies on a sense of 'knowingness' (awareness of others and your links to them) and the self-limiting obligation best summarized as stewardship. In sociological terms community land trusts owe far more to Durkheim than they do to Marx or Smith. (CFS, 2007a, p2)

The challenges facing CLTs are considerable and relate to four main aspects. First, CLTs need to be able to harness their local communities to address local needs and housing markets, and select the organizational and legal models that best meet their needs. Second, they need to be able to carry out feasibility studies and identify sites for development. Third, they need to be able to acquire land and buildings at nil cost through opportunities provided by local authorities, public agencies and private benefactors. Finally, they need to be able to secure the range of permissions required to obtain planning permission and secure an appropriate mix of public and private funding. All these represent significant but not insuperable obstacles, as demonstrated by the examples of GLP and the Higher Bickington Community Property Trust, which are both likely to proceed in modified form.

If these difficulties can be overcome, the potential benefits will be considerable. There is no reason why CLTs should not be fully integrated into local regeneration strategies, so that they can help meet local housing needs through the development of housing and genuinely sustainable communities. Many of the rural areas with emergent CLTs also face escalating house prices and declining community infrastructure through, for example, the closure of village post offices and local shops.

CLTs aim to create a virtuous circle by promoting community engagement, developing democratic systems of governance to manage resources and providing affordable housing and related community services. If sustainable development is the desired output, social sustainability is the broader set of outcomes that result from harnessing resources to meet local needs and engaging local communities over time. CLTs now need to secure the support of government at all levels and demonstrate their effectiveness by delivering successful developments comparable in terms of cost and quality with traditional social and affordable housing. Legal, technical and financial support will be needed in the early stages, but the model has the advantage of being flexible enough to be replicated in all parts of the UK (CFS, 2008). For too long housing has been seen solely as a technical process of funding and delivery – the eco-centric approach. CLTs represent a real opportunity to develop a far more sustainable, anthropocentric (people-centred) model (Kearns and Turok, 2004). This may take longer and require more public investment, but could deliver substantial benefits in the longer term.

References

CDS Co-operatives (2005) *A Simple Guide to Mutual Home Ownership*, CDS Co-operatives, London, www.communitylandtrust.org.uk/, accessed 8 December 2007

Champlain Housing Trust (2006) www.champlainhousingtrust.org, accessed December 2007

Communities and Local Government (2006) *Code for Sustainable Homes: A Step-Change in Sustainable Home Building Practice*, CLG, London

Communities and Local Government (2007) *Homes for the Future: More Affordable, more Sustainable*, CLG, London, p110

Communities and Local Government (2008) *Community Land Trusts: A Consultation*, CLG, London

Community Finance Solutions (2006) *Community Land Trusts: Affordable Homes, in Sustainable Communities*, CFS, Salford

Community Finance Solutions (2007a) *Community Land Trusts: A Practitioners' Guide*, CFS, Salford, www.communitylandtrust.org.uk/, accessed 8 December 2007

Community Finance Solutions (2007b) *Stonesfield Community Trust, Oxfordshire*, www.communitylandtrust.org.uk, accessed 13 December 2007

Community Finance Solutions (2008) *Placeshaping: A Toolkit for Urban Community Land Trusts*, University of Salford, www.communityfinance.salford.ac.uk/pdf/Urban_tools_complete.pdf, accessed 23 June 2008

Conaty, P. (2007) 'A History of Community Land Trusts', www.communitylandtrust.org.uk/documents/history_and_background.pdf, accessed 10 December 2007

English Partnerships (EP) (2007) 'Cashes Green – Statement in Response to GLP Release', 1 November

Gloucestershire Land for People (2007) Press release: 'Cashes Green, Stroud', GLP, 2 November

Hall, P. (1994) *Cities of Tomorrow*, Blackwell, Oxford

Kearns, A. and Turok, I. (2004) 'Sustainable communities: Dimensions and challenges', ESRC/Office of the Deputy Prime Minister Postgraduate Research Programme, Working Paper, ODPM, London

Kintrea, K. (2007) 'Policies and Programmes for Disadvantaged Neighbourhoods: Recent English Experience', *Housing Studies*, vol 22, no 2, pp261–282

MacFadyen, D. (1970) *Sir Ebenezer Howard and the Town Planning Movement*, Manchester University Press, Manchester

Northern Housing Consortium (2007) *Building Strength Through Community Ownership*, Northern Housing Consortium, Sunderland

Office of the Deputy Prime Minister (2003) *Sustainable Communities: Building for The Future*, ODPM, London

Planning Inspectorate (2006) 'Land at Little Bickington Farm, High Bickington, Umberleigh, Devon: Application by High Bickington Parish Council', Report to the First Secretary of State, 13 February 2006

4

Neighbourhood Asset Management: Life Cycles and Learning for Social Sustainability

Judith Allen and Tony Lloyd-Jones

Managing neighbourhood assets is a crucial, but often neglected, element in achieving sustainable communities. Within an overarching UK policy framework, English policy[1] defines sustainable communities as 'places where people want to live and work, now and in the future' (Defra, 2005, p121). In terms of the built environment, the policy focuses on the physical development of new communities and the large-scale renovation and replacement of worn-out places. There is no coherent vision about managing the built environment during the period between building and renovating it, although two important components of such a vision do appear in the current English strategy document: cleaning and greening neighbourhoods; and meeting the decent homes standard for social housing.

Thus, despite enjoining planners to think about the *future*, both strategy and practice tend to be *present* oriented, forgetting that there is likely to be little associational life among the group of strangers who initially come to live in new or fully renovated places. A second problem with the current strategy is that, while it emphasizes the provision of new community facilities, it tends to focus on facilities directly related to services provided by the state, which sits oddly against an emphasis on the contributions that can be made by local voluntary groups.

Most people, however, live in areas that fall between new provision and re-provision of the built landscape. Meanwhile, the social landscape varies from being a complete group of strangers, who come to live in new areas, and the associational life that characterizes longer-settled places. In these in-between places, there is always the problem of (socially) managing and (physically) maintaining the neighbourhood. Looked at in these terms, the key problem becomes one of building supportive organizational frameworks for managing and maintaining the built fabric, whether owned by the state or other actors.

Several chapters in this book discuss aspects of this general problem: Suzy Nelson looks at the initial provision of facilities, Tony Manzi considers arguments for and against socially mixing residents in new neighbourhoods, and Nick Bailey discusses community land trusts, which provide one way to manage and maintain facilities.

This chapter explores the dynamic connections between the physical life-cycle of built assets and the social life-cycle of the communities that use them. These connections are contingent, so the underlying purpose of this chapter is to provide a tool for diagnosing when, where and how to step in to facilitate the management and maintenance of built assets.

Asset management in the global dialogue

Discussions of sustainability are rooted in a transnational global dialogue in which developed countries have as much to learn from lesser-developed countries as the other way around. Thus, the notion of community-based neighbourhood asset management draws from two ideas rooted in discussions about socio-economic development in the global South. One is the idea of asset-based development and the other is the idea of sustainable livelihoods.

In Western economic thought, assets are seen as owned by a juridical or natural person, who has the right to benefit from their use. This concept abstracts from the social context within which assets are used and is firmly located within the framework of *private* property ownership and the rights of *individuals*. In sustainable-development theory, the idea of asset takes on a broader meaning, oriented to the use and conservation of resources over time. It treats all resources – biological, natural, human, social and cultural, physical and financial – in terms of their current and future use. In this context, an asset is anything that is useful and of value. This definition sees assets as a store of immediate and future value and wealth, and thus as a form of capital.

The most commonly used 'five-capitals model' distinguishes natural, social, human, manufactured or physical and financial capitals (Rakodi, 2002, p13; Porritt, 2006, p113). Porritt develops a method for assessing stocks and flows of these five capitals, relating them to each other in order to evaluate strategies for intervention in specific places. The five-capitals approach is designed to be applicable in a wide variety of social, political and economic contexts, and requires the analyst to specify explicitly the nature of the linkages among the different forms of capitals/assets. By using the notion of social capital, the five-capitals model questions the easy elision between natural and juridical persons found in Western economic thought. Thus, it questions how different societies, national or local, ascribe and circumscribe rights associated with decisions over the use and benefits from physical capital.

The second strand of development theory that informs this chapter is the notion of sustainable livelihoods and sustainable livelihoods approaches in international development, which developed alongside and in association with the five capitals model (Lloyd-Jones, 2002). The question behind it is: How can poor communities become more resilient in the face of exogenous shocks and stresses? Initially, the sustainable livelihoods approach focused on sustainable farming practices to conserve the natural resources available to poor communities over the longer term (Carney, 1998). It was a short move to question whether and how the social assets of villages might be developed to manage and maintain physical assets such as schools, libraries and health centres, then look at urban settlements more generally. The remainder of this chapter explores how the lessons learned in developing countries can be extended and adapted to the British context.

Social assets or just social capital?

The assets-based and sustainable livelihoods approaches use a more nuanced and multi-level concept of social capital than is found in English urban policy. However, using the ideas of social capital outlined in Chapter 1 raises a number of questions for assessing specific situations:

- What socially bonded groups exist? To what extent do individuals broker bridges between groups across social strata or interests? (Putnam, 2000)
- How is social capital distributed across social strata? To whom is it attributed? What are the usual ways of doing things? What sustains the usual ways of doing things? To what extent and how can habitual actions be brought to consciousness, challenged and changed? To what extent and how will changing the usual ways of doing things lead to sustainable change and/or development? (Bourdieu, 1989)
- How do institutional and organizational frameworks sustain or inhibit, facilitate or limit the activities of networks of socially bonded individuals? (Coleman, 1988)

These questions guide the analysis of neighbourhood-asset management in this chapter.

Physical assets and social processes

As physical entities, buildings are subject to natural scientific laws. Their material characteristics change over time 'naturally'. However, they are only intelligible as assets, useful and productive of value, when seen through the lens of human intentions and activities. This intertwining of social and natural processes can be clarified by considering one of the most common ways of describing the building life cycle: build, manage, mend, and extend, replace or abandon. The initiation and length of each of these stages are a consequence of some form of social decision-making, whether by individuals or more collectively. These social processes are embedded in a localized context, which determines who (individually or collectively) is (usually) responsible for taking and acting on decisions about the building and who is affected by these decisions. Furthermore, they are also influenced by the regulatory and governance institutions of the state. In short, a physical entity only becomes a physical *asset* when embedded within social practices that mean it is of use and value to *someone*. However, this is not a one-way process. The specific material characteristics of the building also determine what decisions need to be made and when, in order to sustain its use value.

Case studies

This section of the chapter presents three case studies, at various scales and in different places, in order to draw out some lessons for socially sustainable ways of managing the assets of a neighbourhood. They include a set of small projects in India and sub-Saharan Africa, a slum neighbourhood in Jakarta and Soho in central London. The final section of the paper summarizes the lessons from these examples.

Community asset management in rural communities

Community assets are a subset of neighbourhood assets. They can be defined as a physical asset, land or buildings or other forms of infrastructure, used *communally* by members of a localized community for their own purposes – meeting places, religious buildings, local schools, health clinics, and so on. Two features are important in defining community assets. The first is that they support the formation and activities of self-defined groups within localized areas; and the second is that they are subject to the normal stages in the life-cycle of physical assets: build, manage, mend, and extend, replace or abandon. This chapter explores the relationship between the social and associational life that structures a community and the material life of the facilities which support community activities. It is based on research carried out by the Max Lock Centre (an international sustainable development planning unit at the University of Westminster), which extended the sustainable livelihoods approach to investigate whether and how the social assets of villages might be used to manage and maintain physical assets in rural villages in India, Kenya, Malawi and South Africa (Theis et al, 2003; Brown et al, 2005).

The research was stimulated by the outcome of an innovative school-building programme in Andhra Pradesh in the 1990s. This programme was designed to develop a cost-effective construction technology that would make use of local materials, skills and labour. By adapting familiar vernacular technologies, low-income communities in villages and towns could become more self-reliant and less dependent on distant local government public works departments for the long-term maintenance of the buildings. The question was, then, how to move towards a more generalized idea of communities taking 'ownership' of physical assets through managing and maintaining existing facilities provided by the Government or other external agencies? The idea of community asset management was born.

In India, a pilot project was carried out in Orissa by a partnership between the Max Lock Centre and the Human Settlements Management Institute, the research and training arm of the Indian government's Housing and Urban Development Corporation. The aim was to restore a dilapidated school in a poor neighbourhood of the city of Bhubaneshwar (Theis et al, 2003). A set of linked programmes were created to train local government engineers to work cooperatively with the local community, while the resources and skills of the community were pooled and directed, with technical training where necessary, towards restoration and maintenance activities. Trusted members of the community were trained in basic accounting techniques. Money from the Orissa State Government for the project was put into a dedicated bank account, and methods were developed to ensure that all financial transactions were fully transparent to the community and the authorities.

The pilot project provided a framework linking the physical life-cycle of buildings with key social or organizational questions (see Table 4.1). This framework shaped further research on community asset management practices in sub-Saharan Africa, which included primary schools in Kenya, South Africa and Malawi, a wholesale and retail market in Kenya, a community-based library in Malawi, and two community centres and a medical centre in South Africa (Brown et al, 2005).

All these cases illustrated an ongoing tension between capital and revenue funding. Community buildings represent a considerable capital outlay and normally involve sources of finance beyond the community itself. In many cases this is the local authority, more often than not drawing on central or provincial government funds with strings attached. In the African examples, there was a range of sponsors, including international development agencies, religious bodies, charities and various non-governmental organizations (NGOs). Outside donors are frequently involved in the financing of social and community facilities, adding to the complexity and potential conflicts of interest among the range of partners involved in developing the building, and in its maintenance and management once the building has been finished and occupied. Usually, outside agencies focus on the building stage. Their interest ends once a project is set up and running, in a new building. Thus, in most

Table 4.1 *Physical life-cycle of buildings and key social questions*

Stage in life-cycle	Key social questions
Build	Was localized or 'foreign' technology used in design?
	What was the build quality?
	What materials were used?
	Who provided the building?
Manage	Is the building being used as planned and/or for different uses?
	Who has decided on changes in use and users?
Mend	Is it possible to use local skills or are specialized skills required?
Replace, extend	Who makes this decision and how?
or abandon	Is it an explicit decision or a decision by default as the building deteriorates physically?

cases, there were problems with ensuring management and maintenance of the buildings over time.

In many cases, village communities were waiting for the local authorities to assume ownership and solve the problems. However, as also happened in the Orissa case, local authority ownership could plunge the buildings into a highly contested political context, often based outside the village and using the buildings as pawns in a larger game. In such cases, buildings continued to deteriorate, services based in the buildings were threatened and there was a stand-off between local and more distant partners, which prevented continuing management and maintenance.

However, the picture was not entirely bleak. Community involvement in maintaining local assets occurred when five conditions were met. First, if buildings used local technologies, similar to the houses people lived in, then there was a higher level of local skills available for mending them. Second, multiple uses of the building, in addition to what was often a single planned use, created a wider interest in managing and mending buildings. Additional uses also often meant that the building became a factor of production in local economic activity. Funds generated by economic activities located within the buildings remained within the local area and could create cash resources for maintenance. Third, when local actors used a building regularly, they were more likely to notice specific maintenance problems and have a direct interest in the building's upkeep. In particular, where there was an annual cycle of religious or cultural festivals, preparations for these events provided a systematic moment for assessing what repairs needed to be done and putting them in hand. Fourth, far-away local government departments had no effective way of monitoring the state of repair of the buildings. Overall, where management and maintenance were not dependent on actors outside the village (landlords, government engineering departments, NGOs), the building was more likely to be maintained by the local community. Fifth, sufficient local residents needed to be involved who could contribute time to managing and maintaining the building, while at the same time recognizing that self-employed people and smaller households, with three or four members, did not have sufficient time to contribute.

Finally, it should be said that community asset management is not primarily intended to be a method for cost savings by local authorities, but a method for achieving the sustainability of physical assets. Nevertheless, it is likely to be more cost-effective in cases where funds budgeted for maintaining schools and other public buildings are wasted, as now happens in many developing countries.

The notion of social sustainability that characterizes these small examples is strongly focused on single buildings, set within a small-scale social context comprising building users. Three conclusions can be drawn from the example. First, community assets can be maintained in circumstances where it is possible to organize a local group to take responsibility for the buildings, deploying Putnam-type social capital in the process. Second, however, it all depends on the wider organizational framework within which the task is set. Following Bourdieu, where specific actors (landlords, local authority works departments, local politicians and even some NGOs) use provision and/or control over community assets to maintain their social standing or position, then it is entirely contingent whether the assets can be managed or maintained over any long period of time. Third, social position is not independent of the formal organizational framework within which management and maintenance of community assets is set. Coleman's work suggests that forging and sustaining an organizational frame that links the community and 'its' assets is necessary. The next example in this section of the paper illustrates one approach to this problem proposed for an area within Jakarta.

Neighbourhood-asset management: organizational frameworks in Jakarta

Karet Tengsin is a *kampung*, or low-income informal settlement, on the edge of the Golden Triangle commercial district in downtown Jakarta. It has a residential population of about 12,000. Its boundaries run between a river, which regularly floods part of the area, and a main road into the Golden Triangle. Unlike squatter settlements, where residents lack security of tenure, *kampungs* are characterized by a complex mix of tenures, including small landowners who rent out properties, owner-occupied buildings, low-cost rooming and lodging spaces for students and office workers in a variety of buildings, and some council-built and owned replacement housing. There is mixed residential and business use of many premises, involving families who run their own businesses. Other small businesses own or rent space in the area. An additional layer of complexity arises from the wide variety of land tenures in Indonesia, mainly various forms of short-term leasehold, while many notional freehold landowners do not have full certificates of ownership. Informal settlements such as Karet Tengsin, which have grown through the subdivision and development of once-peripheral agricultural land, are more common in cities in developing countries than squatter settlements.

The Max Lock Centre first studied Karet Tengsin in 1997 as part of a multi-national project on Good Practice in Core Area Redevelopment (Max Lock Centre, 2001). By this time, a major commercial developer had purchased a large part of the commercially attractive part of the site, above the floodplain and adjacent to the main road. These purchases were made on a piecemeal basis. However, site consolidation was prevented because many small landowners refused to sell, either because they did not want to move or because they were waiting for a better offer as land prices rose sharply.

The aim of the research was to explore ways in which low-income informal settlements in central locations could be redeveloped through land sharing, which would allow existing residents to be re-accommodated within the area. Usually, in order to realize the potential commercial value of central sites, there are strong pressures to relocate resident communities to peri-urban locations far from the current source of their livelihoods. The Karet Tengsin study showed that, by increasing density and releasing part of the site for commercial development, designing a win–win situation was potentially feasible. Such a solution would also mean that existing residents and businesses could continue to provide valuable, low-cost services to the central area of Jakarta, contributing to the sustainability of the city as a whole.

The proposal for commercial redevelopment was hit by the Asian financial crisis in 1997 and has not yet fully recovered. Meanwhile, in the poorer area around the floodplain, the Jakarta Municipal Government plans to rehouse existing occupants on- or off-site in high-rise tower blocks. More than ten years has passed since the first study and little has happened except for the recent construction of 200 new flats (many promised to outsiders) in a 12-storey block, and the continued deterioration of existing five-storey council-owned blocks due to neglect of basic maintenance, uncertainty about the ownership status of the residents living in the flats and a rent strike by tenants.

The Max Lock Centre revisited Karet Tengsin in 2006/07 on behalf of the UN-Habitat Slum Upgrading Facility (Lloyd-Jones et al, 2007). The aim was to design an organizational structure to harness private capital for low-income development and floodplain infrastructure works, and provide a framework within which it would be possible to mediate the trading of existing rights of occupation for secure tenure within new or improved housing and business units. An additional aim was to find a way to provide long-term management of the physical assets in the neighbourhood, particularly housing and community assets. In a *kampung* like Karet Tengsin, there are many communities of interest, and the differences among them make it difficult to find common ground for resisting pressures for wholesale redevelopment and gentrification. Thus, any proposed organizational structure would need to be both robust and flexible in order to be sustainable.

The project explored an overarching organizational model that could be described, in English terms, as a combination of a community land trust and a community-based housing association. It was designed to bring together the variety of actors whose support would be necessary to make the previously identified win–win physical development scenario feasible. It can be seen as a formal organizational framework for integrated neighbourhood governance, bringing together public, private and community interests to realize shared common objectives (see Figure 4.1).

The redevelopment of Karet Tengsin continues to be on hold for political reasons. The public–private ownership of the development company means that there are minimal costs associated with deferring development. This provides time to search for and set up an organizational model that captures common interests sufficiently to move from a stand-off to a win–win situation. This search reflects Coleman's idea that social capital brings together *both* an organizational framework *and* a community of interest. It also raises questions implicit in Coleman's work about the extent to which an organizational framework can, in

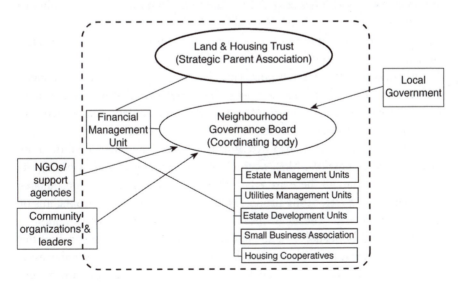

Source: Max Lock Centre, 2006

Figure 4.1 *Integrated neighbourhood-governance model*

the right circumstances, *create* a community of interest from disparate and/or conflicting interests in the community. The Karet Tengsin proposal also draws on Bourdieu's insights in that it seeks to create an organizational structure that harnesses and/or creates sufficient status positions within it to offer the chance of change from the existing fragmented set of positions.

In Karet Tengsin, the overall notion of social sustainability has three elements. The first has to do with maintaining an existing group of residents, businesses and workers within a specific locality in the metropolitan area. The second element has to do with rebuilding the existing physical environment, including substantial infrastructure works. The third is creating an organizational framework for neighbourhood governance that ensures social and physical objectives can be met.

The next example is drawn from Soho, in central London. In this case the problem is to improve the environmental sustainability of the physical buildings and infrastructure in an area in which relatively few user groups have a long-term commitment to staying there.

Environmental sustainability: retrofitting buildings in Soho for energy efficiency

Research on retrofitting buildings in Soho, to improve their energy efficiency and environmental sustainability, explored how the different time horizons of key actors add another dimension to social organizational aspects of achieving sustainability (Lloyd-Jones et al, 2008). The research outlined a simple physical cycle for individual buildings (see Table 4.1). In practice, buildings are more complex than this. Major building elements have different life-cycles which, in turn, frame the time horizons associated with the manage-and-mend stage of decision-making. At the same time, complex tenure relationships introduce a different set of time horizons for actors. The problem is that the time horizons associated with tenure strongly determine the time horizons associated with managing and mending.

Soho is a conservation area that aims to preserve the physical fabric of the area as much as possible. Most of the buildings are considered as having historical merit, although there are relatively few listed buildings within the area. This means that a retrofitting proposal has the potential to improve the 'historical look' of the area. The single most cost-effective environmental solution for the area would be installing a single district heating, cooling and power network. Even if a way is found to make this long-run investment proposal feasible, it would still need to be combined with a detailed way of managing the appearance of the buildings in the area.

Soho shares some characteristics with Karet Tengsin. For much of its 300-year lifetime, it was primarily a low-income, mixed-use area, home to immigrants and a variety of small-scale trades and services, and stubbornly resistant to gentrification. Its mixed-use character remains, although the area is now dominated by high-value creative industry, entertainment and tourism-related businesses. Also, like Karet Tengsin, it was developed piecemeal through the subdivision and selling of agricultural land. As a result, there is a complex pattern of land ownership and tenure in Soho, and most buildings have multiple, small and medium-size businesses and/or residents as their occupiers. There are relatively few large freehold owners in the area, including the Crown Estate in Regent Street, Shaftesbury plc in Chinatown and the Carnaby Street area, and the Raymond family's Soho Estates. Soho Housing Association owns a number of developments fitted into courtyards behind street buildings. There are no formal associations representing business interests in the area, aside from the Chinese Chamber of Commerce, and only a handful of residents' associations. The overall picture is one of extreme social fragmentation. In effect, the social capital associated with residents and businesses in the area is not focused on the neighbourhood itself, but is oriented towards the larger 'outside' world, despite local networks within some of the business communities. There is no overarching organizational framework to knit a plethora of loosely organized, outwardly oriented networks together to focus on the neighbourhood itself.

The basic problem of retrofitting arises from the structure of tenure relationships. Small building owners are unwilling to upgrade their buildings if the benefits accruing to occupiers through reduced fuel bills are not recouped, through increased rents, to finance the works. At the same time, occupiers pay higher fuel costs as a consequence of landlords' unwillingness to invest. Larger building developers and commercial landlords typically look for a payback period of between ten and 25 years, depending on the type of building, the market associated with it and the risk of loss of income if buildings stand empty. Variations in payback periods have a major impact on the cost-effectiveness of sustainable renovation measures. If these measures are to be retrofitted during the payback period, landlords have the added complication of fitting them around occupancy cycles. Upgrading the building envelope can be carried out while buildings are occupied. But other measures, such as replacing windows and internal insulation, are likely to be disruptive to building users, as are works to internal building systems that involve changes to layouts, adding new services, fittings and fixtures, redecorations, and so on. Major landlords can offer their tenants alternative premises during a rolling programme of works, but this adds to the costs, especially if there is any business disruption for the tenant. In practice, renovation in Soho is more likely to be done on an ad-hoc basis as tenants vacate and leases end.

The first part of Table 4.2 shows the time horizons for various elements of the physical capital in Soho. The second part shows time horizons linked to the institutional structure of real property. These disjunctions in time horizons are

Table 4.2 *Timescales in Soho*

Item		Timescale (years)	Responsible actors
Built elements	Buried utilities and street infrastructure	30–150	Utility companies and local authority
	Soho buildings and plots	30–300	Owners
	Replaceable building elements	20–50	Owners
	Major building refurbishments	20–30	Owners
	Boilers, plant, appliance replacement	10–20	Owners/occupiers
	Internal fittings replacement	1–20	Occupiers
Social organizational elements	International/cross-party agreements	5–25	Governments/political parties/civil society
Agreements between owners and occupiers	Commercial leases	Up to 25	Owners/occupiers
	Commercial leases: breaks and/or reviews	5	Owners/occupiers
	Residential leases	Up to 100	Owners/occupiers
Length of use	Business occupancy turnover	1–10+	Owners/occupiers
	Dwellings: owner-occupied turnover	10–20 (median = 15)	Owners/occupiers
	Dwellings: tenanted turnover	<1–10+ (median = 5)	Owners/occupiers
Future orientations	Municipal, public agency and NGO plans	1–10	Local authority/public agency/NGOs
	Governmental plans	1–10	Government/civil service
	Business organization plans	1–10	Occupiers
	Household plans	1–20	Occupiers

Source: Lloyd-Jones et al, 2008, Appendix 6: Timescales and decision-making cycles (authors' adaptations)

a function of each actor pursuing cost-effective strategies within the present legal and institutional framework. The most important disjunction is that there is presently no single actor strongly enough associated with the neighbourhood and with an effective time horizon long enough to consider the very long-run proposal for a combined district heating, cooling and power scheme. In addition, while it is possible to indicate the time-spans associated with the manage-and-mend cycle, much more detailed survey information linking built and social organizational components would be necessary to proceed on a detailed building-by-building basis.

Both the Soho and Karet Tengsin examples suggest that, in thinking about how to create socially and environmentally sustainable communities in the normal run of 'in-between places', it is necessary to think dynamically about how to get from here to there. In other words, how is it possible to create strategies for managing neighbourhood assets that bring some order into the messiness of social structures and processes, specific organizational and institutional arrangements, divergent interests and time frames?

Social sustainability and managing neighbourhood assets

Neighbourhoods can be thought of as physically delimited spaces within urban settlements, bringing together residents and businesses who live and work in them, and organizations, from within or without, concerned with managing the people and buildings in the area. So far, this chapter has focused on the physical life-cycle of buildings and used the notion of social capital to link them to social and organizational processes. The remainder of this chapter aims to outline a diagnostic approach to identify where, when and how to step in to develop strategies for managing and maintaining neighbourhood assets.

In order to do this, the perspective needs to shift to a more social concept of places and their dynamics. Massey's (2005) concept of space as a place in which there is a multiplicity of intersecting life trajectories, creating at any one point in time a simultaneity of 'stories-so-far', provides a useful metaphor for looking at neighbourhood dynamics. The question of strategy becomes one of how individual, group and organizational life-trajectories intersect, and how the stories-so-far have developed and will develop over time.

Within this perspective, it is possible to imagine how neighbourhoods in different places may be characterized by distinctive meta-stories. Three broad variables underlie the as-yet-unfinished stories in the neighbourhood: identities, interests and issues (shown in Table 4.3).

Following Bourdieu, it is important to recognize that social divisions and parallel lives are built into social structures. Following Putnam's view, local divisions may reflect strong bonding social capital within each of the groups, but a

Table 4.3 *As-yet-unfinished stories in the neighbourhood space*

Identity	What are the social and demographic characteristics of low-status and high-status groups? How are specific identities linked to local organizational structures and wider institutional frameworks?
Interests	How do different groups relate to the neighbourhood-space? Do residents see it as 'home' or a 'gateway' to another place, or a 'trap' which they cannot leave? To what extent and how are businesses tied to the locality or are they free to move?
Issues	How does the conjunction of identity and interests relate to the way local neighbourhood assets are managed and maintained?

lack of bridging social capital between them. However, divided neighbourhoods do not necessarily imply strategies based on notions of bridging social capital. There are other ways to create bridging capital, using Coleman's ideas about the organizational and institutional frameworks within which social capital can be formed. Furthermore, externally implemented policies, in practice, usually involve introducing richer people or more successful businesses into the neighbourhood. They have the effect of socially downgrading the people who were in more localized, if limited, status hierarchies.

Linking neighbourhood and external organizations

Figure 4.2 thus provides a template that can be used to identify the linkages among actors relevant to neighbourhood-asset management. It was used in this way to examine deprived residential neighbourhoods in 14 European countries between 1997 and 2002, in European Commission DG XII research programmes on 'Targeted Social and Economic Research' and 'Cities of Tomorrow'. In that case, it allowed the identification of two sets of strong linkages within most neighbourhoods. The first was among local residents groups, service delivery workers and (if present) community workers. The second network linked framework setters, politicians and wider organizations and institutions. The normal operation of intra- and inter-organizational relationships functioned both to separate the neighbourhood from the decision-makers who set the broad framework for what happened within it, and to confine relationships between residents and agencies working within the neighbourhood to issues of service delivery.

The key point is that community development workers, if they were present in the neighbourhood, provided a means for spanning the gap between the neighbourhood, on the one hand, and external agencies, organizations and interests, on the other hand. This template can be extended to cover linkages

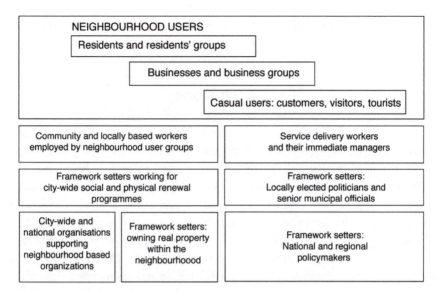

Note: The top two levels indicate actors who are located within the boundaries, arbitrary or natural, of the neighbourhood. The bottom two levels indicate significant actors outside the neighbourhood who have the authority to set the frameworks within which service delivery workers in the neighbourhood carry out their jobs.

Figure 4.2 *The actors who may have a presence in neighbourhood spaces*

between different types of neighbourhood users in more mixed-use neighbourhoods and to explore the extent to which and how different users make linkages with framework setters. In particular, introducing questions about social capital creation into an analysis using this template implicitly raises questions about the extent to which framework setters attend to the creation of neighbourhood-friendly organizational frameworks and processes.

In conclusion, the master-narrative for all neighbourhoods' meta-narratives can be succinctly summarized. Publicly visible and active neighbourhood-based groups wax and wane, come and go, as part of a normal social process. In addition, the pattern of activity by neighbourhood groups is shaped, but not determined, by the range of services delivered locally and how these may change over time. Offsetting the normal division between the neighbourhood and the organizational and institutional framework within which it is set is the strength of feeling about local issues, which in turn is partly shaped by the pattern of social and demographic change in the neighbourhood and partly by the actions of framework setters.

Each place has its own specific meta-narrative, drawing together the not-yet-finished stories of those whose paths cross it and cross within it. This multiplicity of paths generates a not-yet-finished narrative of the place. Neighbourhood meta-narratives can be holistic or fragmented but, whatever their nature, they provide a way of imagining different pathways to further chapters in these as-yet-unfinished narratives.

Conclusions

Within an extended concept of assets, this chapter has focused on neighbourhood assets, the physical built environment and the people who use it. Three different concepts of social capital have been used to explore how social and physical processes become intertwined in managing and maintaining community assets. Three case studies show some of the organizational complexities raised by managing and maintaining community assets. The different concepts of social capital have been used to tease out the significance of organizational issues in supporting neighbourhood-asset management. The final part of the chapter addresses these issues by taking a dynamic and open-ended view of the social processes characterizing small areas within urban settlements, in order to explore strategic questions about when and how to intervene. The chapter concludes that strategic views depend on imagining further chapters in the as-yet-unfinished meta-narrative of a neighbourhood.

These conclusions can also be stated in more pragmatic terms. Building the social capability for neighbourhood-asset management is not a simple process of defining skills and supplying training. Rather, it depends on a conjunction of factors – social, organizational and institutional, physical – all of which are constantly changing. This implies three things. First, the meaning of social sustainability is not the same for every neighbourhood; it is necessary to make the idea explicit for each specific area. Second, decisions about where, when and how to step in require systematic analysis. Third, capability and/or organizational building are not once-and-for-all interventions, but need to be thought of in terms of taking neighbourhood narratives-so-far forward in a set of intermittent (although not necessarily brief) interventions based on imagining further chapters in the narrative.

Acknowledgements

The research on which this paper is based was funded by the UK Department for International Development, UN-Habitat Slum Upgrading Facility and the European Union. The authors are grateful for the opportunity to bring lessons from developing countries to bear on the experiences of developed countries.

Note

1   Because Parliament in Westminster makes both 'national policy' and 'English policy', but not Scottish policy nor devolved aspects of Welsh policy, it is sometimes easy to confuse national policy and policy for England. In this chapter we refer to government policy for England as 'English policy'.

References

Bourdieu, P. (1989) 'Social Space and Symbolic Power', *Sociological Theory*, vol 7, no 1, pp14–25

Brown, R., Kalra, R. and Theis, M. (2005) *Community Asset Management in Africa: Vol 1*, Max Lock Centre, University of Westminster, London

Carney, D. (1998) *Sustainable Rural Livelihoods: What Contribution Can We Make?*, DFID, London

Coleman, J. (1988) 'Social capital in the creation of human capital', *American Journal of Sociology*, vol 94, Supplement, ppS95–S120

Department for Environment, Food and Rural Affairs (2005) *Securing the Future – Delivering UK Sustainable Development Strategy*, Cmnd 6467, TSO, London

Lloyd-Jones, T. (2002) 'Preface: The Sustainable Livelihoods Approach and the Department for International Development', in Rakodi, C., with Lloyd-Jones, T. (eds) *Urban Livelihoods – A People-Centred Approach to Reducing Poverty*, Earthscan, London, ppxiv–xvii

Lloyd-Jones, T., Bouchard, B., Theis, M., Mulwan, B., Winarso, H., Amri, M., Rifayantina, I. and Djohanputro, B. (2007) *UN-Habitat Slum Upgrading Facility: Field Testing Design Instruments in Indonesia*, Max Lock Centre, University of Westminster, London

Lloyd-Jones, T., with Eldridge, A., Mulyawan, B. and Theis, M. (2008) *Retrofitting Soho – Improving the Sustainability of Historic Core Areas*, MLC Press, University of Westminster, London

Massey, D. (2005) *For Space*, Sage, London

Max Lock Centre (2001) *Guide to Good Practice in Core Areas Development: Summary Technical Report*, University of Westminster, London, http://home.wmin.ac.uk/MLprojects/Core_Areas/MainReport/Techreport.pdf, accessed 21 December 2009

Max Lock Centre (2006) *Development of a Housing Association model of Housing Management for Jakarta – Pilot Project Proposal for Kampung Karet Tengsin: Interim Report*. London: Max Lock Centre, University of Westminster

Porritt, J. (2006) *Capitalism: As If the World Matters,* Earthscan, London

Putnam, R. (2000) *Bowling Alone: The Collapse and Revival of American Community*, Simon and Schuster, London

Rakodi, C. (2002) 'A Livelihoods Approach – Conceptual Issues and Definitions', in Rakodi, C., with Lloyd-Jones, T. (eds) *Urban Livelihoods – A People-Centred Approach to Reducing Poverty*, pp3–22, Earthscan, London

Theis, M., Sarin, G. and Kalra, R. (2003) *Building Capacity for Community Asset Management: Main Report/Final Report*, Max Lock Centre, University of Westminster, London

University of Westminster (2008) 'Retrofitting and Sustainability for City Centres: Soho Pilot Study', www.wmin.ac.uk/sabe/page-1156, accessed 21 December 2009

5

Women's Social Networks and Their Importance in Promoting Sustainable Communities

Catalina Gandelsonas

Introduction

The purpose of this chapter is to trace out some of the gendered aspects of social sustainability. It does this by first reflecting on three examples, drawn from developing and developed countries. This reflection is filtered through three lenses: the question of women's specific needs; the notions of social networks; and questions of governance. It illustrates how gender-specific needs drive particular forms of networking activity, including, notably, the communication of particular forms of information and knowledge. It argues that the resulting social capital both empowers women and contributes to more general social sustainability at the community level. Questions of governance at different levels determine both how this social capital is formed and how it is preserved and reproduced. Gender mainstreaming in national policies and institutions can help establish the preconditions for incorporating greater gender equality into the concept of social sustainability.

The significance of studying gendered aspects of social sustainability was signalled by the Fourth World Conference on Women, held in Beijing in 1995. In summarizing the outcome of this international meeting, the UN Division for the Advancement of Women (UNDAW) stated:

> The fundamental transformation that took place in Beijing was the recognition of the need to shift the focus from women to the concept of gender, recognizing that the entire structure of society, and all relations between men and women within it, had to be re-evaluated. Only by such a fundamental restructuring of society and its institutions could women be fully empowered to take their rightful place as equal partners with men in all aspects of life. (United Nations Division for the Advancement of Women, 2000)

The first two examples below illustrate very different approaches to a common problem: women's responsibilities for the management of domestic water. As UN DAW puts it:

> Women have long been a focus in the domestic water sub-sector; their central place based primarily on the idea of their 'natural' role as household managers. For many years women have been identified as the main drawers of water; the primary promoters of hygiene behaviour among children and those most likely to benefit from improved water supplies in terms of alleviation of the burden of their domestic tasks. (United Nations Division for the Advancement of Women, 2005)

Both these examples illustrate the importance of women's solidarity, built through local or neighbourhood networks among them. The third example is very different and raises questions about creating the broader social and organizational infrastructures that support women in taking power.

Women taking power: Pakistan, Argentina and Spain

Lahore, Pakistan

Pakistan's culture and traditions can be traced to the beginning of Islam in the Indian subcontinent. Although there are smaller groups of Hindus, Sikhs and Christians, the majority of the population is Muslim, and Islamic culture and religion affects all aspects of the daily lives of both men and women.

This example involved women's social seclusion in the Old District of Lahore, where women's needs related to their desire to have social contact with each other, in order to communicate and to exchange knowledge relating to their households, child-bearing and other matters of general interest. A study was made in the Choona Mandi sub-area of the Old City of Lahore in 1995 by the Development Planning Unit students (at University College London), in collaboration with local students of architecture of Dawood College of Engineering and Technology, the University of Engineering and Technology and the National College of Arts in Lahore Pakistan (Development Planning Unit, 1995). The study looked at a busy, mixed-used district located in the north-eastern part of the Walled City.

A survey of about 60 families, based on interviews and questionnaires, confirmed that women suffered similar problems to Western women in relation to practical, physiological, strategic and developmental needs, but also severe spatial seclusion (Development Planning Unit, 1996). It confirmed that gender restrictions were severe for working-class women; for example, in the Walled

City, 49 per cent of women never left their homes and had no contact with the outside world. The remainder had some contacts but much less than Western women, as they were allowed to use public space only when accompanied by male family members and were confined to socializing within their houses (domestic space) or on the external terraces of their dwellings (semi-public space). The only chance they had to socialize with other women was when collecting water from public wells and, in order to maintain these social encounters, they rejected the possibility of having piped water facilities in their homes (Gandelsonas, 2000). Similar social networks still prevail in the countryside of Pakistan, while most of the social networks of the Walled City disappeared with the installation of drinking water.

Barrio San Jorge, Argentina

This case study (from Schusterman, 2000) involves the project of a women's social network, part of a low-income community living in a peri-urban settlement in Argentina, designed to address the lack of drinking-water provision in their homes and to clean up the squalor of their area. The women were motivated by the need to protect their children from various diseases, triggered by the lack of hygiene in minimum survival conditions.

In most low-income settlements, women are responsible for water-related activities and, in collecting, consuming and disposing of water, they have a different use and perception of the spaces where these activities take place to those of men. The various systems devised to improve the provision of drinking water and sanitation changed the gender division and use of space, particularly for women who were originally confined to their private domestic space. Where originally water had to be carried in buckets by women and children from the outskirts of the *barrio* to their homes, thanks to the formation of social networks based on community participation, a sanitation and water project was implemented. This project allowed women to gain more time to do other things in the time they previously spent in carrying water, thus improving the quality of their lives.

The Argentinean case study is an example of women forming social networks and creating social capital embodied in a particular project – where they took the responsibility of finding financial solutions, negotiating their problems with the local government and, finally, building the water infrastructure (sewers and drinking-water system) without the help of husbands, partners or local men, making a major contribution to the sustainability of and healthier living conditions for their community.

Other projects in Argentina and in other Latin American countries replicated this experience with very positive outcomes, as women became more visible as paid labour for the construction of shelter and water-related infrastructure (Schusterman, 2000; Hardoy et al, 2002). This triggered a change in gender relations in their households and the community as women dared to carry out tasks traditionally restricted to men, often providing the only monetary income to their households (Schusterman, 2000).

Each of these examples concern the significance of local networks, in this case formed around the task of drawing water from public wells. However, the Pakistan case study illustrates the importance of the network that needs to be preserved to maintain the social capital established through communication between a group of women based on common interests and needs. The Argentinean case study illustrates how a network can develop into a specific project. Both rest on the importance of communication and solidarity among women. Both are concerned with basic needs that arise, in these cases, among low-income groups in urban settlements in developing countries. Women's specific needs do not disappear with economic development. They do, however, change in nature. Under progressive forms of governance, economic development can free up state resources to support meeting women's needs, as illustrated in the following example from Spain.

Instituto de la Mujer, Spain

After the death of General Franco in 1975, Spain's governance, social norms and character underwent a dramatic transformation, and the country has experienced rapid economic development since then. As an applicant to the European Union (EU), this took place in the framework of the *Acquis Communitaire* (the EU law acquired thus far). Spain became an applicant country in 1977, acceding to the EU in 1986. EU policy was expanding from a specific concern with 'women as workers' to the more fully developed equalities concept which is now adopted as formal 'policy'. The original Treaty of the European Union obliged member states to promote equality between women and men and this was reinforced in subsequent legislation, with the policy of gender mainstreaming being introduced in the 1990s (Office of the Equal Opportunities Ombudsman, 2006).

This case study concerns formalized women's networks and partnerships, created to support those who suffer physical violence, sexual abuse and lack of information about access to education and employment. The data was collected from interviews by the author with Sr Jose Luis Burgos, head of research at the Instituto de la Mujer (National Institute for Women), Madrid, in May 2007 and February 2008. It was complemented with information provided by Ms Paloma Candela, equality civil servant from Madrid, in June 2009, and from various reports published by the organization (Instituto de la Mujer, 2004b).

Despite the existence of informal women's networks, it was only in the late 1970s, after 40 years of Franco's dictatorship, that the Spanish socialist government decided to promote gender equality. In 1978, legislation was enacted that recognized women and men's equality, and the Instituto de la Mujer was set up by the Ministry of Work and Social Affairs. Its most important task has been to promote equality between women and men and help women in need. It aims to accomplish this by promoting women's participation in the Spanish cultural, political economic and social life, which did not exist before 1978. The institute has consistently maintained that gender is a social construct defined by roles, beliefs, behaviour and values, which depend more on cultural aspects than on biological differences between sexes (Valle Amparo, 2001).

In 2004, the national government strengthened previous legislation by enacting 'The organic Law of Equality', with the creation of the Secretary for Women. This was followed by the establishment of the Ministry of Equality in 2007. All of these resources were aimed at empowering the work done by the Instituto de la Mujer, acting at regional and local levels. At the same time, drawing on regional and European funds, new local government jobs under the title of equality officer (*funcionario de igualdad*) were created, aimed at coordinating and supporting women's informal social networks and partnerships at local levels. Additional subsidies were released to support existing networks and new associations (non-governmental organizations, social networks and formal partnerships) at local levels. These were established to create and reinforce social capital to provide access to local knowledge about community issues, health matters, training or education, financial possibilities, legal advice for divorce and other related issues.

The Instituto de la Mujer provides 24-hour information and support to local and immigrant women in rural and urban areas on various subjects, including the law (marriage, divorce, rape, free legal aid), general health (cancer, menopause, anorexia, bulimia, disability and age-related health concerns), family planning and pregnancy, jobs and training. It has opened shelters for homeless or bullied women and offers psychological support to victims of physical violence and sexual abuse. It also has relationships with partnerships of women and non-governmental women's networks of lawyers and business women, who help with legal problems relating to residence status, housing and employment (Instituto de la Mujer, 2004a).

This case study illustrates the impact that a framework of 'good governance' (see below) at the national level can have in encouraging the formation of local networks and organizations that can help empower women. It is not an objective evaluation of the programme, as it is based on data obtained from the Instituto de la Mujer and not on a direct survey of the associations themselves. Nevertheless, the Institute's reports suggest that the programme has had widespread success in the creation of lasting social capital.

These examples point to some key general concepts that are examined in the rest of this chapter, which then seeks to integrate them within a theoretical 'model' or conceptual framework. The concepts include:

- The significance of women's networks and the communication between women that gives rise to them.
- Two key aspects in the creation of social capital: the significance of communication in creating networks of trust, on the one hand, and the social organizational characteristics and questions of governance, on the other. Where there is a supportive policy and institutional framework at the national level, this can help promote more formal, durable and potentially better and more transparently managed types of social organization at the local level. Arguably, these two levels of governance are interlinked and mutually reinforcing (for better or worse).
- Social sustainability: women's empowerment and its social benefits in the longer term may require a persistent organizational framework that allows different things to happen as appropriate. It might be unrealistic to expect 'project-based' network-level organizations to persist: accomplishing one's ends is a success. The requirement is to allow lots of women's networks to form and pursue appropriate ends, but not to force their emergence; rather, to support it with appropriate policies and institutions.

Sustainability, social sustainability, social capital and social networks

The Brundtland Commission idea of sustainable development as 'development that meets the needs of the present without compromising the ability of future generations to meet their own needs' concisely encapsulated the social, economic and environmental dimensions. There remained, however, two distinct interpretations of sustainable development: the classic interpretation emphasized economic and environmental issues, and the long-term perspective on availability of natural resources and environmental impacts; the other interpretation focused on social sustainability and was related to achieving 'social sustainability' through a more balanced distribution of economic and social goods, and wider access to social capital.

As discussed elsewhere in this book, a further important contribution to the developing concept of social sustainability came from Bourdieu (1986), who distinguished between three forms of capital: economic, cultural and social (see discussion on social capital in Chapter 1). The definitions of social capital and social sustainability were further refined by Goodland (1992), Portes (1998) and others. Thus, while Goodland states that social capital requires shared knowledge, values and information provided by community, religious and cultural interactions, Portes distinguishes four sources of capital and emphasizes its positive role in social control and family support derived from extra-familial networks, mentioning also examples of its negative consequences. Positive social capital (as opposed to negative social capital resulting from harmful or violent behaviour by members of a community) was defined as the access to human support and information that women and men may get from their relationships with members of social networks. This type of 'social capital' was defined by Portes (1998, p6) as 'the ability of actors to secure benefits through membership in networks and other social structures'. It has also been defined as:

> investments and services that create the basic framework for society and requires cohesion of community for mutual benefit, connectedness between groups of people, reciprocity, tolerance, compassion, patience forbearance, fellowship, love, commonly accepted standards of honesty, discipline and ethics. Commonly shared rules, laws and information. (Goodland, 1992, p2)

All of these things promote social sustainability.

Social networks and issues of governance

Social networks are a persistent theme in urban sociology and anthropology, dating from the German sociologists Durkheim, Tönnies and Simmel from the late 19th century onwards (Freeman, 2004). Simmel was the first to use an explicitly social networking approach by looking at the effect of network size on interaction between individuals and the likelihood of interaction in loosely knit, overlapping networks (Simmel, 1964; Wellman, 1988).

In the 20th century, social network theory, developed as an explicit approach through the empirical study of small community, tribal, kinship, class and work-based and other local groups by sociologists and urban and social anthropologists in the USA and UK, led to a network-based social structure theory (Radcliff-Brown, 1940; Barnes, 1954; Nadel, 1957; Berkowitz, 1982; White, 1992; Freeman, 2004). In the USA and Canada, social network theory has taken on considerable momentum in a much wider range of fields within and beyond sociology, with the adoption of quantitative and computer-based methods (mathematical graph theory, statistical methods) and the growing importance of the Internet as a medium of social communication.

In this theoretical discourse there has been little or no attention to gender-related issues, nor is it clear how gender-related power relations sit within a social-network theory framework. Some clue as to how this might be interpreted can be found in French post-structuralism, particularly in the ideas of Foucault, who envisaged power as having a network-like structure, vested not in particular organizations or individuals, but in the relationships between them (Foucault and Gordon, 1980, p98). At the household level, the focus in theories of 'co-operative conflict' in the development discourse (Sen, 1990) has been on intra-household, gender-based power relations within patriarchal households, with a relative neglect of networks and of the recognition of different types of household and their existence as sub-systems within wider sets of social relation (Ruwanpura, 2006).

Social networks can be identified by:

- The way they are generated, including gender- and age-based networks, kinship associations, neighbourhood-based groupings, origin-based networks, politically based networks, religious and ethnic, cooperative credit groups, employment-based networks, linkages with NGOs and other organizations (Gandelsonas, 2002; Phillips, 2002). It is important to understand how to gain access to a particular network, as the possibility of meeting a single network member can provide key access to the rest of the social network.
- Their continuity or lack of continuity in communicating information or knowledge in connection to a particular topic, as most social networks may lack continuity, which seriously triggers the loss of valuable information or social capital (Mullins, 2006; McShane and Von Glinow, 2007).
- Their structural characteristics, including network size, density, clustering and centrality, which determines the morphological and functional characteristics of networks (see Kuper and Kuper 1985). This type of quantitative analysis was not undertaken in the case studies being reviewed in this chapter.

Social networks are normally socially related groups of women and men such as friends, relatives, neighbours or colleagues at work (Gandelsonas, 2002; Phillips, 2002). Local women's networks or associations operating on a largely informal basis may get as far as initiating or even operating projects, as described in the examples above. However, in undertaking such activities, they will need to draw on resources (e.g. a meeting place, vehicles, tools) that require financial transactions. The more large-scale and continuous this is, the more likely they are to need formal machinery and be constituted as a legal body. They may become charities or trusts, receive legacies and donations, acquire property and/or take on paid officers. Such formal associations need to be transparent and operate under a regime of effective organizational governance (using governance in the sense that it is used, for example, in corporate social responsibility in the business world), with a clear purpose, roles, timeframes and rules of conduct, all of which are broadly necessary to manage common resources (Greengage International, 2002). There is a wide-ranging terminology to describe this form of local organization depending on the context: community-based organizations, 'popular' or grass-roots organizations, local NGOs, civic societies. Community development trusts and other 'third sector' organizations are explored by Nick Bailey in Chapter 3. However, many these of terms give no clue as to their degree of formality, legal definition or form of governance.

The issue of internal governance raises questions about potential conflicts between effective management and transparency: whether more informal and open forms of association are better at generating and maintaining trust within communities and social networks than more formal and closed types of organization, where decision-making is channelled through representative or paid individuals. The following is a brief outline of how this problem sits within a framework of governance at a range of levels.

If trust is the basic substance of social capital, then we need to consider the role of governance in ensuring the transfer of social capital by social networks or more formal bodies in a particular context. Practice suggests that the various stakeholders involved at all levels should operate under internationally agreed principles of 'good governance'. Governance is a broader concept than government. According to the United Nations Development Programme (UNDP): 'It comprises the mechanisms, processes and institutions through which citizens and groups articulate their interests, exercise their legal rights, meet their obligations and mediate their differences' (UNDP, 1997). Although this is normally applied at the national level, the same concept clearly has an application to many different types of organization at the local level. Principles of 'good governance' include fairness, decency, accountability, transparency, efficiency and rule-of-law for all the stakeholders involved (Rakodi with Lloyd-Jones, 2002; Lloyd-Jones and Taylor, 2004). Other key principles include subsidiarity of authority and resources to the lowest or 'closest' appropriate level, participation and equity of access to decision-making (UN-Habitat, 2002, pp19–24).

Case studies in urban governance and development were undertaken in India by the author (Gandelsonas et al, 2005), together and by other members of the Max Lock Centre research team in Pakistan, Kenya, Tanzania and Brazil, as part of the Department for International Development (DFID)-funded research of 'Localising the Habitat Agenda' between 2001 and 2004 (Lloyd-Jones and Auramaa, 2005). These showed that, typically in developing countries, as in urban regeneration projects in the UK and developed world countries, local community organizations including grass-roots women's organizations enter into partnerships with local authorities, funding agencies, NGOs and other civil society organizations to realize projects that contribute to the infrastructure of social sustainability.

This introduces a second layer of governance, intermediate between the community-based organizations and the activities of the formal governmental system. To enable partnerships to work, all partners involved need to have access to knowledge and information relating to the social capital embedded in the particular project or programme that the partnership is pursuing. For a partnership to succeed, trust and mutual respect between partners must exist or be promoted.

According to Greengage International (2002), the following principles need to be established and followed for the survival of healthy partnerships:

- Getting the right people involved.
- Creating inclusive meetings.
- Facilitating the climate and norms within the group.
- Building a commitment to action.
- Ending every meeting 'in action'.
- Creating good housekeeping and administration systems.

Obviously, such aims cannot be exactly replicated in each partnership but provide guidance to achieve partnership permanence. Roberts (2003) points out that, to achieve continuity, partnership members need to be aware of the need to constantly improve the way in which their partnership works and to have the willingness to achieve conflict resolution resulting from good and bad relationships between partners. Thus, partnership members need to develop the ability to use conflict as a means of improving their way of working together to transfer social capital.

Social networks, formal community-based organizations and partnership associations have their advantages and disadvantages. As social networks may lack permanence and structural continuity, formal bodies including partnerships appear to be more reliable organizations for the transfer of valuable social capital. However, if social networks are already operating, they and the social capital they embody may be easier to access for outsiders than formal organizations, where such access may only be possible with the consent of their members. What formal organizations gain in durability they may lose in terms of the trust that forms the bedrock of social capital. The problem of accessibility may be best addressed, as shown by the example of the Instituto de la Mujer in Spain, through gender mainstreaming and a progressive institutional and policy framework. Thus, while the problem of social networks is that once their purpose is accomplished, they are likely to disappear, triggering the loss of valuable knowledge and information as social capital (Gandelsonas, 2007), partnerships and other formal organizations may only be accessible to the wider community if good governance is in place.

Partnerships will most likely operate better than social networks if the above-mentioned good governance principles are followed particularly by central and local governments, as they may ensure the permanence of projects and internal good governance, enabling the transfer of social capital. This is because such organizations are formally conceived and managed, which may guarantee that the aim/purpose of their projects do effectively transfer social capital over a steady period of time, as in the case of the Instituto de la Mujer.

Women and men's needs and motivation

Women and men have different needs relating to their different gender roles. Despite this, classic psychology and development theories group men and women's needs together in a single category that makes the differentiation of their individual gender needs difficult (Evans, 1992; Gandelsonas, 2000). Gender theories, however, have established the importance of defining women and men's differences, as only when their differences are understood can their 'needs' possibly be resolved (Evans, 1992).

Psychological theorists following Maslow (1943, 1987) categorize needs from the most pressing physiological survival needs of air, water, food, warmth and shelter to psychological needs, which are equally important but not fundamental to survival. Survival is a basic human need, followed by safety and security that relates psychological and physiological components. From a temporal point of view, both needs are pressing. Once safety and security have been met, other important psychological needs have to be satisfied, including a sense of affiliation (men and women need to feel that they belong to a group), esteem (men and women need to be valued and loved by themselves and by others), and cognitive, actualization and aesthetic needs, which are needed to fulfil one's capacities.

While various theories address a 'human needs' hierarchy', gender theories describe men and women's particular practical and strategic needs (Moser and Peake, 1987; Gandelsonas, 2000). Needs are definitely different as:

> in many parts of the world, women carry a heavier burden than men, resulting from their productive and reproductive roles. Whilst men generally hold the single role of income earner, women may suffer the combined burden of bearing and caring for children, undertaking domestic tasks as well as providing for their families, all of which puts them in a very vulnerable position. Furthermore, the obligations and workloads of women and men vary according to the different roles they play in their life-cycles, all of which are subject to the different belief systems of their cultures. (Gandelsonas, 2007, p106)

While practical needs are water, shelter, healthcare and employment, strategic needs, which vary in each socio-political context, include alleviation of domestic tasks that refer to the burden of childcare, land ownership, equal pay, legal rights and access to employment. Practical and strategic needs are clearly related to the concept of social capital, which is crucial to achieving social sustainability. This is because, while practical needs include childbearing, child rearing, general family health and organization of the household, strategic needs are associated to work information, education, self-development and community or political roles (which also relate to improving living conditions). Both practical and strategic needs are related to the ability to access knowledge and information about community social capital.

Women and men's needs vary in different cultures and locations in the world. While the needs of women and men from Europe, the USA, Japan and other developed countries relate mainly to education, employment, safety, spatial barriers and mobility (Cavanagh, 1998), in many Islamic countries women also suffer severe spatial seclusion (Gandelsonas, 2000). Furthermore, in Latin America, Asia and Africa, large groups of low-income women and men fall into dramatic poverty traps, lacking all the above needs but particularly basic practical and physiological needs such as shelter, drinking water, food and sanitary facilities (Moser and Peake, 1987; Gandelsonas, 2000).

Thus, it may be assumed that in most cases, women and men's needs and interests differ, and will, therefore, have different motivations in pursuing specific roles. Once needs have been clearly identified, motivation will trigger actions that are the driving force necessary to achieve desired goals. To fulfil basic needs, women and men must communicate with the environment and with each other.

Communication issues

Communication needs to be understood as a complex cycle. It involves people (a sender and receiver), actions (coding, decoding and sending a message), a message and the vehicle or media. It also includes 'an effect', which refers to people's reactions when they receive the message and their willingness to react or answer the message received. Thus, a successful communication cycle requires a mode/media or vehicle for transmitting the message between sender and receiver, and vice-versa (Watson and Hill, 2000; Gandelsonas, 2002). The communication *vehicle* or *media* may be a social network, a partnership and/or an intermediary. Also, the vehicle or media for communicating knowledge may be published posters, handouts, leaflets, radio, TV and Internet (Max Lock Centre, 2000).

The aim of a communication cycle is to establish that the receiver or recipient of the message has a clear understanding of the contents or meaning of the message. In communication generally the recipient does not have to agree with the message but, in the context of social networks, when people attempt to communicate, they are trying to establish a connection or commonness, and effective communication will hopefully result in agreement, unity, common good and common concern (Reilly and DiAngelo, 1990, p139; in Newell, 2001).

In this sense, the message or knowledge/information is the 'social capital' needed to fulfil women and men's basic practical and physiological needs. Thus, social networks or socially related groups of people may function as an effective media for communicating or transferring knowledge about social capital, when their members deliver messages to each other that have a 'shared meaning' (which is possible when women and men have similar needs and share similar beliefs, level of education and culture). Furthermore, organizational behaviour and gender theories establish a difference between 'superficial' and 'deeper' levels of 'meaning', both embedded in the message transferred in a communication cycle initiated by women or men (Newell, 2001; Wilson, 2001; Mullins, 2006; McShane and Von Glinow, 2007).

This is accomplished through active listening, the most effective communication skill associated with women, because good communication happens when meaning is shared, which is best done through active listening (McKenna, 1994; Newell, 2001). McKenna identifies a number of criteria to assess active listening, including eye contact, nodding, paraphrasing, and showing a clear interest by avoiding interruptions and distracting actions. Differences between male and female communication styles, endlessly discussed by feminists, partly explain the effectiveness of women's social networks and partnerships (Newell, 2001; Wilson, 2001). Feminists basically recognize that these differences result from the different socialization processes experienced in childhood by girls and boys, which lead to different gender identities and differences in styles of communication (Newell, 2001; Wilson, 2001).

These factors explain the importance, uniqueness and effectiveness of women's social networks and partnerships (in contrast to women and men's social networks or men's social networks) as an active communication media that may help to successfully transfer social capital. One of the important aspects of social capital relates to encouraging poor families or single women or men who have recently moved into a community to get in touch with existing social networks, relationships and organizations used by poor people as a starting point. The support women achieve from women's social networks and partnerships is crucial in achieving social sustainability, as larger percentages of single-women-headed households hold both productive and reproductive roles, either because their husbands have migrated to urban areas to improve their income or because they suffer from feminization of poverty occurring, that is, 'as poverty among women is rising faster than poverty among men' (Wach and Reeves, 2000, p6; Phillips, 2002; Rakodi, with Lloyd-Jones, 2002).

A theoretical framework combining the above concepts

The various concepts that have been discussed above may be combined to formulate a theoretical and practical framework, which here is used to analyse three case studies: two based on secondary information relating to women's social networks and a further study based on primary data regarding women partnerships and governance.

Figure 5.1 describes a sequence whereby women and men's needs trigger the motivation required to communicate with each other, by communicating or transferring messages, information or knowledge. Thus, social networks, community-based organizations and partnerships are utilized here as media to transfer social capital related to a relevant need or problem, which may be resolved through the acquisition of particular information–knowledge of social capital. Such networks and organizations may have a positive impact on the sustainability of a community, as they can generate positive social capital, which may help other community members or women and men to fulfil their basic needs.

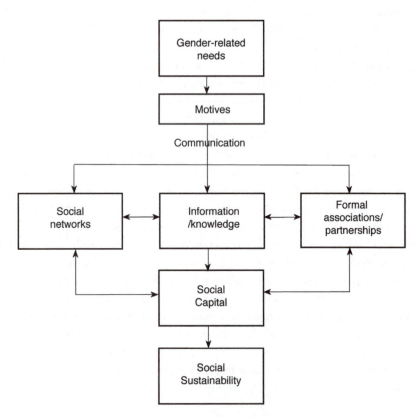

Figure 5.1 *Conceptual model*

Conclusions

In summary, in addressing the gendered aspects of social sustainability, this chapter has:

- Highlighted the importance of women's social networks, community-based organizations and partnerships for creating and transferring social capital.
- Shown how the resulting social capital both empowers women and contributes to more general social sustainability at the community level.
- Shown how forms of organization and the effectiveness of governance at different levels determine both how this social capital is formed and how it is preserved and reproduced.
- Illustrated how gender mainstreaming in national policies and institutions can help establish the pre-conditions for incorporating greater gender equality into the concept of social sustainability.
- Discussed how gender-specific needs drive particular forms of networking activity, including, notably, the communication of particular forms of information and knowledge critical to the formation of social capital (including access to basic needs related to shelter, water, sanitation, health, education and employment).
- Noted the differences between women and men's productive and reproductive needs, and shown how these trigger the 'motivation' required for forming social networks and other forms of local association.
- Highlighted the differences between male and female 'communication styles', resulting from different socialization processes and how, in the case of women, these can enhance the effectiveness of women's social networks.
- Illustrated with case studies how women are able to use their motivation to rally themselves through informal networks and/or formal organizations to fulfil their various productive and reproductive needs.

Women's productive and reproductive needs and their particular way of communicating enable them to form effective networks, community-based organizations and partnerships. Depending on the framework of governance, these can be effective media for preserving and transferring information and knowledge relating to their needs, and underscoring their empowerment.

References

Barnes, J. (1954) 'Class and Committees in a Norwegian Island Parish', *Human Relations*, vol 7, pp39–58

Berkowitz, Stephen D. (1982) *An Introduction to Structural Analysis: The Network Approach to Social Research*, Butterworth, Toronto

Boissevain, J. (1985) in Kuper, A. and Kuper, J. (eds) *The Social Science Encyclopaedia*, Routledge & Kegan Paul, London

Bourdieu, P. (1986) *The Forms of Capital*, Greenwood, New York

Cavanagh, S. (1998) 'Women and the Urban Environment', in Greed, C. and Roberts, M. (eds) *Introducing Urban Design: Interventions & Responses*, Addison Wesley Longman Ltd, Harlow

Department for International Development (2000) *Sustainable Livelihoods Guidance Sheets*, DFID, London

Development Planning Unit (1995) *Report of Fieldwork in Lahore*, DPU, University College London, London

Development Planning Unit (1996) *MSc Workshop: An Introduction to Gender in Policy & Planning*, DPU, University College London, London

Evans, A. (1992) 'Statistics', in Ostergaard, L. (ed.) *Gender and Development: A Practical Guide,* Routledge, London

Foucault, M. and Gordon, C. (1980) *Power/Knowledge: Selected Interviews and Other Writings 1972–1977*, Harvester Press, Brighton

Freeman, L. (2004) *The Development of Social Network Analysis*, Empirical Press, Vancouver

Gandelsonas, C. (2000) 'The Development and Application of a Gender Sensitive Urban Design Methodology', in *Open House International Journal* special issue 'Gender and Space', vol 25, no 4, DPU, University College London, London/Eastern Mediterranean University Mersin 1, Turkey

Gandelsonas, C. (ed.) (2002) *Communicating for Development*, ITDG, London

Gandelsonas, C. (2007) 'The Importance of Communication in the Design Management Process', *The International Journal of Interdisciplinary Social Sciences*, vol 1, issue 4, pp155–168

Gandelsonas, C. (2008) 'Women's Social Networks and Sustainability', *The International Journal of Interdisciplinary Social Sciences*, vol 2, issue 6, pp107–111

Gandelsonas, C., Sagoo, I. and Khosla, R. (2005) 'Case Study in India', in Max Lock Centre, *Localising the Habitat Agenda for Urban Poverty Reduction*, vol 3, Annex 3A, 'Country Reports', Max Lock Centre, University of Westminster, London

Goodland, R. (1992) 'Sustainability: Human, Social, Economic and Environmental', draft report, World Bank, Washington, DC, later published as part of: Munn, T. (2001) *Encyclopaedia of Global Environmental Change,* John Wiley & Sons Ltd, Chichester, UK

Greengage International (2002) in Max Lock Centre, *Localising the Habitat Agenda for Urban Poverty Reduction*, vol 4, Annex 4I, 'Workshop presentation, Partnerships Workshops, London, 10 October 2002', Max Lock Centre, London

Hardoy, J., Mitlin, D. and Satterthwaite D. (2002) *Environmental Problems in an Urbanizing World*, Earthscan, London

Instituto de la Mujer (2004a) *Agrupacion de Desarrollo del Projecto 'Diversidad Activa'*, '*Manual de Igualdad de Oportunidades*', Madrid, Spain

Instituto de la Mujer (2004b) Reports on Health, Finances, Legal Aid etc., Madrid, Spain

Lloyd-Jones, T. and Auramaa, I. (2005) 'Case Studies Summary', in Max Lock Centre, *Localising the Habitat Agenda for Urban Poverty Reduction*, vol 1, Annex 1B, Max Lock Centre, University of Westminster, London

Lloyd-Jones, T. and Taylor, W. (2004) 'The Concept of Urban Governance', in Max Lock Centre (2005) *Localising the Habitat Agenda for Urban Poverty Reduction*, vol 2, Annex D, Max Lock Centre, University of Westminster, London

Maslow, A. (1987 [1954]) *Motivation and Personality*, 3rd edition, revised by Frager, R., Fadiman, J., Reynolds, C. and Cox, Ruth, Harper, New York

Maslow, A. H. (1943) 'A theory of human motivation', *Psychological Review* 50(4), pp370–396

Max Lock Centre (2000) *Knowledge Transfer Guidelines*, University of Westminster, London

McKenna, E. (1994) *Business Psychology and Organizational Behaviour*, Lawrence Erlbaum Associates Ltd, Hove, UK

McShane, S. L. and Von Glinow, M. A. (2007) *Organizational Behaviour*, McGraw-Hill, Irwin, London

Moser, C. and Peake, L. (eds) (1987) *Women, Human Settlements & Housing*, Tavistock Publications, London

Mullins, L. (2006) *Essentials of Organizational Behaviour*, Prentice Hall, London

Nadel, S. F. (1957) *The Theory of Social Structure*, Cohen and West, London

Newell, S. (2001) 'Communication', Chapter 4, in Wilson, E. (ed.) *Organizational Behaviour Reassessed: The Impact of Gender*, Sage, London

Office of the Equal Opportunities Ombudsman (2006) 'Gender Equality in the European Union', Gender Equality Creates Democracy, Social Innovation Fund, Kaunas, Lithuania, www.gender-equality.webinfo.lt/presentations/Liudos.ppt, accessed 21 December 2009

Phillips, S. (2002) 'Community Development and Social Networks', in Rakodi, C. and Lloyd-Jones, A. (eds) *Urban Livelihoods*, Earthscan, London

Portes, A. (1998) 'Social Capital: Its Origins and Applications in Modern Sociology', *Abstract Annual Review of Sociology*, vol 24, pp1–24

Radcliffe-Brown, A. R. (1940) 'On Social Structure', *Journal of the Royal Anthropological Institute*, vol 70, pp1–12

Rakodi, C. with Lloyd-Jones, T. (2002) *Urban Livelihoods: A People-Centred Approach to Reducing Poverty*, Earthscan, London

Roberts, I. (2003) 'UK Pilot Partnerships Workshop Report' (draft), in *Localising the Habitat Agenda for Urban Poverty*, Annex B, DFID, London

Ruwanpura, K. N. (2006) 'Shifting Theories: Partial Perspective on the Household', *Cambridge Journal of Economics*, vol 31, no 3, pp525–538

Schusterman, R. (2000) 'Crossing Borders: Water, Gender and Space in Buenos Aires', in *Open House International Journal*, Special issue: *Gender and Space*, vol 25, no 4

Sen, A. (1990) 'Gender and Co-operative Conflicts', in Tinker, I. (ed) *Persistent Inequalities: Women and World Development*, Oxford University Press, New York, pp123–149

Simmel, G. (1964) *Conflict and the Web of Group Affiliations*, translated by Wolff, K. (ed.), Free Press, Glencoe, IL

UN Development Programme (1997) 'Governance for Sustainable Human Development, a UNDP Policy Document', UN Development Programme, January, http://mirror.undp.org/magnet/policy/, accessed 3 May 2009

UN Division for the Advancement of Women (2000) 'Beijing +5 – 2000: Gender Equality Development and Peace for the 21st Century', www.un.org/womenwatch/daw/followup/session/presskit/hist.htm, accessed 3 May 2009

UN Division for the Advancement of Women (2005) *Women and Water*, Division for the Advancement of Women, UN Secretariat, New York

UN-Habitat (2002) *Principles and Realities of Urban Governance in Africa*, Global Campaign on Urban Governance and Regional Office for Africa and the Arab States, UN-Habitat, Nairobi

Valle Amparo, O. (2001) 'Teoria y analisis de Genero: Guia Metodologica para trabajar en Grupos', Madrid, Spain

Wach, H. and Reeves, H. (2000) *Gender and Development: Facts and Figures*, Report No. 56, Institute of Development Studies prepared for DFID, London, UK

Watson, J. and Hill, A. (2000) 'Dictionary of Communication and Media Studies', 5th edn, Arnold, London/Oxford University Press, New York

Wellman, B. (1988) 'Structural Analysis: From Method and Metaphor to Theory and Substance', pp19–61, in Wellman, B. and Berkowitz, S. D. (eds) *Social Structures: A Network Approach*, Cambridge University Press, Cambridge

White, H. C. (1992) *Identity and Control: A Structural Theory of Social Action*, Princeton University Press, Princeton, NJ

Wilson, E. (ed.) (2001) *Organizational Behaviour Reassessed: The Impact of Gender*, Sage, London

Section 2

The Role of Place and Connectivity in the Urban Socio-Physical Environment

Introduction to the section

The provision of adequate social infrastructure, services and amenities is an important criterion for social sustainability at both the micro- and meso-scale of urban planning. In this context, debates about the 'compact city' (Jenks et al, 1996) have become a prominent feature of urban policy, with proposals to develop housing at higher densities; however, less attention has been devoted to the appropriate level of social infrastructure provision needed to support thriving communities.

Recent research (Silverman et al, 2006) stresses the importance of health and education in attracting families into new developments. The role of transport in linking people to jobs, public services and other amenities such as shops is also a vital component of the wider social infrastructure, and it is increasingly recognized that this must include a range of viable alternatives to the car in order for urban areas to become both environmentally and socially more sustainable. These are the primary considerations of this second section.

In Chapter 6, Suzy Nelson evaluates this provision through case studies of education and health provision in Southwark and Hackney, and raises the important issue of how effective the planning system has been in developing new communities in inner London. She advocates effective partnerships, using creative joint asset management strategies and better use of the land-use planning system to identify new sites, and new models of integrated provision, which use land efficiently. She argues that such an approach requires the development of coordinated Social Infrastructure Plans and robust forecasting of population change to anticipate the likely demands on social infrastructure in the future. She identifies that the monitoring of the implementation of plans for new social infrastructure is a further important feature in developing sustainable communities. The approach involves regular assessment of whether the provision of school places and primary healthcare facilities are keeping up with demand, involving the use of qualitative as well as quantitative data.

Chapter 7, by Karen Lucas and colleagues, provides a detailed discussion of the opportunities and constraints offered by transport policies. This is an important but often neglected feature in discussions of sustainability. Their case study examples show that accessibility planning is a necessary but not sufficient condition for identifying the transport sustainability of new and existing developments. They argue for the early development of effective multi-agency approaches and for the effective involvement of professional stakeholders and local communities that are best placed to identify local accessibility needs.

In Chapter 8, Peter White and his colleagues consider the important role of new information technology and the impact that this might have on individuals' activity patterns, as well as the knock-on effects for local communities looking at the particular example of teleworking. This is a significant development in a digital world, where access to electronic communications can facilitate integration, but, conversely, lack of access to computers and digital technology can serve to increase marginalization and social exclusion for some sectors of the population. The authors find that teleworking can potentially make an important contribution to physical sustainability by reducing the total volume of travel, involving reductions in energy, pollutants and transport capacity costs. They suggest it may also reduce commuting times and thereby assist individuals to interact more effectively with their families and local neighbourhoods. However, they also warn that it can produce negative consequences, where the main beneficiaries are likely to be higher-income, higher-status individuals whose jobs are best suited to this form of working.

References

Jenks, M., Burton, E. and Williams, K. (1996) *The Compact City: A Sustainable Urban Form?*, London: Routledge

Silverman, E., Lupton, R. and Fenton, A. (2005) *A Good Place for Children? Attracting and Retaining Families in Inner Urban Mixed Income Communities*, Coventry: Chartered Institute of Housing and Joseph Rowntree Foundation

6

Residential Intensification, Family Housing and Educational Provision

Suzy Nelson

Introduction

Since the 1990s the UK government has espoused the concept of the compact city and adopted a policy of absorbing growth within existing urban areas. This approach is resulting in an increase in residential densities in areas of high demand. The focus of government policy has been on building new homes, but there are concerns about shortfalls in the provision of family housing and of infrastructure to meet the needs of the expanded population. This chapter focuses on the provision of family housing and school places, which are key factors in attracting and retaining families with children in dense urban areas and which will thus have an impact on social sustainability.

The Labour government, shortly after coming into office in 1997, commissioned the Urban Task Force to make recommendations on how to improve the quality of English towns and cities, at the same time as providing an additional four million homes over a 25-year period to meet the projected increase in the number of households (Urban Task Force, 1999). The members of the task force, in their report *Towards an Urban Renaissance*, advocated a compact and well-connected city. They proposed intensification of development to reduce the amount of land required and to reduce car use. They argued that transport hubs and town centres could support higher population densities and a more diverse mix of uses, and pointed out the importance of getting the right balance of uses and a good mix of households in terms of income and tenure.

The Sustainable Communities Plan (ODPM, 2003) is a key strategy document in implementing the urban renaissance policy agenda. It sets out the Government's strategy of managing housing growth in areas of high demand in the south of England and of managing decline in areas of low demand elsewhere in England. It defines sustainable communities as 'Places where people will want to live and will continue to want to live' (ODPM, 2003, p5). The plan does not explicitly consider how to accommodate the needs of people at different stages of their lives, but puts forward a policy of creating mixed-income communities in order to overcome the problems resulting from concentrations of disadvantaged people. However, in practice, the realization of sustainable mixed-income communities will depend upon making provisions for people at different stages of their lives, but there is some debate about the attractiveness of dense urban living to families with children. Recent research (Bromley and Tallon, 2004; Allinson, 2005; Nathan and Urwin, 2006) suggests that households with children are not being attracted to the core areas of provincial cities. Allinson argues that the policy challenge is to broaden the appeal of cities to groups at different stages of their life-cycle.

Silverman et al (2006) specifically focus on the issue of attracting and retaining families in urban, mixed-income communities. In their view, families, particularly better-off families, are key to the success of mixed-income communities, because a more mixed school intake creates opportunities for interaction across income groups, and because people with children tend to be the most active in community groups, as they have a high stake in their neighbourhoods and services. Silverman et al argue that, if mixed-income communities are to retain middle-class households when they have children, there needs to be an adequate supply of family-sized homes and good local schools.

Following the argument put forward by Silverman et al, this chapter assesses the social sustainability of housing growth and the intensification of development by examining the provision of family-sized homes and local schools. It focuses on London, where a high demand for homes has been stimulated by economic growth. London is an interesting case because it already has a higher population density than other urban areas in the UK, but there is evidence that some high-density neighbourhoods in London are attractive to people with a range of lifestyles, including families with children (Burdett et al, 2004). The chapter looks at two London boroughs and examines the extent to which the planning of growth is addressing the issue of family housing and the provision of local schools. Before presenting these research findings, the recent history of population growth in London and the policy of continuing growth are outlined.

Housing and population growth in London

Until the mid-1980s, London's population was in decline, but it has subsequently grown at an increasing rate (ODPM, 2006). Between 1997 and 2003 the annual rate of change in London was +0.82 per cent. This growth in population corresponded with a substantial expansion in the housing stock. The Greater London Authority Housing Provision Survey shows that more than 421,458 new homes were provided in London between 1987 and 2005; an annual rate of more than 23,000 new homes (GLA, 2005a). The growth has not been spread evenly across the capital. Inner London boroughs, particularly those in the eastern part of the city, experienced particularly high levels of growth.

The London Plan 2004 set ambitious targets for continuing growth. It incorporated targets for regional housing growth set by the UK government; a total of 457,959 additional homes were to be provided for the period 1997–2016, with an annual monitoring target of 23,000 homes, which was the same as the average rate of growth in the previous two decades (Mayor of London, 2004). These targets were based on the London Planning Advisory Committee's Housing Capacity Study (2000). However, they were subsequently revised as a result of a further housing capacity study (Mayor of London, 2005a). The revised target for new homes for the period from 2007/08 to 2016/17 became 305,000 new homes and the annual target increased to 30,500 new homes (Mayor of London, 2006a), a 33 per cent increase on the previous target.

These housing capacity studies assessed the availability of land for housing development, but there are concerns that this approach does not consider wider issues of urban capacity. Gunn (2006) criticizes the UK government guidance on how to carry out these assessments for concentrating on identifying opportunities for future housing development without considering whether the existing infrastructure is over- or under-used. The expert panel that examined the Draft Early Alterations to the London Plan (Examination in Public Panel, 2006) expressed concerns about whether the necessary transport and social infrastructure would be provided to support the increased population. In the panel's view, there was not a clear mechanism for determining infrastructure requirements stemming from a large number of small developments.

Central government targets for housing growth concentrate on the overall number of homes to be produced, but do not specify the type of housing to be produced. The Mayor of London's planning policy, as well as setting overall targets, included requirements relating to the affordability of new homes and the mix of unit sizes. In order to address the problem of high market prices in the capital, the London Plan 2004 included a strategic policy that 50 per cent of housing provision should be affordable. The Supplementary Planning Guidance to the London Plan on Housing (Mayor of London, 2005b) addressed the issue of providing family housing by including guidance on the mix of housing required at the regional level. Overall, 32 per cent of the requirement is for one-bedroom units, 38 per cent for two or three bedrooms and 30 per cent for four or more bedroom units. A report commissioned by the Greater London Authority on housing space standards (Drury et al, 2006), published after this guidance had been produced, shows that an increasing proportion of new dwellings in London are small flats. In 1996/97 equal numbers of flats and houses were produced in London, but by 2004/05 more than 80 per cent of dwellings were flats, and fewer larger flats were being produced. There had been a significant reduction in the number of three-bedroom units built and a corresponding increase in the number of two-bedroom units. In 2004/05 80 per cent of dwellings produced were one- or two-bedroom units. Drury et al highlighted that this trend to the production of flats with fewer bedrooms contrasts with London's demographic profile, as the average household size in London is above the national average.

Housing and population growth in the case study boroughs

Two case studies were undertaken by the author in 2007 to investigate to what extent the needs of families were being considered in planning and implementing residential intensification in London. The boroughs of Southwark and Hackney were chosen for this research because they had high existing population densities, high levels of growth in population since the late 1980s, linked to significant increases in housing capacity, and high targets for future growth, a high proportion of which was to be on small sites. Southwark is opposite the City on the south bank of the Thames and Hackney is immediately to the north of the City. Both boroughs have experienced deindustrialization and some of the land for new housing was previously used for industrial and industry-related purposes. In 2003, Hackney was the third most densely populated London borough and Southwark the eighth (Office for National Statistics, 2003). The recent population growth of both boroughs was higher than the London average. Between 1997 and 2003, Southwark was the London borough with the fourth largest number of new homes; Hackney had the sixth largest number of new homes (GLA, 2005a). In the London Plan 2004, Southwark's annual target was 1480 new homes and Hackney's was 720 new homes; in the early alterations to the London Plan, Southwark's target was increased to 1630 new homes and Hackney's to 1085 (Mayor of London, 2004, 2006a). Thus, both boroughs faced considerable challenges in terms of managing the process of growth and providing an environment which would be attractive to families with children.

Between 2003 and 2006, the rate of completions of new homes in Hackney was consistently above both the original and revised London Plan annual targets, but in Southwark the original target was not met in two out of three years and the revised annual target was not realized (Mayor of London, 2005c, 2006b, 2007). During this period, 4109 new homes were completed in Hackney and 3321 were completed in Southwark.

The case study research involved the review of planning documents produced by key local stakeholders and interviews with the coordinators of Local Strategic Partnerships (LSPs), local politicians, local authority planners and officers responsible for planning school places.

Community strategies and the role of the local strategic partnerships

Since 2000, local authorities in England have had a duty to prepare community strategies 'to improve the economic, social and environmental wellbeing of each area, and to contribute to the achievement of sustainable development in the UK' (DETR, 2001). Local authorities are required to involve LSPs, which should include representatives of the public and private sectors and local communities, in the preparation of community strategies. Given that achieving sustainable development is intended to be one of the objectives of community strategy, one would have expected community strategies to address the issue of managing growth, including the specific needs of households with children. However, Southwark's and Hackney's community strategies (Southwark Alliance, 2006; Hackney Strategic Partnership, 2006) both strongly focused on the issues of social justice and reducing inequality without any consideration of managing growth. Southwark's strategy also included an objective of delivering quality public services that are accessible, well-integrated, customer-focused, efficient and modern (Southwark Alliance, 2006), but it did not refer to the need to provide services for a growing population. Hackney's strategy (Hackney Strategic Partnership, 2006) acknowledged a problem of high population turnover and the tendency for well-off people to move out when they start a family, and it therefore stressed the importance of improving the quality of educational provision in order to create a more stable community.

Although Southwark's community strategy did not address the issue of managing growth, the coordinator of the Southwark LSP (interview, 13 February 2007) did recognize population growth as an important issue for the borough. The LSP had set up a unit to analyse demographic data. This unit is managed by one of the LSP partners, the Primary Health Care Trust (PCT); it is working on issues of deprivation to ensure that resources are effectively targeted, but is also studying population change so services can be effectively planned to meet the needs of the changing population (interview with Southwark PCT officer, 13 February 2007). It saw population growth as being driven by housing growth, but also viewed increasing overcrowding, particularly in the private rented sector, as an issue. Southwark has a high turnover of population, and the unit was comparing data from a range of sources to build up an understanding of who was moving into the borough and who was leaving.

The director of Hackney LSP (interview, 27 March 2007) said that managing growth was not on its agenda, but acknowledged that perhaps it should be. Hackney LSP was also sharing data between organizations, but was not looking at demographic change. A priority for the LSP partners was to provide better integrated services. Although the initial focus of this initiative had been an integrated service for telephone enquiries, this was leading to a discussion about a joint strategy for managing community assets.

Spatial planning

The UK government's current policy is to integrate land-use planning into a wider system of spatial planning, involving greater collaboration and coordination between public and private stakeholders in order to achieve more sustainable development. The Planning and Compulsory Purchase Act 2004 introduced a new system of spatial planning in England. It requires existing development plans to be replaced by Local Development Frameworks (LDFs) (CLG, 2006a). As part of the process of creating development frameworks, Local Planning Authorities (LPAs) have to produce core strategies consistent with the Regional Spatial Strategy, which for the case study boroughs is the London Plan. The legislation also focuses on the implementation of plans and requires LPAs to produce annual monitoring reports (ODPM, 2005a,b).

A planning issue that has been the subject of considerable recent policy discussion is contributions by developers to infrastructure provision (Barker, 2004; CLG, 2006b). Current government guidance (CLG, 2006c) permits LPAs to make the granting of planning permission conditional on developers entering into planning agreements requiring them to contribute to infrastructure provision necessitated by the development.

The extent to which LDF core strategies and other planning documents in the two case study boroughs addressed the provision of family housing and schools is discussed below. The monitoring of the provision of new housing and the role of developers' contributions in the provision of schools are then reviewed.

LDF core strategies

Hackney was in the process of developing a new core strategy. However, when the new system of spatial planning was introduced in 2004, Southwark Council was already well advanced in producing a new Unitary Development Plan under the old system. As Southwark Council considered that the policies in this plan were up-to-date, it decided to continue with the process of adopting this plan instead of preparing a new statement of core policies (Southwark Council, 2005). The revised draft Southwark Plan (Southwark Council, 2006a) and the draft Hackney Core Strategy (Hackney Council, 2006a) gave prominence to the issue of growth; both included housing growth targets from the London Plan 2004 (Mayor of London, 2004). The Hackney Plan anticipated that the resultant growth in population would be 1 per cent a year over the forecast period (2002–16), a total of 14 per cent. The plans both noted that their boroughs had young and expanding populations, with a bulge in the 20 to 39 years age group; this is the age band in which people are most likely to have children. The Hackney)lan also noted a bulge in the 0–4 years age group.

In line with the London Plan 2004, both the Southwark and Hackney plans included a policy target of 50 per cent of all new housing being affordable. They also included targets relating to the size of dwellings to be produced, but these did not directly relate to the London Plan's Supplementary Document on Housing 2005. The Southwark Plan stated that the majority of dwellings should have two bedrooms. However, as private-sector homes tend to be under-occupied, private-sector two-bedroom flats will frequently not be occupied by families with children (GLA, 2005b). The Hackney Plan identified a problem of families living in overcrowded accommodation and states that the borough has a greater requirement for family-sized accommodation than other London boroughs. It required one-third of all new housing to be family accommodation with three or more bedrooms. While Hackney's requirement for providing larger units was more ambitious than Southwark's, it was still below the requirement set out in the London Plan's Supplementary Housing Guidance (Mayor of London, 2005b).

Monitoring of new homes produced

LDF annual monitoring reports for Southwark and Hackney showed that both boroughs were falling well short of their target of 50 per cent affordable housing in 2006. In Southwark in 2004–05, 42 per cent of new homes were classified as affordable housing, and in 2005–06 the figure was only 27 per cent (Southwark Council, undated a and b). In Hackney in 2004–05, 30 per cent of new homes were classified as affordable housing, and in 2005–06 this had been reduced to 19 per cent (Hackney Council, 2006b). Both boroughs failed to realize their targets for a net increase in the number of affordable homes, in part because of estate demolitions, which resulted in a loss of affordable housing. No information on the size of completed units was available in the Hackney monitoring reports; and Southwark Council reported only data for 2005–06, when 50 per cent of completed homes had two bedrooms and 12 per cent had three bedrooms or more. In the London region as a whole there was a continuation of the trends identified by Drury et al (2006); in 2005/06, 85 per cent of new dwellings were one- or two-bedroom units (CLG, undated a). Possibly Hackney's stronger policy on family housing may have resulted in more large homes being produced, but it is probable, as in Southwark and in London as a whole, that most of the new homes produced were one- or two-bedroom flats for the private market.

Developer's contributions

In both plans, the discussion of infrastructure provision, including the provision of additional school places, was considered mainly in the context of developers' contributions to the funding of new provision. Both boroughs produced guidance on planning contributions (Southwark Council, 2006b; Hackney Council, 2006c) that partially codified planning obligations. Formulae were introduced to calculate developers' contributions to the cost of providing additional capacity in schools, where there is a projected shortfall in school places. These contributions are based on child yield rates for new developments and the average capital cost of a school place. Child yield rates, provided by the Greater London Authority, indicate the average number of children of school age occupying different sizes of units in new social and private housing (GLA, 2005b). However, they are based on a relatively small sample of occupants of new housing and have been challenged by some developers (interview with Southwark Council Officer, 4 March 2007). The practice of including contributions for schools in planning obligations was relatively new and the scale of the funding they would provide relative to the amount of investment in schools needed to provide for an increased population was not yet clear. The All Party Urban Development Group (2007) envisaged that developer's contributions on their own would not provide enough resources to fund the new facilities required in growth areas.

Planning school places

London boroughs have, since 1990, had responsibility for education. Until 2004, Local Education Authorities (LEAs) were obliged to produce School Organization Plans, which assessed the need for school places on the basis of demography and other data. These were prepared by School Organization Committees, which brought together key partners in education provision locally, and were intended to inform decisions about the development of new schools and the closure of existing schools. These plans covered all state-aided schools: both community schools, whose admissions are controlled by the LEAs; and voluntary-aided faith schools, whose admissions are controlled by their governing bodies. Since the Children Act 2004, LEAs have no longer been required to produce School Organization Plans. They are now subsumed into Children and Young People's Plans, which are intended to provide a more integrated approach to the provision of children's services. However, in practice, neither Southwark's nor Hackney's plans, produced by their Local Strategic Partnerships, included any analysis of projected changes in school population (Young Southwark, undated; Team Hackney, undated). The most recently published School

Organization Plans, which were for the five-year period 2003–08, therefore provide useful baseline information on the supply and demand for school places in the two boroughs (School Organisation Committee for Hackney, undated; Southwark Council, undated c). Both these plans used data on projections for the school population in their boroughs provided by the Greater London Authority and their own analysis of the child yield of large regeneration schemes.

Primary school provision

The Southwark report showed a decrease in the projected primary school population for 2003 and 2005, but an increase thereafter, and, although there was 11 per cent surplus capacity, when the report was written, a deficit of reception places was forecast for 2007–08 (Southwark Council, undated c). The Hackney report indicated a 9 per cent surplus in primary school places at the beginning of the plan period and anticipated the primary school population would rise by 4.5 per cent between 2003 and 2008 (School Organization Committee for Hackney, undated).

Children are expected to attend primary schools relatively close to their homes; Southwark Council has an explicit policy objective that children should be able to walk to primary school (Southwark Council, undated c). The capacity of primary schools therefore needs to be considered at neighbourhood level, as well as in terms of overall capacity within the borough. In both boroughs, existing surplus capacity was unevenly distributed across the borough and did not necessarily correspond with areas of anticipated growth. Parental choice also affects the distribution of spare capacity, with the result that some schools were oversubscribed, while nearby schools had as much as 50 per cent surplus capacity.

Since the publication of these School Organizsation Plans, there had been some change in the provision in both boroughs; unpopular schools had been closed and provision was being expanded elsewhere. Southwark Council had decided not to dispose of the site of a closed school because of possible future increase in demand and in the meantime was using the building for decanting existing schools that are being rebuilt (interview with Southwark Council Officer, 4 March 2007). It was reviewing primary provision in the borough and it was anticipated that some expansion of capacity would be needed. In Hackney, the Learning Trust, an independent not-for-profit organization that delivers education services including school-places planning in the borough, considered that some of the projected increase in demand was inflated and was therefore not planning to expand capacity in primary schools (interview with the Learning Trust officer, 29 March 2007). However, if there were to be an increase in demand, it was confident that it could fairly easily increase capacity by expanding existing community schools.

Secondary school provision

The planning of secondary school provision is more complex because of the relatively high proportion of students who travel to secondary schools outside their boroughs and the changing nature of secondary provision. As well as community and voluntary-aided faith schools, there is a new form of state-funded secondary provision in both boroughs. The Government has a programme of creating new schools, known as academies, to challenge the culture of low educational attainment (see Department for Children, Schools and Families, 2007). Academies are privately-sponsored state schools in disadvantaged areas. They are independent of LEAs and are directly funded by central government and eligible for high levels of state funding to invest in their premises. Both Hackney and Southwark, as areas in which secondary schools have performed poorly, and are beneficiaries of the Academies Programme. The Hackney School Organization Plan (School Organization Committee for Hackney, undated) anticipated considerable changes in secondary school provision, with some existing schools being closed and reopened as academies. The projected net effect of these changes was a significant increase in secondary places in the borough and a decrease in the number of children needing to travel outside the borough to school. Similarly, the Southwark School Organization Plan anticipated that the opening of two new academies would reduce cross-borough movement (Southwark Council, undated c).

In 2004, the Government introduced a major programme of investment in all secondary schools, Building Schools for the Future (BSF) (2007). This ambitious programme aimed to rebuild or substantially refurbish all secondary schools within 15 years. Early waves of investment were targeted at areas with the poorest educational standards, including Hackney and Southwark. This programme is being delivered through a new form of public–private finance initiative (PFI), involving new partnerships between central government, local authorities and the private sector. The introduction of BSF means that all secondary schools should in due course receive the level of investment in their premises that was previously only available to academies.

In Southwark, the BSF programme has had a radical impact on school-places planning (interview with Southwark Council officer, 4 March 2007). Work on school-places planning has been undertaken in close collaboration with the Partnership for Schools, the government agency that has been set up to deliver BSF. This process has been much more rigorous than previous school-places planning. To obtain BSF funding, LEAs have to make a strategic business case justifying their investment plans; this needs to include detailed information on projected school rolls over a ten-year period (interview with BSF consultant, 21 May 2007). The preparation of these projections involves close collaboration between various departments within local authorities to capture local knowledge. In Southwark, the school-places planning officer worked closely with colleagues in planning and regeneration to estimate the impact of new housing in the borough (interview with Southwark Council officer, 4 March 2007). However, it remains difficult to translate housing growth into increased demand for school places, because the Greater London Authority (GLA, 2005b) guidance on child yield rates is based on limited research. Southwark and the Partnership for Schools made considered judgements about the anticipated impact of improvement in standards in Southwark schools on cross-border movement of pupils and on the numbers of children being sent to independent schools. Southwark's involvement in this process has changed its approach to the planning of primary school places. In Hackney, as the LEA continues to own the educational estate, it is directly managing the BSF pro-gramme with the result that there has not been close collaboration between the Learning Trust and the Partnership for Schools on school-places planning. Thus, BSF has not had the same impact on primary school-places planning in Hackney as in Southwark.

The availability of land for new secondary schools had been problematic in Southwark, but not in Hackney. In Hackney new academies have been built on sites of schools that had been closed. In Southwark difficult decisions about sites for the development of new schools needed to be made (interview with Southwark Council Cabinet member responsible for regeneration, 11 June 2007) . One school in the north of the borough was being built on land that was partly formerly Open Metropolitan Land. This controversial decision was made by members, although there was local opposition to the loss of public open space in an area of increasing population density.

Sufficiency of school places relative to future demand

The priority being given to investment in secondary schools was clearly driving forward the process of school-places planning at secondary level. A more rig-orous process has been developed, and the time period considered is ten years rather than the five-year period considered in School Organization Plans. Also, in both Hackney and Southwark, the intention was to increase the overall num-ber of places to reduce the number of pupils travelling outside of the borough for education. If the BSF programme proceeds as planned, it would therefore seem unlikely that there will be a shortfall in secondary school places in either borough in the next decade.

There is not currently the same scale of resources available for investment in primary schools. Primary school-places planning has therefore not been driven by investment planning as in secondary schools. In Southwark, the process of planning primary school places has been reinvigorated as a result of the involvement in the more rigorous approach required by BSF. In Southwark, the officer responsible for school-places planning recognized that there was likely to be a need for additional provision in the near future. In Hackney, the officer responsible for school-places planning did not anticipate a need to expand capacity further in the next few years, which was somewhat surprising given the rate of increase in the number of dwellings in Hackney in recent years and the projected further increases, and the high proportion of children below school age in the population noted in the draft LDF Core Strategy (Hackney Council, 2006a). In both boroughs, there is also the question of the availability of places sufficiently close to where children live and, in the context of the UK government policy of parental choice, whether these places are in schools that parents want their children to attend.

Conclusions

Although the UK government's Sustainable Communities Plan (ODPM, 2003) aimed to encourage well-integrated sustainable development, there has been inadequate recognition of the contribution that families with children make to social sustainability and of the need to make provision for them; the case studies show that the implementation of policy is in practice somewhat dis-jointed. In areas such as Southwark and Hackney, where development is being intensified in a piecemeal way on relatively small sites, it is important that all those involved in making and delivering public policy understand the impact of this incremental development on their communities and on the demands for services. Too much of the focus appears to have been on the number of new homes to be produced. The evidence presented above suggests that there will be a growing shortfall in the number of homes large enough to accommodate families with children. This is likely to increase problems of overcrowding and encourage more mobile, generally better-off families to migrate to outer bor-oughs or out of London. Because Labour governments have prioritized investment in secondary education, there should be sufficient secondary school places to meet the needs of an expanded population, but there may possibly be local shortfalls in the provision of primary school places. Any shortages in pri-mary school places are also likely to encourage families to move out of the boroughs. Unless a better-integrated approach to providing for the need of fam-ilies with children is adopted in dense urban areas, there is a danger of increasing population churn, with residents lacking long-term commitment to these localities.

Providing for the needs of families with children needs to be recognized as crucial to managing housing growth and creating sustainable communities; it needs to become a central part of community strategies. More robust planning policies on the provision of family housing are clearly crucial, as is effective monitoring of their implementation. There needs to be investment in primary schools as well as secondary schools in order to retain families. There needs to be more analysis of local population change, such as is being undertaken in Southwark, in order to effectively forecast demand for school places and other services. There is a specific need for more research on the occupants of new housing in order to be able to more accurately predict the child yield.

In order to create socially sustainable communities, a more proactive approach is needed in the planning of social infrastructure. Southwark and Hackney, and other growth areas, could benefit from considering the practice of social infrastructure planning being developed in a number of other London boroughs. The London Borough of Barking and Dagenham, for example, commissioned a social infrastructure plan in 2006 that involved mapping all existing social infrastructure, assessing its capacity and demand over a 20-year period and producing costed plans for future provision (EDAW and Bevan Brittan, 2006). The plan also explored the potential for co-location and integration of services. To realize such plans, all stakeholders, including central government, will need to work together to ensure that adequate funding and land is available to implement the plans. This will need to involve creative joint asset-management strategies that view land in public ownership as a shared resource, to utilize the land-use planning system effectively to identify new sites, and to develop new models of integrated provision that use land efficiently.

Since the case study research was undertaken in 2007, recession has reduced the number of new homes produced nationally and in London (CLG, undated b). However, the new draft London Plan (Mayor of London, 2009) emphasizes the importance of planning for growth and includes further increases in the annual target for additional homes in London. The plan states that priority should be accorded to the provision of affordable family housing, but leaves it to the boroughs to set targets in their Local Development Frameworks. The plan also recognizes the need for additional and enhanced education facilities to meet the needs of the growing population. Whilst this strategic recognition of the importance of providing family housing and educational facilities for a growing population is a positive development, the case study research suggests that there remain significant challenges in developing and implementing local planning policies which will meet the needs of households with children.

References

Allinson, J. (2005) 'Exodus or Renaissance? Metropolitan Migration in the Late 1990s', *Town Planning Review*, vol 76, no 2, pp167–189

All Party Urban Development Group (2007) *Loosening the Leash: How Local Government Can Deliver Infrastructure with Private Sector Money*, http://www.allparty-urbande-velopment.org.uk/reports.html, accessed 28 May 2007

Barker, K. (2004) *Delivering Stability: Securing our Future Housing Needs*, Final Report Recommendations, HMSO, London

Bromley, R. D. F. and Tallon, A. R. (2004) 'Exploring the Attractions of City Centre Living: Evidence and Policy Implications in British Cities', *Geoforum*, vol 35, pp771–787

Building Schools for the Future (2007) http://www.bsf.gov.uk, accessed 21 June 2007

Burdett, R., Travers, T., Czischke, D., Rode, P. and Moser, B. (2004) *Density and Urban Neighbourhoods in London*, Enterprise LSE Cities, London

Communities and Local Government (2006a) *Preparing Core Strategies: Spatial Plans in Practice – Supporting the reform of local planning*, Department of Communities and Local Government, London

Communities and Local Government (2006b) *Changes to Planning Obligations: A Planning-Gain Supplement Consultation*, Department of Communities and Local Government, London

Communities and Local Government (2006c) *Planning Obligations Practice Guidance*, Department of Communities and Local Government, London

Communities and Local Government (undated, a) *Table 254 Housebuilding: permanent dwellings completed, by house and flat, number of bedroom and tenure, England*. http://www.communities.gov.uk/housing, accessed 21 June 2007

Communities and Local Government (undated, b) *Table 253 Housebuilding: permanent dwellings started and completed, by tenure and district*, http://www.communities.gov.uk/housing, accessed 22 December 2009

Department for Children, Schools and Families (2007) 'Academies – Welcome', http://www.standards.dfes.gov.uk/academies, accessed 21 June 2007

Department of the Environment, Transport and the Regions (2001) *Local Strategic Partnerships*, *Government Guidance*, DETR, London

Drury, A., Watson, J. and Broomfield, R. (2006) *Housing Space Standards*, HATC/Mayor of London, Greater London Authority, London

EDAW and Bevan Brittan (2006) *LB Barking and Dagenham Social Needs Assessment Final Report*, www.barking-dagenham.gov.uk, accessed 12 June 2007

Examination in Public Panel (2006) 'Early Alterations to the London Plan – EiP Panel Report', www.london.gov.uk/mayor/strategies/sds/eip-report06/index.jsp, accessed 12 June 2007

Greater London Authority (2005a) 'London Housing Provision Survey Figures 1987–2005', http://www.london.gov.uk/gla/publications/housing.jsp, accessed 25 June 2007

Greater London Authority (2005b) *'Child Yield, Data Management and Analysis Group Briefing 2005/25'*, Greater London Authority, London

Gunn, S. (2006) 'The Changing Meaning of Urban Capacity', *Town Planning Review*, vol 77, pp403–421

Hackney Council (2006a) *Core Strategy Preferred Option for Consultation,* London Borough of Hackney, London

Hackney Council (2006b) *London Borough of Hackney LDF Annual Monitoring Report 2005/06*, London Borough of Hackney, London

Hackney Council (2006c) *Planning Contributions Supplementary Planning Document,* London Borough of Hackney, London

Hackney Strategic Partnership (2006) *Mind the Gap: Hackney's Strategy to Reduce Inequalities and Poverty, Community Strategy 2005–15, Review and Update,* London Borough of Hackney, London

London Planning Advisory Committee (2000) *London's Housing Capacity,* Greater London Authority, London

Mayor of London (2004) *The London Plan, Spatial Development Strategy for Greater London,* Greater London Authority, London

Mayor of London (2005a) *2004 London Housing Capacity Study,* Greater London Authority, London

Mayor of London (2005b) *The London Plan Supplementary Housing Guidance,* Greater London Authority, London

Mayor of London (2005c) *London Plan Annual Monitoring Report 1,* Greater London Authority, London

Mayor of London (2006a) *The London Plan, Spatial Development Strategy for Greater London, Housing Provision Targets, Waste and Minerals Alterations,* Greater London Authority, London

Mayor of London (2006b) *London Plan Annual Monitoring Report 2,* Greater London Authority, London

Mayor of London (2007) *London Plan Annual Monitoring Report 3,* Greater London Authority, London

Mayor of London (2009) *The London Plan, Spatial Development Strategy for Greater London, Consultation draft replacement plan,* Greater London Authority, London

Nathan, M. and Urwin, C. (2006) *City People, City Living in the UK,* Institute for Public Policy Research, London

Office of the Deputy Prime Minister (2003) *Sustainable Communities: Building for the Future,* OPDM, London

Office of the Deputy Prime Minister (2005a) *LDF Monitoring: A Good Practice Guide,* ODPM, London

Office of the Deputy Prime Minister (2005b) *Circular 05/05 Planning Obligations,* 18 July, ODPM, London

Office of the Deputy Prime Minister (2006) *The State of English Cities,* ODPM, London

Office of National Statistics (2003) *Population Density, 2002: Regional Trends 38,* available from http://www.statistics.gov.uk/STATBASE/ssdataset.asp?vlnk=7662

School Organisation Committee for Hackney (undated) *School Organisation Plan 2003 to 2008,* The Learning Trust, London

Silverman, E., Lupton, R. and Fenton, A. (2006) *A Good Place for Children? Attracting and Retaining Families in Inner Urban Mixed Communities,* Chartered Institute of Housing/Joseph Rowntree Foundation

Southwark Alliance (2006) *Southwark 2016,* Southwark Council, London

Southwark Council (2005) *Local Development Scheme,* March, Southwark Council, London

Southwark Council (2006a) *Emerging Southwark Plan,* Southwark Council, London

Southwark Council (2006b) *Section 106 Planning Obligations Draft Supplementary Document,* Southwark Council, London

Southwark Council (undated a) *Southwark LDF Annual Monitoring Report 2*, Southwark Council, London

Southwark Council (undated b) *Southwark LDF Annual Monitoring Report 2*, Southwark Council, London

Southwark Council (undated c) *School Organisation Plan for Southwark for the Period 2003–2008*, Southwark Council, London

Team Hackney (undated) *Hackney's Children and Young People's Plan 2006–09*, London Borough of Hackney, London

Urban Task Force (1999) *Towards an Urban Renaissance: Final Report of the Urban Task Force*, chaired by Lord Rogers of Riverside, Spon, London

Young Southwark (undated) *Children and Young People's Plan, 2006–07 to 2008–09*, Southwark Council, London

Transport Planning for Sustainable Communities

Karen Lucas, Derek Halden and Sarah Wixey

Introduction

The issue of adequate transport provision within communities, and at the more strategic level of connectivity to link them to each other and to key activities such as employment, education, healthcare, shopping and leisure and social opportunities, is an important one in the social sustainability debate. We all live, work and play in a highly mobile society, which often requires us to travel to a number of different destinations in any one week just to carry out our basic activities. Many of us automatically do this by car, without thinking of the environmental consequences of this on our local and global environment, or what impact it might have on other forms of transport or the lives of other people.

This chapter broadly considers some of these consequences in the light of the UK government's plans to create more sustainable communities. It asks what this might mean for future transport and local service planning and provision, using the example of the East London section of the Thames Gateway, one of the Government's chosen growth areas. It goes on to consider how people's future transport and activity needs might be better anticipated by extending the method of *accessibility planning* to these new development areas. Finally, it offers two case studies to demonstrate how *accessibility planning* might contribute to the creation of more socially sustainable urban environments in the future.

The key issues for transport and social sustainability in the UK

Both car ownership and use in the UK has grown dramatically over the last 50 years. It has progressed from being a minority form of transportation for the privileged few to become the main way in which most people now travel. The average person in the UK travels ten times the distance in a year than they did

50 years ago. In total, traffic volumes increased by 79 per cent between 1980 and 2003, from 277 to 495 billion vehicle kilometres. The majority of this growth has been in car traffic, which has gone up by 83 per cent since 1980, from 215 to 393 billion vehicle kilometres (Department for Transport, 2004). Although trip lengths have got longer, the number of trips and the time spent travelling has remained roughly the same (RAC Foundation, 2003).

Most often these travel trends have opened up new opportunities and widened our choice of where we live, work and play. Cars allow people to carry out far more activities in a day, over far greater distances than they did 50 years ago. They have also had a role to play in women's increased participation in the labour market and have helped many older drivers maintain their independence for longer. On the downside, the increased ability to travel and increased dependence on the car has encouraged dispersed and car-orientated patterns of development. In turn, this has led to more travel-intensive lifestyles, so that it is increasingly necessary to drive to carry out basic daily activities.

More traffic has meant less safe and more polluted local environments, and many people are afraid, or find it undesirable, to walk and cycle. One of the biggest social changes in childhood in the last 50 years has been parents' unwillingness to allow their children to walk or cycle alone for fear of accidents or assaults. It is possible to assert that increased car use has eroded opportunity and choice for pedestrians and cyclists. In many places, mass car ownership has served to undermine the viability of the public transport network. In 1950, buses and coaches accounted for 40 per cent of total UK passenger transport. This figure had fallen to 6 per cent in 2000 and there has been a related decline in the frequency, reliability and quality of services. It is also evident that, while the cost of motoring has remained fairly constant over the past 30 years, the cost of public transport has risen dramatically over the same period.

Bus deregulation has encouraged competition on the more profitable routes, but local authority funding for buses has fallen since deregulation, and many services on the less commercial routes, particularly evening and weekend services, have been run down or abandoned. Some rural areas do not have any regular bus service and many urban areas are without evening and weekend services. Public transport networks have largely failed to adapt to new land-use patterns, meaning that those relying on them have less opportunity to access key goods and services. The average number of occupants per car has also fallen (in 2002/03, 61 per cent of cars on the road had only one occupant (Department for Transport, 2004)), which has further contributed to vehicle kilometres increasing more than passenger kilometres over the same period and reflects increasing car ownership.

These transport trends are exacerbated by accompanying changes in land use. Despite the policy rhetoric of integrated transport and land-use planning in the UK (e.g. various planning policy guidance notes and statements), many new major developments continue to be located in out-of-town and dispersed locations as a result of various loopholes in the regulations. Furthermore, many neighbourhoods have lost local shops as the big retailers have taken over their customer base. For example, between 1991 and 1999, the number of households living more than a 27-minute walk from a shopping centre doubled from about 40 per cent to 90 per cent of all households. Similarly, in 1991, approximately 72 per cent of households lived within a 27-minute walk of a doctor's surgery, whereas this had dropped to 40 per cent by 1999 (from an analysis of National Travel Survey statistics, 1989/91 and 1998/99). These deficits in local services are rarely identified by local plans and there are few mechanisms for directly addressing a lack of essential services within an area through the land-use planning system.

While the problem is often described in terms of land-use planning, the solution is often out of the hands of land-use planners to affect. Wider partnerships are needed to influence the activities undertaken from each location, not just the built environment. Land-use and transport agencies may not be in a position to influence the location decisions of public agencies and private companies that may not hold the interests of transport and accessibility at the forefront of their decision-making. Planners are also regularly forced to accept that less than optimal development should proceed, since each part of the country is competing for job creation and efficiency savings and the profitability of large local companies is often high on corporate priorities of authorities.

For instance, hospital services have been and are continuing to be rationalized into fewer, larger units serving wide areas, located in places that are difficult to reach without a car. They are often located on the sites of old sanatoriums and as such do not require planning permission, or the service providers claim that urban sites offer insufficient space for their needs. The introduction of planned 'poly clinics', centralized health centres offering specialist health services, will only exacerbate these accessibility challenges, unless high-quality public transport services are introduced to support the clinic's appointment hours.

For similar reasons, many post-16 colleges are in places that are hard to access by public transport. Added to this, the new 14–19 curriculum means that pupils are no longer receiving their education at a single site. This requires many students not only to undertake home to school travel, but also needs them to travel considerable distances between lessons.

However, many of the demographic, economic and social trends that have contributed to these dispersed settlement patterns and increased travel growth over the last century have now peaked. It is unlikely that per capita vehicle ownership or the amount of time individuals are prepared to spend travelling to access basic activities will increase significantly in the future.

In his analysis of future trends in transport, Litman (2004) recommends that, in affluent societies, reductions in per capita vehicle travel should offset any growth in the number of households that occurs over the next 50 years. However, he also identifies that car ownership and use will probably increase among some sectors of the population within these countries, in particular among people transitioning from poverty to wealth.

A recent Social Exclusion Unit (SEU) study in the UK (2003) identified that past transport and land-use policies have significantly contributed to and reinforced social exclusion. Transport can be a significant barrier for jobseekers attempting to access work and has also been linked with low participation in post-16 education and college drop-outs. Studies show that travel to hospital is particularly difficult for people who have to rely on public transport services. Poor transport can also lead to missed GP appointments and later health interventions.

Poor transport affects people's participation in a range of other activities; for example, in an Office for National Statistics (ONS) Omnibus survey for the SEU study, 16 per cent of non-drivers found it difficult to get to a supermarket and 18 per cent had difficulties visiting friends and family. This is a particular issue for older people and it has negative implications for their quality of life. There is also a clear link between social class, road traffic accidents and exposure to air and noise pollution from road traffic, with the highest incidents occurring in the most deprived areas.

The changing age structure of the population is likely to have a major influence on both people's activity needs and wider UK travel trends over the next 50 years. By 2020, the number of over-50-year-olds will have grown from the current 20 million to a projected 25 million, meaning that by this time more than half of all adults in the population will be over 50, and the number of over-65s will have reached 12.5 million. In general, women tend to live longer than men, which implies the number of women within the future population will be higher.

Disabilities and long-term illnesses are also most concentrated among this sector of the population. Migration also affects the age structure of the population, both in terns of those who move out of areas and those who are left behind, meaning that the geographical spread of these population changes will be felt differently in different parts of the country. For example, older people are more likely to retire to coastal areas and in smaller market towns and villages, whereas bigger cities, particularly in the south-east of England, are attracting younger people.

Older people tend to make less trips overall; on average, people of between 60 and 69 years of age make only 82 per cent of the trips of 30- to 49-year-olds (Department of Transport, 2004b), and the proportion of trips made by car also declines significantly from age 60. However, this is partly a cohort effect, as many of today's older people have never driven a car. The next generation of older people are much more likely to be established car drivers and will therefore be more likely to continue driving for as long as possible. There is research evidence to suggest that many older drivers are already choosing to hold on to their cars for longer in order to retain their independence (Lucas et al, 2001).

Clearly, these outcomes have strong implications for a wide range of key areas of government delivery, most notably those encouraging welfare into work, reducing health inequalities, raising educational attainment and participation in post-16 education, crime reduction, accessible housing and neighbourhood renewal. There is also a wider implication: in terms of future UK travel trends, low-income households offer the greatest potential to increase their car ownership and use.

There is clear evidence that many of the people on very low incomes own cars out of necessity rather than choice. This is demonstrated by the willingness of car-owning households on extremely constrained incomes to pay out large proportions of their income on motoring expenses, when clearly there are other important demands on this money. Many people are unable to rely on public transport for their travel needs and an increasing number of low-income households need to own and drive cars as the only way to secure their social inclusion. On the basis of current trends, it would be reasonable to anticipate that car ownership will continue to grow.

Although the current poorest car-owning households tend to use their cars much less than average households, they are more likely to own older and thus less energy-efficient and more polluting vehicles. This suggests that, unless low-income households are provided with access to high-quality public transport or cleaner and more efficient cars, the correlation between polluting vehicles and socially deprived communities will continue. This is not to say that poor people should be denied the right to own and drive cars in the future; indeed, in many instances it might provide the key to their social inclusion and should be encouraged. However, unless we are fully aware of these trends, they will not be accounted for in our forward planning and could undermine other policy aims, such as those currently being put forward to create sustainable new communities in the south of England.

How do we move towards more socially sustainable transport futures?

Partly in recognition of the fundamental economic, social and environmental challenges we face in the delivery of socially inclusive and environmentally sustainable transport, in 2004 the Department for Transport introduced a statutory requirement for local transport authorities in England (outside London) to submit Accessibility Plans as part of their five-year Local Transport Plans (DfT, 2004a). The key aims for this accessibility planning are:

1   To ensure that local decision-makers have improved information on the areas where public transport access to key services is poorest.
2   Improved understanding of the barriers to accessibility from the perspective of the people who are living there.
3   To create a more transparent, integrated and equitable process for transport and land-use decisions.

Transport planners are being encouraged to 'think outside of the box' and work more collaboratively with their partner agencies, ensuring that a wider range of solutions to accessibility problems can be identified and greater value for money achieved through their combined and synchronized efforts. The guidance identifies that the process of accessibility planning should entail:

• Assessments of local need against a set of predefined national indicators to identify and analyse accessibility to the key services.
• Option appraisal and identification of existing and potential financial and other resources across the partnership agencies (e.g. land, staff time, information) that may be available to address the problems that are identified.
• A joint action plan that sets out how transport and land-use planners, those involved in the location and delivery of other local services and other relevant local bodies will improve the gaps in accessibility identified by the needs audit.
• Implementation and monitoring to ensure that delivery is consistent with objectives and that future plans can build on success and learn from failure.

In response to local authority concerns about the pace of change, the first round of accessibility plans were scaled back so that only accessibility strategies were required. Rather than the costed deliverables with timescales for action originally envisaged, the strategies were instead statements of how the authority proposed to approach the preparation of the plans. Although good progress has been made with the strategies, their practical delivery has taken several years to be adopted into council plans. Since April 2008, Local Area Agreements directly link funding to delivery of improved accessibility, so with resources being made available it can be expected that the rate of delivery will increase.

Although accessibility planning was specifically designed to improve the inclusion of low-income and largely non-car owning sectors of the population in key economic and social activities, it has also been successfully used as a planning tool to assess the level of public transport connectivity and pedestrian access of locations more generally. This is becoming an increasingly important consideration in determining both the long-term economic vibrancy and social and environmental sustainability of housing and business locations across the

UK. For this reason, it is the authors' contention that accessibility planning should become an integral part in the planning of all new and regenerated housing developments across the UK. This is particularly pertinent in the case of the Government's Sustainable Communities Plan for the South East.

Recognizing the role of transport in planning sustainable communities

According to the Sustainable Communities Plan, sustainable communities are:

> places where people want to live and work, now and in the future. They meet the diverse needs of existing and future residents, are sensitive to their environment, and contribute to a high quality of life. They are safe and inclusive, well planned, built and run, and offer equality of opportunity and good services for all. (Department of Communities and Local Government, 2003, p6)

In terms of transport, the plan recommends that sustainable communities should be well-connected, with good transport services and communication linking people to jobs, schools, health and other services. It places an emphasis on good public transport connectivity, safe walking and cycling facilities and traffic demand management, so as to encourage reduced reliance on cars. Several noteworthy commentators of the plan have recommended that for growth to be successful:

> There will need to be a shift of mode away from car... It is the modal shift which is critical, because if its scale is insufficient, then even with new road space it will be highway capacity that will force a limit on development potential. (Llewelyn Davies et al, 2003)

The plan also recognizes the need for good local access to key services (commonly referred to as 'local accessibility') of these growth communities. For example, it recommends that to be properly sustainable, communities should be well served by well-performing local schools, further and higher education institutions, and other opportunities for lifelong learning. They should also have high-quality local healthcare and social services, which are integrated where possible with other services, high-quality services for families and children (including early years child care) and a good range of affordable public, community, voluntary and private services, which are accessible to the whole community.

However, the Sustainable Communities Plan does not offer a consistent or systematic method for determining whether the proposed locations for these new communities are sufficiently well served by public transport or local serv-ices to be considered 'sustainable' in transport terms, neither is there any practicable guidance for developers or planners in this respect. This is well illus-trated if we consider the key proposed regeneration areas in the Thames Gateway region.

Sustainable communities in the Thames Gateway

The Thames Gateway region stretches along the estuary from Canary Wharf in London to Southend in Essex and Sittingbourne in Kent, therefore encom-passing three sub-regions: east London, south Essex and north Kent. Its strategic location on major transport links to Europe and its close proximity to London creates an ideal location for significant development and regeneration. Of the 160,000 new homes to be delivered in the Gateway, almost 110,000 will be accommodated by just ten developments. Five key sites in east London will deliver just over 72,000 new homes, two developments in south Essex will deliver almost 19,000 and three developments in north Kent are set to deliver a further 17,500 (see Figure 7.1).

The Gateway has been granted an allocation of £446 million to be spent over the three-year period of the action plan. The Government's aim for the region is to generate 225,000 new jobs and 160,000 new homes by 2031. This substantial increase in both housing and business development implies a

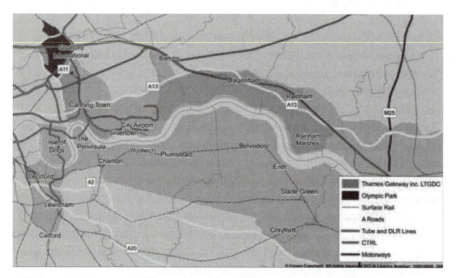

Figure 7.1 *Location of key transport routes in the east London region of the Thames Gateway*

massive growth in travel activity across the region. A crucial question in this respect is whether people living, working and undertaking economic and social activities in planned new developments in the Thames Gateway will be able to do so in an environmentally and socially sustainable manner, now and in the future.

Much of the existing public transport infrastructure in this section of the Gateway is already severely overloaded and it is doubtful whether the planned upgrades to the system will cater for the existing demand, let alone the massive increases that are likely to arise from incoming populations to the area.

In his presentation to the Royal Institute of British Architects (RIBA) at the special Transport Development Areas conference in 2008, Stan Hornagold, Director of Marstan Group change advisers, was less than optimistic about the future transport fortunes of the Gateway. He recommended that existing train services to the east are already over capacity and are poorly connected to the planned locations for new communities, which necessitates the provision of more bus and tram services. He suggests this will not happen without significant upfront government investment in the public transport network and faster delivery structures to deliver new transport initiatives in tandem with new housing provision.

In the 2005/06 session of the House of Commons Housing, Planning, Local Government and the Regions Committee; Affordability and the Supply of Housing, Keith Mitchell, Leader of Oxfordshire County Council, recommended of the Thames Gateway:

> I do not see the Department for Transport signed up yet to linking housing need to transport need and to the funding, I just do not see that. We need more joining up.

The Thames Gateway Delivery Plan paints a much brighter picture in terms of the progress with new transport infrastructure, as this 2006 quote from Stephen Jordan of London and Continental Railways demonstrates:

> Real progress is being made on the ground – we opened our new international station at Ebbsfleet last week. Already, this and existing and the emerging new communities are linked by an award-winning bus rapid-transit system which is stretching road capacity and achieving a modal shift of 19 per cent from cars. Even more transport infrastructure can be phased in to support yet more homes and jobs thanks to an innovative 'roof tax', arrangements for which have been brokered by Kent Thameside partners and Judith's team. Ebbsfleet is ready to go and will create a transformational step-change for the Gateway. (HM Government, 2007, p14)

Nevertheless, many of the proposed schemes to date are road-based, with £432 million of new government expenditure committed to roads but only £15 million to public transport, and there is already an over-reliance on private cars and long-distance commuting across the region. Clearly, large increases in car-based travel and an insufficient supply of public transport do not fit with the claimed ethos of promoting sustainable communities in terms of economic, social or environmental well-being.

What are the key issues in terms of transport and social sustainability in the Thames Gateway?

As a first principle, achieving a low-carbon economy needs to be at the forefront of all planning decisions if the Thames Gateway is to be economically, environmentally and socially sustainable (Department for Transport, 2007). Even if vehicle technologies improve dramatically over the next 10–20 years, this will have to mean some level of reduction in overall car travel among the UK population. Private travel is now one of the greatest single contributors to climate change from the domestic sector and emissions from the transport sector are still growing. However, the Sustainable Communities Plan does not include any over-arching strategy or set specific targets for reducing carbon dioxide emissions from the transport sector. Clearly, unless people have the opportunity to switch to lower emission vehicles, as well as better options to use less-polluting public transport modes, this situation will not change and the Thames Gateway will fail to achieve its core sustainability aims.

In the first place, it is essential to ensure a high level of strategic access to work and other major destinations such as hospitals, secondary schools and colleges is provided by non-car modes. The issue of public transport provision is poorly considered within Social Infrastructure Plans, even when these do exist. Even if new homes and employment are co-located, there is no guarantee that people will choose to live and work in the same place. It is therefore vital that any longer distance travel they need to undertake (particularly into and out of London) can easily be facilitated by public transport. The location of many new homes in the Thames Gateway on old brown-field sites is a major challenge in this respect. While such sites can be considered sustainable in land-use terms (because they do not infringe on undeveloped green spaces), in many instances these are often old mineral extraction and other ex-industrial sites, which are situated in isolated locations with relatively poor connectivity to the public transport network and local services.

Ensuring public transport is affordable and that a reasonable balance between house and travel prices and private and public transport is achieved is also essential. Many people will be making a trade-off between more affordable house prices in the urban periphery and longer commuting trips. If public transport is unavailable, inconvenient or places a high burden on the household budget, people will choose to use cars for these journeys. This will result in higher levels of congestion and also undermine the Thames Gateway Plan's aspirations for a low-carbon economy. It may also reduce the viability of other transport modes and will become increasingly untenable for many lower-income households in the light of fuel scarcity and rising fuel costs.

New communities also need to offer a good level of access to key local public services. Ideally, people should be able to walk or cycle to many everyday activities such as the doctor's surgery, primary schools, community facilities and food shopping. This also helps to build and support social networks and community cohesion. It is evident that many existing communities on the outskirts of London can barely claim to be this, as they display few or none of the attributes that bind people together in mutually supporting ways. There is evidence that inadequate public transport has given rise to reduced social networking and reduced independence among older people. It also reduces the opportunity for young people to participate in after-school activities and can lead to higher incidences of anti-social behaviour and a breakdown of social cohesion.

Finally, it is important to provide not only for the transport needs of communities now, but also in the future. Many of the people that move into the new homes in the Gateway are likely to be young single people or couples without children or with young families. At present, they are likely to be self-sufficient private vehicle owners, who rely only on themselves and their cars for most trips. Over time, however, they may become unable to drive due to growing older and will need to rely on public transport. Similarly, as young children grow older and more independent they will need to use public transport, in order to secure a healthy level of autonomy from their parents.

If planners and developers follow these basic core principles for transport and access in the design and development of the planned new housing in the Thames Gateway and elsewhere in the UK, there is every opportunity for them to become well-connected, thriving, vibrant and socially sustainable communities. If they fail in this respect, it is likely that they will become the disconnected, run-down, unpopular urban slums of the future.

Could accessibility planning provide planners with a new way forward?

The Transport White Paper 2000 set in motion a new national framework for producing a fairer and more inclusive system of transport in the UK. In line with this new policy remit for transport, in spring 2001 the prime minister gave the SEU the task of making evident the links between transport and social exclusion, and identifying the extent of the problem and its implication for other areas of welfare policy delivery. Accessibility planning was a key recommendation arising from the SEU study (2003). It is a method to assess the ability of different disadvantaged groups to access key destinations such as employment, healthcare services, education centres and food shops. These assessments should include consideration of the availability, affordability and accessibility of local public transport, the design, location and delivery of non-transport services and the ability of the community to reach those services by foot or cycle. The key features of the method are:

- Strategic and local accessibility audits – identifying accessibility problems in relation to key activities.
- Engagement of key influencers of travel and local stakeholders and decision-makers, such as employers, primary care and hospital trusts, local education authorities and local strategic partnerships.
- Reality checks with local residents.
- A resource appraisal to assess what is available for tackling the problems across the different key stakeholder agencies.
- A joint action plan with the key stakeholder agencies to identify initiatives to improve accessibility and implementation.
- Monitoring and evaluation against a set of nationally and locally defined indicators.

The flow chart in Figure 7.2 identifies the key stages involved in the accessibility planning process. It was adopted as a core feature of the Local Transport Plans (LTPs) of all local transport authorities in England (outside of London) in 2006. The Department for Transport recommends that it should be set in the context of the wider local authority vision and objectives for a given area and aim to improve accessibility for all, but particularly for disadvantaged groups and areas. Currently, however, it is primarily used in the context of existing communities and is not a specific requirement in the planning and development of new communities. There are, however, a few working examples of its application in these instances, to considerable effect in terms of improved public transport and/or better local access to facilities.

Case study examples of the use of accessibility planning in the development process

Although it is not a statutory requirement for local authorities to undertake accessibility assessments of their strategic or local development plans, there are a number of good-practice examples of where this approach has been applied,

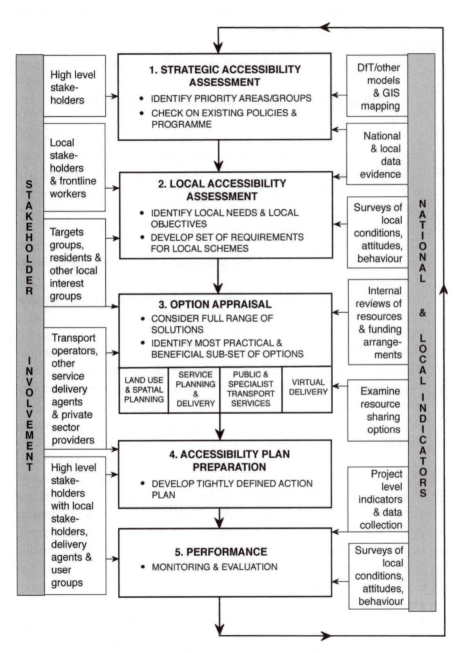

Figure 7.2 *Main stages of the recommended accessibility planning process*

with some considerable gains in terms of reducing the need for people to travel by car, while at the same time improving accessibility to essential activities. Three of these examples are briefly outlined here to offer a flavour of what can be achieved once a systematic analysis of transport and land-use interactions is available.

Edinburgh Structure Plan case study example

The population of Edinburgh and the Lothians is more than 750,000, and is experiencing among the fastest population and employment growth of any part of the UK. Five development scenarios were identified by the land-use and transport planners in the area and the accessibility impacts of these on people and places assessed. The five scenarios were:

1   Committed Development: This included population and employment change, based on the latest audits of housing and employment including development under construction.
2   City Expansion: A development approach that emphasizes the development of brown-field sites, reinforcing Edinburgh as a compact city with a high-density core.
3   Green Belt Development: Development within the long-standing continuous green belt around the city, but linked to existing transport networks.
4   Development of the Landward Towns: Major expansion of existing towns in the Lothians, particularly towns in need of regeneration.
5   Development in New Settlements: New communities in the Lothians with a balance of housing and employment.

Travel times for car and non-car available households were tested for employment, shopping, education, healthcare and access to population. The analysis showed significant differences largely related to the location of future housing supply and growing road congestion. Under all scenarios accessibility improved, showing that for the options being considered the proximity of proposed housing locations to key destinations was better than the average for the present situation. However, there were also significant differences between the scenarios, as shown in Table 7.1.

It can be seen from the table that there are important differences of scale between the impacts for car and non-car accessibility. In absolute terms, the changes in accessibility resulting from the development scenarios are generally more than ten times greater for car than for non-car accessibility. However, in relative terms, the non-car accessibility changes are generally two or three times those for the car accessibility changes.

Table 7.1 *The five development scenarios for Edinburgh, with a summary of their likely impacts on accessibility*

Scenario	Summary comments
City expansion	Maximizes car and non-car accessibility within the city, but has the least impact outwith the City. Nevertheless, destination accessibility changes outside the city, particularly to the south and east, are still substantial.
Green belt	Maximizes car and non-car accessibility for zones around the city bypass, but the effects spread more widely to the Lothians for car accessibility, particularly destination accessibility.
Landward towns	Lower level of both car and non-car accessibility within the city, but higher level of non-car accessibility in some landward towns.
New settlement	Similar pattern as for the landward towns scenario, but the impacts are greater in Mid and East Lothian. The largest impacts for car and non-car destination accessibility are in East Lothian, but origin accessibility for these zones is only marginally different from other options.

Aggregating the results of the accessibility indicators for each trip purpose and traveller group allowed a composite indicator of accessibility to be calculated, as shown in Table 7.2. This shows that development in the green belt to cater for new housing helps to keep the additional time that people need to spend travelling to a minimum, but that expansion of the landward towns where there are good public transport links is also an efficient option. The poorest option is the city expansion scenario, where the new housing is in peripheral city locations poorly served by public transport and where congestion is also growing fastest.

On the basis of these accessibility assessments, the decision was taken for some of the proposed housing developments to go ahead on the sites that were most accessible. Unfortunately, however, the Structure Plan failed to get approval by the Scottish Parliament (then Executive) for a number of reasons

Table 7.2 *Comparison of overall changes in accessibility*

	Committed	City expansion	Green belt	Landward towns	New settlement
Change from base development level (generalized minutes $\times 10^6$)	−1.46	−4.87	−5.22	−5.15	−5.04

and the final agreed version of the Structure Plan was less good from the accessibility perspective. However, it is of note that all of the planned development scenarios improved accessibility, which is a stark contrast from previous structure plans. The fact that accessibility was being considered and measured ensured that only housing locations consistent with this goal were brought forward. The less-than-optimal approach was, however, only a few per cent worse than more optimal development locations. Land use only changes at about 2 per cent a year, but the impacts of a ten-year development plan build up over time and can result in a large increase in trips generated.

Warrington Borough Council healthcare provision case study example

Warrington's development as a New Town has left a legacy of dispersed facilities and activities that are often in out-of-town locations. This pattern of development means that many key services and facilities are difficult to reach without a car, especially from deprived central wards. Early assessment of the strategic issues identified access to healthcare as a particular issue, especially in light of a number of proposed changes to the way that health services are planned and delivered.

Work with health partners began in summer 2005 with a presentation by the transport planning team to Warrington Primary Care Trust's (PCT's) executive board. This highlighted a range of common issues and objectives in relation to transport and health, and emphasized the opportunities for working more closely to improve access to health services. The PCT was very receptive and provided a letter of support to the council, which was included in Warrington's Provisional LTP in July 2005.

In January 2006, a one-day health and transport workshop was held, involving a range of partners from the council, health, transport and community sectors, and covered issues such as common strategic objectives, access to healthcare facilities and access to fresh food. This workshop led to a detailed action plan being developed. A key action was to look at the accessibility implications of several new community health facility proposals in the borough. This work is now well under way and has helped to gain a better understanding of the accessibility implications of reconfiguring health services in Warrington.

An initial strategic accessibility mapping exercise of healthcare facilities in Warrington and neighbouring boroughs, focusing on access to GPs, dentists and hospitals, was undertaken; this helped to identify borough-wide issues and deficiencies. The PCT also had information from various public consultations that indicated the location of services was a key issue for the public. Following further discussion with the PCT, more detailed local analysis of accessibility issues relating to proposed new community health centres in west Warrington and south Warrington was also undertaken. This work involved mapping more local area accessibility mapping to services, local area audits of different modes of transport and analysis of local public consultation exercises.

Accessibility maps were produced for two site options in south Warrington. The maps clearly illustrate the differences in accessibility between these two sites (see Figures 7.3 and 7.4). Discussions were also held with a number of key stakeholders such as Warrington Borough Transport, council planning officers and PCT representatives. A draft accessibility questionnaire was also developed and applied, to highlight to decision-makers the accessibility implications of health facility proposals and potential improvement measures to ensure that new facilities are accessible, particularly for those without a car. This is designed to help decision-makers in the health sector ensure that they consider all the relevant accessibility issues when evaluating future proposals for health service location and delivery. It is likely to become formalized as part of the PCT process for evaluating all new healthcare proposals in Warrington. It is also proposed that the checklist be used to assess the accessibility implications of other development proposals in the borough.

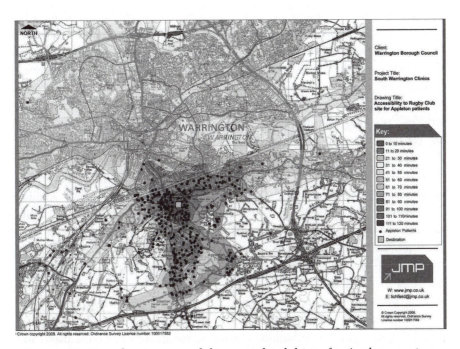

Figure 7.3 *Map showing accessibility to rugby club site for Appleton patients*

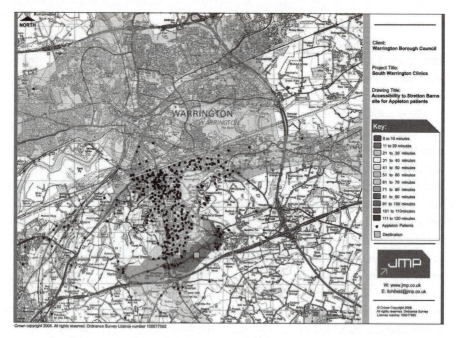

Figure 7.4 *Map showing accessibility to Stretton Barns site
for Appleton patients*

A report into the west Warrington case study highlighted a range of accessibility issues associated with the proposed healthcare facility in west Warrington, which is being developed as part of a new urban village development. A number of different health service delivery options were considered within this report, including options for relocating some specialist services from Warrington Hospital to the new facility. Although no decision has yet been made by the PCT, the report was well received and is helping the PCT to determine the type and range of health services that might be delivered in the new health centre, and what accessibility improvements may be necessary.

Through this process of accessibility planning, Warrington Borough Council and the PCT have developed a much greater understanding of mutual priorities. Common objectives have become clear in many areas and the borough council is now being involved in PCT health-centre proposals much earlier in the process, and there is an open channel for exchanging ideas to improve proposals prior to site selection and planning application. In addition, some proposals that would not necessarily need planning approval, such as service relocation into existing buildings, are now more likely to be discussed and the accessibility issues considered.

Conclusions

This chapter has considered the issue of local transport planning for more economically, socially and environmentally sustainable communities. This is particularly relevant in the increasingly evident imperative to move to reduce people's need to travel by car in the move towards a lower carbon economy. Planning Policy Guidance 13 (DfT, 2004a) introduced a requirement for all planning applications to be accompanied by an assessment of the accessibility impacts and this requirement has now been developed to require delivery of these accessibility goals through the site Travel Plan. Travel Plans outline the steps that will be taken to ensure that the traffic implications of a new development are limited at the point of source as much as possible and that all travel needs can be met. Commonly, the accessibility analysis and demonstration that accessibility needs are being met has been poorly delivered, and further improvements are needed to enforce this requirement. We have presented the case for the requirement for a process of accessibility planning to be undertaken in the development of all new communities, with particular emphasis on applying this in the case of the Government's Sustainable Communities Plan.

As we have demonstrated, some local authorities are increasingly recognizing the benefits of using accessibility planning techniques to assess the accessibility of their sites in the context of their strategic and local development plans. This information has then been successfully used as the basis for early negotiations with key service providers and developers about their future location and land-use decisions.

We would argue that, in order to be fully sustainable, all future communities need to be planned so that they provide a high level of public transport and pedestrian accessibility to key economic and social activities such as employment, health visits, education, shopping and leisure. This will not only help to secure the greater social inclusion and participation of low-income, non-car owning households, but will also encourage greater community vibrancy and cohesion more generally as a result of the increased opportunity for people to meet and interact.

It is clear from our two case study examples that, although *accessibility planning* is a useful tool for identifying the transport sustainability of new as well as existing developments, it is not in itself a decision-maker. For this reason, it is vital that a multi-agency approach is adopted at an early stage in the development or regeneration of communities. This should include the involvement of key professional stakeholders but also communities themselves, as it is usually local people who are best placed to identify their own local accessibility needs.

References

Department for Transport and Local Communities (2003) *Sustainable Communities: build-ing for the future*, http://www.communities.gov.uk/documents/communities/pdf/146289.pdf, accessed 14 December 2009

Department for Transport (2004a) *Planning Policy Guidance note 13*, DfT, London

Department for Transport (2004b) 'Transport Trends 2004', DfT, London, www.dft.gov.uk, accessed 7 May 2008

Department for Transport (2004c) 'Guidance on Accessibility Planning in Local Transport Plans', DfT, London, http://www.dft.gov.uk/pgr/regional/ltp/accessibility/guidance/gap/accessibilityplanningguidanc3633, accessed 3 July 2008

Department for Transport (2007) 'Towards a Sustainable Transport System: Supporting Economic Growth in a Low Carbon World', http://www.dft.gov.uk/about/strat-egy/transportstrategy/hmtlsustaintranssys, accessed 9 July 2008

HM Government (2007) *The Thames Gateway Delivery Plan*, http://www.communities.gov.uk/documents/thamesgateway/pdf/565039.pdf, accessed 14 December 2009

Litman, T. (2004) *The Future Isn't what It Used To Be: Changing Trends and their Implications for Transport Planning*, http://www.vtpi.org/future.pdf, accessed 7 May 2008

Llewelyn Davies and Steer Davies Gleave, with Roger Tym & Partners and Atkins (2003) *Relationship between Transport and Development in the Thames Gateway*, http://www.communities.gov.uk/documents/thamesgateway/pdf/158154.pdf, accessed 14 December 2009

Lucas, K., Grosvenor, T. and Simpson, R. (2001) *Transport, the Environment and Social Exclusion*, Joseph Rowntree and York Publications, York

Office of the Deputy Prime Minister (2003) *Sustainable Communities: Building for the Future*, ODPM, London

RAC Foundation (2002) *Motoring Towards 2050*, RAC Foundation for Motoring, London, UK

Social Exclusion Unit (2003) *Making the Connections: Transport and Social Exclusion Final Report*, http://www.cabinetoffice.gov.uk/social_exclusion_task_force/publications_1997_to_2006/making_transport_summary_2003 per cent20pdf.ashx, accessed 7 May 2008

8

The Impacts of Teleworking on Sustainability and Travel

Peter White, Georgina Christodoulou, Roger Mackett,
Helena Titheridge, Roselle Thoreau and John Polak

Introduction

Considerable attention has been devoted in recent years to the growing potential of 'teleworking', in which a worker avoids the need to commute to a place of work provided by an employer (typically, an office), but instead is able to work from a more convenient location (typically, their home). The widespread provision of broadband connections and powerful PCs has made the required technology largely ubiquitous for the working-age group in the population that may wish to use it.

In theory, this could contribute substantially to environmental sustainability as well as individuals' quality of life. Interpreted in the sense of reducing consumption of resources, it would reduce the need to travel, with resultant savings in use of energy, emissions of pollutants and need for road space. Such reductions would be largely pro rata to total distance travelled. In addition, especially from the public transport viewpoint, useful gains could be made by reducing and/or spreading the highly concentrated peak in demand on current systems. This would enable a reduction in fleet size and staffing requirements, while catering for other existing demand without reducing off-peak service levels. However, the overall net reduction in travel would not necessarily be a simple matter of eliminating home to work travel on certain days, since some additional local trips might be made on those days.

One could also see a contribution being made to social as well as physical sustainability. Present commuting patterns disrupt home life, as one or more members of the household commute to various places five days a week. Especially in large conurbations, notably London and its surrounding catchment area, such journeys may be quite long (e.g. an hour each way), reducing the ability of commuters to play an active role in their local community, except at weekends.

Claims are often made regarding the actual or potential impact of these changes. For example, a survey by the telecommunications business O_2 quoted in *The Times* on 12 August 2008, indicated that many small businesses were shifting from conventional offices, with more than half the companies that had scrapped their offices stating that new technologies such as wireless internet and mobile broadband had meant that they no longer needed a dedicated business base. However, one must be cautious about surveys targeted at particular types of business, or those most likely to favour change. Evidence from comprehensive national surveys of travel patterns, such as that quoted below, suggests a much more gradual rate of change in society as a whole. The actual extent of teleworking may be much less than often imagined.

This chapter examines some of the outcomes of a study undertaken jointly by the University of Westminster, University College London and Imperial College London. The British context was reviewed, principally by analysing data from the National Travel Survey (NTS) and through interviews with organizations in the London area. Comparisons are made with the outcomes of research in the USA and Norway (Choo et al, 2005; Hjorthol and Nossum, 2008).

Defining the volume of teleworking

Many organizations now offer, at least in principle, scope for their employees to telework. However, the actual volumes are often much less than may appear possible in theory. Several levels may be defined:

1   The proportion of organizations permitting teleworking by their staff.
2   Within such organizations, the proportion of workers undertaking the types of work that may be suited to teleworking. Typically, these are tasks which can be accomplished at home (such as writing a report). However, other tasks continue to require the physical presence of the worker (such as office cleaning).
3   Within those eligible types of work, the proportion of staff who take up the teleworking option.
4   Of those staff, the proportion who are based at home as full-time teleworkers and the proportion teleworking on a part-time basis (that is, working from home on some days, but on others at the traditional workplace).
5   From the combined total of work done by the full-time and part-time teleworkers, the proportion of total days or hours worked on this basis.

For example, a study by Waters (2007) of staff at Gloucestershire County Council showed that from 100 per cent of a category who could potentially telework, only 37 per cent would be willing to do so having taken personal factors into account. Organizational factors indicated a potential 69 per cent would be acceptable to management, and cross-tabulation of these last two categories indicated that 27 per cent of staff could potentially convert to home working. Within this group, introduction on a part-time basis was preferred by many respondents, which would further reduce the actual proportion of days worked in this form.

A further distinction may also be drawn between whole-day and part-day teleworking. There is evidence of part-day teleworking, in which some may, for example, avoid the morning peak by checking emails at home, but travel to their workplace later in the day. This does not reduce the total volume of travel, but helps to spread peak demand on the network (Lyons et al, 2006).

Allowing for all these factors, the overall impacts of teleworking on total distance travelled may be small – for example, an estimate of about 1 per cent by Choo et al (2005) for the USA.

The present extent of teleworking in Britain

The NTS enables us to examine the current degree of working at home in Britain, from which inferences about teleworking may be made. It consists of a very large household survey, which has been carried out continuously since 1989. All members of the households responding complete a seven-day travel diary, in which data is collected on each trip made by purpose, mode, length, and so on. In addition, data is collected on each individual (e.g. age, gender, income) and the household (e.g. car ownership). It is thus possible to cross-tabulate travel patterns against these classificatory variables.

In addition to the seven-day diary, the NTS also includes questions on frequency of working at home over the year as a whole, enabling occasional patterns to be identified. A further advantage is that the stability of questions asked and the continuous nature of the survey enable trends to be tracked over time, as well as a sample taken for a defined period. However, there is a limitation in that part-day teleworking is not readily identified.

An annual bulletin is published, highlighting the main NTS results. The most recent travel diary data – for calendar year 2008 (DfT, 2009a, Table 6.11) – indicates that about 4 per cent of the working population always worked from home, but a substantially larger proportion (about 6 per cent) did so on at least one day in the previous week and a further 10 per cent were able to work from home, although had not done so in the previous week.

Taking the respondents in the last two categories, these may be further subdivided, using 2006 data (DfT, 2007, Table 6.14). Of the 15 per cent of respondents who either did work at home in the previous week or were able to do so, 9 per cent of them worked at home three or more times a week, 22 per cent once or twice a week, 44 per cent did so less than once a month but at least once or twice a year. The remaining 25 per cent only worked from home once or twice a year or had never done so.

These data probably encompass some traditional home-working occupations and also small businesses operated from home. However, 79 per cent of those working from home at least once or twice a year indicated that a computer was essential for their work to be conducted at home, and hence this proportion may be considered as a broad proxy for teleworking (it would also cover some home-based small businesses which now use computers, but were previously using less sophisticated technology).

The proportion of those in employment working wholly at home has remained at about 3 or 4 per cent for some years, but the proportion working at least once a week from home has tended to rise, albeit slowly. Those working at least once a week from home average about 2.3 days in this form. In combination, those already working at home, and those doing so at least one day in a week, account for about 5 to 6 per cent of all days worked.

A fuller set of NTS data for the years 2002–04 inclusive was available to the researchers to examine these patterns in more detail. There was evidence of a slightly higher proportion of working at home in London and the south-east, which might be expected given the greater proportion of office-based employment found there. There was also strong evidence of part-week working from home being characterized by higher status, higher-income staff, as might be expected from the nature of the work undertaken.

In the case of Norway, Hjorthol and Nossum (2008) found that 48 per cent of their respondents had the possibility of working at home using information and communication technology, but for these, average days worked at home comprised 1.3 whole days and 3.8 part days per month. Those more likely to telework from home were of higher occupational status and income.

The relationship between teleworking and total distance travelled

A particularly noticeable feature of the NTS data was that the total volume of travel (distance per person per annum) did not fall steadily as the proportion of days worked from home increased. As Table 8.1 shows, it was actually higher for those working one or two days a week at home (about 17,000 miles) than those who worked from home only once or twice a year (about 14,000 miles). Only where three or more days a week were worked at home was the total travel volume lower (about 12,000 miles). All of these figures themselves exceed the average reported by working-age males in 2004 of about 11,000 miles. This apparently surprising result may be explained largely in terms of the status and income of those who telework, since such individuals will tend to have higher car ownership and travel more than the average employed person. It might also reflect occupation, such as that of a travelling salesman working from home. Hence, the effect may be largely that of a correlation, and should not be read as simple cause and effect. A similar result emerged in Norway, those occasionally working full days at home displaying a significantly higher average total travel distance per day than those who did not work at home (Hjorthol and Nossum, 2008, Table 6).

The NTS data also enable a breakdown by number of trips and trip purpose to be made, as shown in Table 8.2.

Table 8.1 *Total distance travelled by frequency the respondents work at home (miles)*

Frequency of working at home	Total distance per year (miles)	Of which, 'commuting' distance per year (miles)
Three or more times a week	11,752	1472
Once or twice a week	17,069	3702
Less than once a week, more than twice a month	16,074	4211
Once or twice a month	15,446	4112
Less than once a month, more than twice a year	14,387	4682
Once or twice a year	13,982	4716

Note: This data is also shown in Figure 8.1

Source: Derived by authors from NTS sample 2002–04

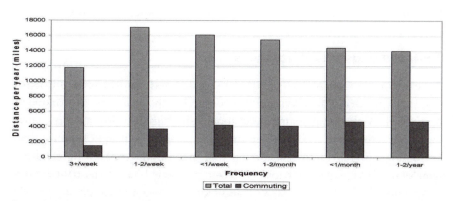

Source: Derived by authors from NTS data, as in Table 8.1

Figure 8.1 *Distance travelled per year by frequency of working at home (miles)*

Table 8.2 *Total trips per year made by frequency the respondents work at home*

Frequency of working at home	Total trips per year	Trips per year reported as 'commuting'	Implied average commuting trip length (miles)
Three or more times a week	1183	106	13.9
Once or twice a week	1211	187	19.8
Less than once a week, more than twice a month	1151	247	17.1
Once or twice a month	1176	275	15.0
Less than once a month, more than twice a year	1332	327	14.3
Once or twice a year	1248	320	14.8

Source: Derived by authors from NTS sample 2002–04

This indicates that the number of 'commuting' journeys fell as frequency of home working increased (as might be expected). However, the total number of journeys did not necessarily vary with frequency of working at home, an average of about 1200 per year being observed, with no systematic variation. There is stronger evidence for a reduction in total distance than in total journeys, as days worked at home increase beyond two per week. The broad stability in trip rates is typical of trends observed over many years, in which the number of journeys per person per day has remained stable (at about three) while distance covered has increased. However, when average commuting trip lengths are calculated, shown in the right-hand column of Table 8.2, it is noteworthy that substantially higher values (about 17–20 miles) are found for the categories who worked at home between 'more than twice a month' and 'twice a week' inclusive.

Evidence of gender differences

A further analysis of NTS 2002–04 data was carried out to examine whether noticeable gender differences exist, associated with frequency of working at home, making the same assumptions about using this as a proxy for teleworking, as described above. In making such comparisons, it is important to avoid attributing differences to teleworking that are found generally by gender – females tend to make more trips per person per year, 1060 versus 1014 in 2006 for example (DfT, 2007, Table 3.6), and more of these on foot, 272 versus 225 (DfT, 2007, Table 4.3). They also made fewer commuting trips, 153 versus 185 (DfT, 2007, Table 4.3), a function of a lower-paid economic activity rate and probably a higher proportion of part-time jobs.

Of the 2193 males providing data on frequency of working at home, 638 did so at least once a week (29.1 per cent of the total). Of the corresponding 1539 female respondents, 397 did so at least once a week (25.8 per cent of the total). By number of trips made, a similar sub-division can be produced.

Overall, gender differences associated with frequency of working from home as such appear small, indicating a slightly lower proportion of females working from home at least once a week, but very little difference between males and females doing so in terms of the distribution within the week. The former difference would be consistent with the higher status/higher income jobs that tend to involve teleworking, as described earlier. In terms of distance, overall average trip lengths by gender indicate lower totals for females, as might be expected from aggregate NTS data. However, a similar pattern of variation in average trip length by frequency of home working can be found (in this case taking all trip purposes combined). For males, the highest commuting average trip lengths were found for those working at home between 'more than twice a month' and 'twice a week' inclusive at about 19–22 miles (higher than the overall commuting averages for these frequency categories in Table 8.2), while for females the highest average trip lengths (at about 14–15 miles) likewise occurred in this category. A fuller analysis of the NTS data and their implications is presented elsewhere by the authors (White et al, 2007).

Who benefits from teleworking?

Interviews were carried out with 19 organizations in the London area – principally based in central London – in both the public and private sectors. In each case, a senior manager (e.g. someone responsible for the estates portfolio or human resources) was interviewed to obtain evidence on the current extent of teleworking and the organization's policies towards it. Given the informal nature of much teleworking, precise estimates of its extent were not available. The proportion of staff with formal teleworking contracts with their employer was very small, usually less than 5 per cent.

From the employers' perspective, possible benefits include:

- Reduced stress for the employee as a result of reduced effort in travel, leading to better quality work.
- Reduced staff turnover (or easier recruitment) through improved working conditions.
- Reductions in costs of office space (such as rentals and heating). This change tends to take a 'step' form when substantial changes in working patterns occur, perhaps enabling downsizing of accommodation, or more staff

to be employed without expanding accommodation. It is associated with the practice of 'hot-desking' (i.e. fewer working desks than staff employed).

- A form of working particularly attractive to younger staff, who are more familiar with electronic methods.

In addition to traditional office-based tasks, a category of 'nomadic' workers was identified by some respondents, comprising staff who are often based at home and travel to activities such as repair work, maintenance, running training courses and selling to clients. In this case, teleworking takes the form of enabling much faster and more accurate communication with staff (e.g. downloading via a laptop), thus improving quality and productivity of work, rather than reducing travel per se.

From the employees' viewpoint, benefits include:

- Reduced personal expenditure on travel, as well as time and stress involved.
- Greater flexibility in timing of work.
- The ability to undertake household tasks during the normal working day (such as childcare or receiving repair staff), completing work at other times.

Hjorthol and Nossum (2008, Table 4) show that those who telework indicated that the most common motives for working at home were work-related (such as 'can work when I want'), followed by family reasons (such as childcare), and transport only third in importance.

From both the viewpoint of the employer and that of the employee, it is necessary that a degree of trust exists between a manager and an employee that work will be undertaken without direct supervision. This is associated with a change in working practices generally toward assessing 'outcomes' of work performed rather than 'inputs' such as hours worked. For this, a certain level of seniority may be needed. In particular, newly recruited or junior staff might be expected to follow a more conventional working pattern until this level of trust has been established. It would also vary according to the attitudes of the line manager concerned.

Wider benefits to society are principally those arising from reduced travel in terms of lower energy use and emissions, and the reduced need for transport infrastructure. The latter is associated with the extent to which demand at peak periods can be shifted or eliminated. A potential danger exists in that certain days of the work may be favoured for working from home (such as Fridays), which could result in peak demand being as high as before on the other working days (and hence even less efficient utilization of transport capacity). However, the NTS data indicate a fairly even distribution over the five-day working week for days worked at home.

Economic evaluation of changes in transport systems indicates that the total value of time saved is typically the largest single element. For example, an improved road or rail link might enable the same journey as before to be made at substantially higher average speed. The resulting time savings can be expressed in monetary terms by using appropriate values of time, based on behavioural evidence. In most cases, travel time comes out of the worker's own personal time, rather than that of the employer, for which a relatively low rate (about £5 per hour) is applicable. However, where an employee is travelling during paid working hours (e.g. between meetings within the working day), a much higher rate is applied, corresponding to the average earnings plus employer overheads.

In the case of teleworking it is not a question of 'speeding up' an existing journey, but of eliminating that journey altogether. In addition to savings in resources (such as energy used), a value can be placed on the resultant time savings. A fairly obvious approach would be to use the values applicable to savings in a person's own time, reflecting greater time available at home. However, if some of the time spent in commuting were used instead for economically productive work, a much higher value of time would be applicable in that case. Without reducing the present amount of free time at home, substantial increases in productive working time could occur. For example, a commuter to central London travelling one hour each way might use that time on days worked at home to telework. In this respect, a much higher value of time would be appropriate (the 'in work' rate) rather than the standard 'commuting' value (personal time spent in home-to-work travel) currently used in evaluation.

This would, of course, represent the extreme case. A more likely scenario is that some workers would be willing to follow this practice, but only on some, not all, working days, while others would not do so at all. A range of scenarios may be envisaged, as discussed elsewhere by the authors (White et al, 2007). Given the high valuation rate for in-work time, this could easily dominate the benefits arising in any overall economic evaluation of teleworking, rather than changes in travel costs per se. Such economic benefits would accrue whether or not the employee was paid additionally for this work. One would assume, however, that a transfer payment could take place between the organization and employee to reflect this.

At the personal level, it could be argued that it is the higher-income, higher-status groups who tend to benefit, since the type of work they do is best suited to teleworking, and they will also be those trusted to work in this fashion. Lower income groups are more likely to occupy those jobs still requiring physical presence at the place of work and thus incur the cost and stress of travel.

The limitations of teleworking

If teleworking has so many advantages, why is it not more widespread?

From the employers' viewpoint, the need to control the quality of work remains important. While continuous supervision is no longer required in many cases, some periodic supervision is often deemed desirable. This also enables staff to be briefed and to interact effectively.

There is also evidence that in some sectors, notably finance and business services, face-to-face interaction at the workplace remains very important, as indicated in the study of response to a flu crisis, mentioned above. It is note-worthy that recent development of office space at Canary Wharf in east London (now employing about 90,000 people) is in many respects a very 'traditional' form of employment, in that there appears to be little teleworking, and employ-ees are largely working a standard weekly pattern. The evaluation by Graham (2007) indicates statistically significant elasticities for economic benefits of 'agglomeration' (i.e. higher output per worker in zones with a high concentra-tion of employment in particular sectors), notably in the financial services and business sectors. Although one major employer at Canary Wharf, the bank HSBC, has indicated an intention of encouraging employers to work from home, other employers continued to expand at that location (Seib, 2007), at least until the current economic recession.

Organizations must consider not only the economic, but also the social implications of teleworking. Having the workforce distributed between home and office may ultimately lead to the loss of teamwork, which may lead to a reduction in the skill level of employees and a lower level in the quality of work that is brought about when people with different skills and aptitudes come together.

From the employee's viewpoint, full-time home teleworking may be unat-tractive, resulting in isolation from colleagues. Interaction at work serves not only a work purpose, but also a social function. Therefore, to uphold or enhance the employee's quality of work-life, the employers would need to ensure that teleworkers feel that they are part of the wider group and are con-tributing to the team or department's overall objective. Furthermore, there is not only the additional costs to the employee in terms of heating, lighting, asso-ciated call and web connection charges and the disruption of home life and space, but the possible loss in salary such as the 'London Weighting' allowance.

Combining these factors, the attractiveness of the part-week teleworking pattern becomes evident. It is also clear that informal patterns of teleworking are commonly associated with this method of working. Flexible working meth-ods may be particularly convenient to those with domestic responsibilities such as childcare and might encourage greater participation in the workforce as a result. However, as noted earlier, gender differences in aggregate appear rela-tively small. Flexible, informal working is also attractive to employers, avoiding the need for formal contracts and retaining a link with the 'traditional' work-place (thus enabling effective supervision of work, and interaction between teleworkers and their colleagues who continue to follow a conventional full-time working pattern).

Other implications of teleworking

Sustaining activity at times of crisis

A benefit both to specific organizations and society as a whole could be the ability to respond to crises that result in a reduced ability to travel, or particular locations becoming inaccessible (indeed, the origins of the internet as part of the US defence system illustrate this). At the time organizations were being interviewed, the threat of bird flu was seen as significant. This could have resulted in substantial restrictions on travel into city centres, for example. There is anecdotal evidence of severe disruption to the Chiltern Railways' commuter services into London for several months in 2005 (caused by a tunnel collapse), resulting in some regular travellers shifting to working from home for this reason (Dark, 2007). However, once travel conditions have returned to normal, this higher level of teleworking may not necessarily persist. Nonetheless, it could offer a valuable safeguard in the event of sustained change (e.g. severe shortages and/or high real prices for oil).

A simulation of how Britain's financial system could respond to a crisis such as a flu pandemic, as reported by Moore (2007), indicated that reduced scale of activity could continue, but nonetheless a strong emphasis remained on the ability to conduct trade 'on site', resulting in reduced trading hours being a more likely outcome than trading from home on a prolonged basis.

How does teleworking affect commuting distances between home and work?

If no change occurs in location of the home, then for a part-week teleworker, reductions in home to work travel are pro rata to frequency of working at home – for example, someone working one day in five at home would reduce such travel by 20 per cent, and so on. However, this assumes that home location remains fixed. In practice, the situation is a dynamic one, and both home and work locations change frequently. In cities such as London, very high housing costs and limited availability make it difficult for new workers to locate in their preferred location, making it necessary to live at a greater distance. Teleworking, while not causing a greater distance to exist between home and work, may nonetheless enable such a response to other conditions such as housing costs. Hence, in the long run, it does not necessarily follow that teleworking for a certain proportion of total working days produces directly proportional reductions in distance travelled between home and work, quite apart from any additional local trips made on teleworking days.

However, detailed studies in Britain have yet to be made, and a study in California by Ory and Mokhtarian (2005) indicates that workers who took up teleworking tended to relocate closer to, rather than further from, their traditional place of work.

Potential longer-run developments

While the impact to date of teleworking appears fairly limited, despite widespread availability of the technology required, there could be more substantial effects in future; given an external stimulus, more jobs could shift to this form of working.

Types of employment currently expanding are typically in the service sector, and the workforce in manufacturing continues to decline. This could favour a shift towards teleworking for certain types of service industry work (such as consultancy and professional services), but not in all cases (e.g. growth in the hotel and catering trade generally involves work at the location where the service is delivered).

Further research evidence

Subsequent to the study described in this chapter being completed, further work elsewhere has updated some trends and examined certain aspects in greater depth. NTS Household Interview data for 2007 (DfT, 2008, pp40–42) confirms that teleworking is closely correlated with income band, the top quintile having the highest ability (33 per cent) and propensity (10 per cent in the previous week) to work at home on a part-week basis, compared with 10 per cent and 3 per cent respectively for the lowest quintile.

A study by Penfold et al (2009), of the National Centre for Social Research for the DfT, examined a sample of 49 teleworkers through qualitative in-depth work. Respondents generally confirmed a preference for part-day or part-week working and welcomed the greater degree of flexibility it permits. Displacement of travel time to less congested periods was found, but not necessarily a reduction in total distance travelled. The importance of part-day home teleworking is also illustrated in the National Centre for Social Research Omnibus Survey in 2008 (DfT, 2009b).

Conclusions

While work described in this paper is specific to Britain, parallels with studies in other countries, especially Norway (Hjorthol and Nossum, 2008), is noteworthy. Even though the Norwegian study used a different approach – based on a large sample of teleworkers as such, rather than inferences from national survey data and interviews with employers – very similar conclusions were reached, notably in the attractiveness of part-week teleworking rather than full-time teleworking from home. This gives confidence that the results are of wider application. Further study of teleworkers in Britain who reduce the amount of time they spend in travel, to examine how they make use of such time savings, would usefully enhance current research evidence.

In terms of physical sustainability, teleworking assists by reducing the total volume of travel, with savings in energy, pollutants and transport capacity costs. In terms of social sustainability, it may reduce the amount of time spent in commuting and enable teleworkers to interact more with their families and local community. However, in other respects it could be divisive, insofar as it appears to be the higher-income, higher-status individuals whose work is best suited to teleworking.

A particular benefit in transport systems would be to spread the peak demand, giving better utilization of capacity. This could be further stimulated by suitable pricing mechanisms (road pricing for cars and a finer degree of peak/off-peak price differentiation in public transport). This could be aided by wider use of smartcards, enabling more sophisticated fare structures to be adopted without undue complexity of operation.

One can already see a blurring between traditional 'work' and 'leisure' activities. Greater flexibility should be beneficial to both the individual and society at large.

The contribution of teleworking of 'sustainability' remains open to debate. In principle, it enables reductions in travel, as identified above. Under conditions imposed externally, such as a severe fuel shortage, it could be adopted much more widely, enabling activities to be sustained under conditions different from those now found, either as an emergency or longer-term solution. However, the rate of spontaneous adoption at present appears relatively low, and will still be subject to constraints, notably in respect of those types of work that still require the physical presence of the worker at the place of production, whether in manufacturing or service sectors.

Acknowledgements

This study was jointly sponsored by British Telecommunications plc (BT) and Transport for London (TfL). We acknowledge the assistance of the British Council for Offices (BCO) and others in identifying a sample of organizations for interview in the London area, and the time spent by managers in those organizations. Prof. Patricia Mokhtarian of the University of California provided helpful comments on the draft report. Use of data from the NTS 2002–04, supplied by the Department of Transport, was of great value. All inferences drawn from data and views expressed in this paper are those of the authors.

References

Choo, S., Mokhtarian, P. and Salomon, I. (2005) 'Does Telecommuting Reduce Vehicle-Miles Travelled? An Aggregate Time-Series Analysis for the U.S.', *Transportation*, vol 32, pp37–64

Dark, J. (2007) 'Chiltern is Finding Light at The End of The Tunnel', *Transit*, 23 March, pp15–17

Department for Transport (2007) 'National Travel Survey: 2006', Transport Statistics Bulletin SB(07)21, September

Department for Transport (2008) 'National Travel Survey: 2007 Interview Data', Transport Statistics Bulletin SB(08)22, September

Department for Transport (2009a) 'National Travel Survey: 2008', Transport Statistics Bulletin SB(09)20, August

Department for Transport (2009b) 'Public Experiences of Home Working and Internet Shopping', January, http://www.dft.gov.uk/pgr/statistics/datatablespublications/trsnstatsatt/homeworkinginternet, accessed February 2009

Graham, D. (2007) 'Agglomeration, Productivity and Transport Investment', *Journal of Transport Economics and Policy*, vol 41, pp317–343

Hjorthol, R. and Nossum, A. (2008) 'Teleworking: A Reduction in Travel or just Increased Flexibility?' *The Journal of e-working*, vol 2, June 2008, pp81–94

Lyons, G., Haddad, H. and Jones, T. (2006) 'Introducing Consideration of Varied-Spatiotemporal Workers to the Study of Teleworking', Conference paper, session 4.8, 11th International Conference on Travel Behaviour Research, Kyoto, August

Moore, J. (2007) 'Banks could be crippled by flu pandemic', *The Independent*, 5 January

Ory, D. T. and Mokhtarian, P. L. (2005) 'An Empirical Analysis of Causality in the Relationship Between Telecommuting and Residential and Job Location', University of California, www.ctc.net/papers/733.pdf, accessed May 2006

Penfold, C., Webster, S., Neil, H., Ranns, H. and Graham, J. (2009) *Understanding the Needs, Attitudes and Behaviours of Teleworkers*, Department for Transport, London

Sieb, C. (2007) 'Work-from-home drive as HSBC aims to sublet HQ', *The Times*, 15 June

Waters, R. (2007) 'Is There a Virtual Solution to Traffic Congestion?', *Logistics and Transport Focus*, vol 9, no 1, January/February, pp31–34

White, P., Christodoulou, G., Mackett, R., Titheridge, H., Thoreau, R. and Polak, J. (2007) 'The role of Teleworking in Britain: Its Implications for the Transport System and Economic Evaluation', *Proceedings of the European Transport Conference*, October, Leeuwenhorst Conference Centre, The Netherlands

SECTION 3

REGENERATION AND ECONOMIC DEVELOPMENT

Introduction to the section

What becomes clear from both of the previous sections of this book is that providing the urban fabric to support sustainable communities will require considerable inward investment (both monetary and organizational). Generating the necessary resources to fund such investment for not just new development, but also the regeneration of existing communities, is obviously, therefore, a crucial issue. In this final section, we consider some of the ways that the resources for providing communities with the social infrastructure they require have been generated in the past, as well as some of the barriers that have been encountered in practice.

While economic growth is seen as a public good within UK policies for sustainable development, the latest orthodoxy views this as not an unconstrained good. The sustainability agenda understands that economic development should be constrained by attention to ecological concerns; a concept that can be particularly problematic for developing countries, but is also relevant in the context of the developed world. One of the key issues in this respect as far as social sustainability is concerned is 'who wins and who looses', or the social equity and fairness of the new urban structures that evolve from policy interventions.

In a recent report for the Home Office, Ledbury et al (2006) recommend seven core criteria against which all government policy intervention should be judged. In addition to the more obvious likely effectiveness against objectives and cost-effectiveness objectives, the authors recommend that policies should not adversely affect already disadvantaged groups and should also not produce any negative unintended consequences.

The next three chapters provide further case studies and evidence about the relative effectiveness of economic policies to stimulate sustainable communities for the future, with a particular focus on their intended and unintended outcomes for social sustainability, including social equity and overall quality-of-life objectives. First, in Chapter 9, Chris Marsh considers the role of planning gain from developers through the planning system in the financing of new social infrastructure projects. He argues that while planning agreements with developers will in general make some contribution to social sustainability, which is their intended role, for the most part they will only provide for *development necessities* rather than additional social infrastructure. They obviously can also only be invoked where considerable additional new development is being brought forward in an area and will not be available where retrofitting existing communities is the main aim.

In Chapter 10, Adam Eldridge considers the way in which some local authorities have promoted the *night-time economy* to stimulate local jobs and the economy and regenerate town centres in run-down areas. This is a highly neglected issue in policy discussions of social sustainability, and Eldridge points out some important tensions within government urban policy. On the one hand, government has been keen to emphasize how cities can be thriving, continental-style café cultures; on the other, the negative externalities of these approaches are often obscured. Eldridge provides research evidence that calls into question the approach of the 'urban renaissance' agenda (Urban Task Force, 2005) to sustainable city centres. He argues that government policy has neglected to understand cities as interconnected social, political and economic networks. Much of the discussion about the night-time economy has been one-dimensional, with the consequence that cities have become highly individualized spaces, based on a model of consumption over production and non-participation. Eldridge argues that sustainable city centres require the active involvement of their communities, rather than the passive acceptance of top-down policy prescriptions about what makes an effective city centre.

In Chapter 11, Andrew Smith examines the use of *mega-event*s and the role that these can play in regeneration of the urban fabric. As local authorities become more involved in a 'place shaping' agenda, such events play an important role in the branding of cities; their success and failure can leave substantial legacies, both positive and negative. Smith argues that an understanding of the spatial dimension of event planning is critical to their success. Venue planning should be aimed at providing services for local communities, rather than simply based around one-off events. The impact of events (even temporary ones) can be spatially significant if based on models that have social sustainability as an explicit objective.

In the final chapter of this section, we draw some broad conclusions about the achievement of social sustainability in the urban fabric thus far, as well as offering some general guiding principles for future practice. The chapter is intended as less of a conclusion in this respect, and more of a stimulus for future discussion and debate within academic, policy and practice circles.

References

Urban Task Force (2005) *Towards a Strong Urban Renaissance*, London: Urban Task Force

Ledbury, M., Mille,r N., Lee, A., Fairman, T. and Clifton, C. (2006), *Understanding Policy Options*, Home Office online report, www.homeoffice.gov.uk/rds/pdfs06/rdsolr0606.pdf, accessed 28 September 2006

9

Planning Obligations and Social Sustainability

Chris Marsh

Introduction

Planning gain, planning obligations and developer contributions are all terms that have been used over the last 30 years to describe the content of contractual agreements (known as 'planning agreements'). Such agreements are normally based on Section 106 of the Town and Country Planning Act 1990 (as amended; HMSO, c1990), but do draw on empowerment from other areas of legislation, perhaps most commonly Section 278 of the Highways Act, 1980 (HMSO, 1980). Agreements between those seeking planning permission (usually property developers) and Local Planning Authorities (LPAs) normally address and seek to mitigate the negative social impacts of new development proposals by providing appropriate community infrastructure. For many councils, revenue from such contributions (in cash or works in kind) has become crucial in providing community infrastructure and meeting the policy objectives of the Government's Sustainable Communities agenda.

Chapters elsewhere in this text consider definitions of social sustainability, some narrower than others. This section adopts a simplistic stance, namely that the product of planning agreements will in general make some contribution to social sustainability – that is their broad role – but for the most part, planning obligations deliver *development necessities* focused on key physical infrastructure requirements, albeit often meeting community needs in parallel. Only occasionally do planning agreements provide *additional* social sustainability objectives.

Clearly, the financial viability of any development proposals will be a key determinant in terms of implementation, and thus local planning authorities are increasingly testing planning policies in terms of their deliverability in advance of their adoption. Similarly, site-specific circumstances, where proven, may limit developer contributions to social sustainability. This does not negate the need for the broadest range of community infrastructure, but it does highlight that in some circumstances, not least an economic and property market downturn, developer contributions may only partially meet infrastructure needs, and thus additional funding sources, including public subsidy, may be necessary to meet any financial shortfalls.

The key themes in this chapter are:

- The development of planning obligations and government guidance.
- The nature and incidence of obligation types using all London boroughs as a case study, with particular reference to the sustainable agenda.
- Potential changes (at the time of writing) to planning obligations with the proposed introduction of the Community Infrastructure Levy, via enabling powers contained in the Planning Act (2008), finally enacted in December 2008, and the possible effects on social sustainability objectives.
- Likely futures, with particular reference to implementation of developments.

The development of planning obligations and government guidance

Councils were empowered from the early planning acts to enter into planning agreements with landowners, which *restricted and regulated the use and development of land*, and were often used to secure, for example, 'gifts' of land for public parks in perpetuity (effectively restrictive covenants). From the late 1970s/early 1980s, however, councils started to explore the wider potential of planning agreements, albeit slowly. Definition was always difficult and Jowell (1977) provided a beginning in his survey as follows:

> [A planning gain is] the achievement of a benefit to the community that was not part of the original scheme (and was therefore negotiated) and that would not of itself normally be commercially advantageous. (Jowell, 1977, p414)

The essence of Jowell's approach to planning gain was sound in its emphasis on community needs, but missed the key point in its reference to gains *not* normally being *commercially advantageous*. At a time when planning gain was in its infancy, Jowell assumed, not unreasonably, that any community gains must be loss-making and thus a cost to the developer, a view still presented by less-enlightened elements within the development industry. The shortcomings in this approach are explained below.

Nevertheless, in the interim, with additional contributions from the professions (and despite the heavily weighted/developer-oriented Property Advisory Group Report; DoE, 1981), basic 'ground rules' did gradually emerge; they can be summarized as follows. Planning gains/obligations:

1   Should be clearly justifiable in planning policy and the law.
2   Should be needed and benefit the community.
3   Should be a direct consequence of the development proposal.
4   May be offered or negotiated.
5   May be commercially advantageous or, indeed, a development necessity.

These basic requirements continue to underpin the planning obligations system (albeit subject to the most recent government proposals described below).

In the early years, however, the difficulties of definition remained. The Government's first attempt, under pressure from the development industry, was Circular 22/83, *Planning Gain*, which stated that planning gain was:

> a term which has come to be applied whenever in connection with a grant of planning permission, a local planning authority seeks to carry out works not included in the development for which permission is being sought, or to make some payment or confer some right or benefit in return for permitting development to take place. (DoE, 1983)

While the tenor of the definition attempted to placate the development industry, privately it also reflected the Treasury's tacit support for a system that delivered community requirements at little or no cost to the Exchequer. In other words, government guidance on the subject kept itself at arm's length from day-to-day practice. Indeed, locally, the system began to gather some (limited) momentum.

On the definitional front, Fordham (1989) then rightly redefined the basis of contributions as 'planning loss'; that is, the cost of *impacts* of new developments on the taxpayer and thus the level of *compensation* necessary to meet those costs. The writer subsequently distinguished between so-called *compensatory* gains and *true* planning gains; that is, those compensations that directly mitigate the impacts of new development proposals, compared with those *additional* contributions that are effectively 'icing on the cake'. Compensatory gains in pure financial terms are 95 per cent of the total. Where compensatory gains are not provided, that failure may be grounds for refusal.

A simple illustration may assist. The residential developer who focuses on family housing is likely to generate a need for additional primary school places among other community facilities. While the cost of an additional school would historically have been met by the taxpayer, the requirement was the result wholly or partially of new developments, and thus the cost should be met by those developments that generated the need. Conversely, a failure to provide the school would also inevitably adversely affect residential sales, and thus there is clearly a *commercially advantageous* correlation (in Jowell's terms) between the provision of community infrastructure and development marketability and its value.

Nevertheless, and not surprisingly, in the light of political window-dressing from the development industry, planning gain/obligations evolved slowly. However, eventually, Circular 16/91, *Planning Obligations*, expanded the agenda, not least in its almost open-ended definition of *legitimate* planning gains/obligations, which can be summarized within the following (paraphrased) quotations from the circular. Planning obligations may be:

1   Social, educational, recreational, sporting or other community provision, the need for which arises from the development.
2   To secure the implementation of local plan policies (e.g. affordable housing).
3   Intended to offset the loss or impact on any amenity or resource present on the site prior to development. (DoE, 1991; Circular 16/91, para. B11)

While embracing the concept of *planning loss*, Circular 16/91 considerably broadened the potential range of planning obligations and also concluded the protracted debate regarding the legitimacy of planning agreements including affordable housing requirements, assuming that a genuine need for affordable housing had been fully demonstrated. Where proven via an up-to-date Housing Needs Study, affordable housing requirements were acceptable. The financial impacts of this recognition were considerable, not least on other areas of obligations, and are addressed later in this chapter.

Following various amendments, Circular 01/97, *Planning Obligations*, primarily a consolidating guidance document, nevertheless addressed two long-standing issues within planning gain/obligations practice, namely:

1   Pro rata payments – The simple notion that while, for example, a single housing development proposal might not generate a requirement for say a primary school in its own right, together with other local housing proposals, an aggregated requirement for such a facility might well arise. Pro rata contributions on such bases had been pursued by some local authorities previously. (DoE, 1997; Circular 1/97 confirmed local practice).
2   Revenue/maintenance payments – Developer contributions had traditionally focused on *capital* payments towards community facilities, subsequent revenue funding usually being left to the recipient council, where they could 'afford' such funding. Circular 1/97 accepted the principle that subsequent 'maintenance' payments may be appropriate, but only applied that principle to public open space. However, some councils, subsequently, gradually expanded revenue applications to other service areas.

For the first time, Circular 1/97 also specified the provision of public transport facilities as a legitimate area of development contributions. The effect was immediate and a wide range of obligations in pursuit of the sustainable transport agenda emerged in planning agreements, including subsidized bus services, cycling and pedestrian measures, green transport plans and car-free schemes.

Indeed, the development of planning obligations has often been characterized by local initiatives, subsequently copied by neighbouring councils and eventually 'adopted' by revised government guidance. Elements of the sustainability agenda are no exception.

Thus, while the development of planning gain/planning obligations was to an extent incremental and certainly gradual, the underlying principles were steadily expanded. If a development proposal generated a 'cost' to the community in social, economic, environmental or sustainable terms, then it was necessary that the community was fully compensated for the cost incurred. This is *not* a tax in the sense of a *'betterment levy'*, previously attempted by various governments, in which a proportion of the increase in land value resulting from the grant of planning permission is returned to the state. Rather, its foundation was embedded in the notion of 'equity' and not dissimilar to the 'polluter pays' principle; that is, the costs of mitigation/remediation are met by the causal party. Predictably, the Government eventually accepted this approach, albeit the Treasury has continued, occasionally, to focus on property magnates as easy taxable targets. The Planning Act (2008) is no exception. Indeed, after much pressure, the Government agreed changes to remove mention of developer contributions on land whose value increases due to permission for development; that is betterment and thus a 'tax'.

Overall, however, the product was a gradual widening of the legitimate scope for planning obligations, and this raised interesting questions in terms of which areas of community infrastructure should be reasonable expectations and, more particularly, whether a rational methodology for the nature and scale of developer contributions could be established and survive potential legal challenge. Inevitably, this leads us to the incidence of planning obligation types and their extent, and thus cost, and thus (potentially) prioritization in current market conditions.

The range and incidence of planning obligations

As noted earlier, Circular 16/91 encouraged the expansion of legitimate planning obligations but, nevertheless, three key prerequisites had to be met:

1   Justified and adopted planning policies were required in Local Development Plans (the current introduction of revised Local Development Frameworks providing LPAs with a particular policy opportunity to upgrade and adopt revised policy bases).

2   Appropriate planning 'standards' were necessary in order to provide a base position for infrastructure requirements from which developer contributions

could be calculated. In some cases, such as school provision, central government lays down standards regarding size of school, scale of facilities and the number of children to be accommodated, and thus the cost of provision. This then enables a calculation of child yield from particular development proposals to be converted into the contribution necessary to meet additional school places required. In contrast, mitigating environmental impacts may be much more difficult to cost. Perversely, government advice (until Circular 05/05 – see below) discouraged local authorities from using formulae to make such calculations, but the reality was the increasing use of standard approaches wherever possible, subsequently acknowledged in Circular 05/05.

3   Traditionally, planning obligations could not be *required* by the LPA until existing spare capacity had been taken up. Thus, to use again the schools example, if spare places existed in the local primary school, the developer could not be required to make an education contribution until that capacity had been taken up, although this approach has always been questionable.

Such requirements continue to evolve and are (eventually) being 'driven' by *accessibility* criteria, increasingly based on walking rather than car-borne trips. Thus, the availability of the school place is not conditioned by spare capacity at the other end of the borough and, as a result, the 'unsustainable' school trip, but on provision within close proximity to the development proposal, which may then generate the requirement for more *local* school places.

Unfortunately, developing requirements are also subject to priorities in a difficult budget climate and market circumstances, further varied by individual planning authorities' preferences, depending on local policies, circumstances and political preferences. The resulting 'pecking order' is determined therefore by a combination of central government guidance, case law (albeit limited), policy requirements, implementation/resourcing plans and local circumstance.

In addition, planning obligations can also be categorized by other key characteristics as follows. Those planning obligations that are:

1   Directly consequential on the proposal.
2   Increasingly formulaic.
3   Requirements without which there are grounds for refusal.

In contrast to those obligations that are:

1   Addressing more general community needs.
2   Offered and/or negotiated rather than formulaic.
3   Not grounds for refusal if missing.

Figure 9.1, compiled by the author in 2003 (Marsh, 2003, p41), classified obligations into a 'pecking order'. Despite its age, it remains a useful benchmark, not least for subsequent developments and changes in priority. In particular regarding obligations, it emphasized:

1   The traditional significance of physical infrastructure factors such as education and transport, which in terms of impact and mitigation were relatively simple to calculate, if restricted to immediate local impacts; less so where strategic issues arise.

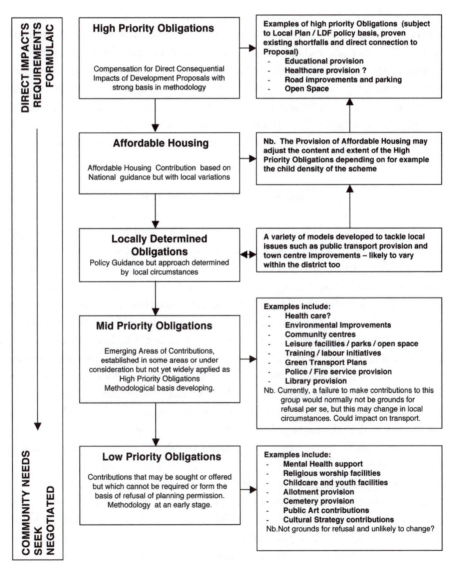

Figure 9.1 *Planning obligations 'pecking order' 2002*

2   The status of affordable housing provision, albeit subject to specific local needs.
3   Those service providers who, via obligations, traditionally were not benefi-ciaries but who have increasingly become included, such as healthcare trusts, police and fire authorities.
4   The continuing dynamic in prioritization, where some contribution areas such as road improvements are losing significance, while in contrast the sus-tainable transport agenda, including public transport contributions, green travel plans, pedestrian and cycling measures, is gaining momentum.

Having said that, developer contributions often occur as works in kind; that is, infrastructure inputs that are not 'commuted' in the sense that the contribution is made over in cash, and then it is up to the local authority or service provider to deliver the community facility required. Often such contributions are deliv-ered directly by the applicant, first because this guarantees that the 'monies' are spent on the required infrastructure, and second because infrastructure deliv-ery can be coordinated with completion of market units, the correlation between infrastructure delivery and commercial advantage being secured.

The London experience

In terms of planning obligations and based on the simple but crude assump-tion that high residential and commercial values must equate (at least theoretically) with high delivery of community infrastructure, it was perhaps not unreasonable to base case-study material in this work on London (and thus London boroughs) as the 'leader' in delivering community infrastructure via planning obligations. While in some cases this may be relevant, the real deliv-ery picture is much more mixed, with a wide variance in London boroughs' performance and, for that matter, some authorities outside the metropolitan areas performing better. Tables 9.1–9.3 summarize performance for each London borough. They are based on MoliorLondon's research monitoring of the content and nature of Section 106 agreements across London boroughs, albeit only in the year up to July 2007, but subject to an online service coming on-stream in early 2009, which will update its planning agreements database continuously.

It should be emphasized that these statistics only represent *completed* plan-ning agreements in the specified time period and are thus only a 'snapshot' at a particular point in time. Further, financial contributions exclude works in kind, which may be significant in particular cases. Nevertheless, despite totalling £168 million in contributions, the product varies noticeably across boroughs.

Table 9.1 *Affordable housing delivery*

London borough	Total units	Private Units	Percent	Intermediate Units	Percent	Social rented Units	Percent
Barking & Dagenham	11,474	6806	59	2235	19	2433	21
Barnet	4439	3205	72	49	1	1185	27
Bexley	666	535	80	35	5	96	14
Brent	1587	1217	77	131	8	239	15
Bromley	1341	933	70	134	10	274	20
Camden	2614	1511	58	369	14	734	28
City of London	127	127	100	0	0	0	0
Croydon	1291	658	51	202	16	431	33
Ealing	503	268	53	104	21	131	26
Enfield	642	445	69	132	21	65	10
Greenwich	5204	3310	64	1000	19	894	17
Hackney	1901	1230	65	236	12	435	23
Hammersmith & Fulham	552	219	40	192	35	141	26
Haringey	85	74	87	11	13	0	0
Harrow	1134	728	64	246	22	160	14
Havering	876	529	60	145	17	202	23
Hillingdon	1499	1129	75	134	9	236	16
Hounslow	581	228	39	64	11	289	50
Islington	3098	1818	59	312	10	968	31
Kensington & Chelsea	362	327	90	27	7	8	2
Kingston upon Thames	131	90	69	14	11	27	21
Lambeth	2962	1648	56	569	19	745	25
Lewisham	1070	746	70	133	12	191	18
Merton	654	430	66	90	14	134	20
Newham	797	319	40	264	33	214	27
Redbridge	842	610	72	76	9	156	19
Richmond upon Thames	262	163	62	34	13	65	25
Southwark	2904	1999	69	391	13	514	18
Sutton	615	389	63	42	7	184	30
Tower Hamlets	4818	3721	77	434	9	663	14
Waltham Forest	337	205	61	67	20	65	19
Wandsworth	2723	2061	76	487	18	175	6
Westminster	1400	960	69	33	2	407	29
Totals	59,491	38,638	65	8392	14	12,461	21

Source: MoliorLondon Database, 2008

Variable product

One, if not the main, criticism emanating from the development industry regarding the planning system is the need for *certainty*, with specific reference to planning obligations, an accusation that has occupied the Government since 2001 in its efforts to reform the process (considered later in this chapter). Put simply, developers, not unreasonably, question why obligation requirements change when crossing the local authority boundary! The explanations are noteworthy:

1   Local planning circumstances and infrastructure requirements vary; some boroughs in, for example, the Thames Gateway area have much higher growth allocations than others.
2   Affordable housing policy requirements in terms of percentage target and tenure split vary from borough to borough.
3   Existing shortfalls in infrastructure capacity also vary, especially in growth areas.
4   Other policy requirements will increase costs, including the Code for Sustainable Homes.
5   Property market circumstances locally both vary and fluctuate differently.
6   Infrastructure priorities evolve.
7   Planners' skills vary.
8   Political preferences shift.

Thus, while Tables 9.2–9.3 may tell one story, the explanations for the variable incidence in planning obligation achievement by London boroughs (and elsewhere) will always require a more considered assessment of local circumstances.

The remaining question in this section therefore is: Where do *social sustainable* objectives sit in the pecking order of planning obligations?

The responses can be summarized as follows:

•   If you accept the broad definition of *social sustainability*, then there is no doubt that many local authorities have steadily increased their expectations and achievements via planning agreements in delivering social infrastructure.
•   If you consider a narrower definition, then it is equally clear that planning obligations continue to focus primarily on basic physical infrastructure provision, albeit a widening definition, while less well-defined aspects of community infrastructure such as cultural development and services struggle to get established.

Table 9.2 *Total Section 106 financial contributions across London*

London boroughs	Total schemes Schemes	Units	Schemes with financial payments Schemes	Units	Amount (£)	Amount per unit (£)
Barking & Dagenham	11	11,474	7	11,047	11,400,000	1032
Barnet	21	4439	10	1136	1,490,314	1312
Bexley	13	666	3	475	363,790	766
Brent	16	1587	11	1200	6,948,433	5790
Bromley	29	1341	3	534	3,883,892	7273
Camden	26	2614	21	2523	25,992,670	10,302
City of London	6	127	1	64	0	0
Croydon	36	1291	29	1149	2,565,663	2233
Ealing	13	503	7	307	1,514,591	4934
Enfield	20	642	4	130	239,556	1843
Greenwich	29	5204	15	4803	20,087,971	4182
Hackney	25	1901	18	1747	4,091,488	2342
Hammersmith & Fulham	5	552	2	483	1,450,000	3002
Haringey	4	85	2	53	94,999	1792
Harrow	22	1134	4	658	1,528,000	2322
Havering	15	876	10	764	1,819,197	2381
Hillingdon	35	1499	28	1335	3,283,243	2459
Hounslow	13	581	6	400	417,754	1044
Islington	32	2803	29	2751	9,797,888	3562
Kensington & Chelsea	14	362	4	172	163,000	948
Kingston upon Thames	4	131	3	115	153,500	1335
Lambeth	43	2962	24	2634	4,778,096	1814
Lewisham	28	1122	8	646	1,514,171	2344
Merton	14	654	9	557	1,464,654	2630
Newham	19	797	9	623	1,942,635	3118
Redbridge	19	842	8	598	1,491,752	2495
Richmond upon Thames	6	262	3	38	156,865	4128
Southwark	34	2904	20	1883	10,356,926	5500
Sutton	19	615	12	447	604,547	1352
Tower Hamlets	44	4818	29	3920	42,807,822	10,920
Waltham Forest	10	337	8	307	363,218	1183
Wandsworth	34	2723	11	1556	1,780,450	1144
Westminster	28	1400	16	1186	3,627,455	3059
Totals	687	59,248	374	46,241	168,174,546	3637

Source: MoliorLondon Database, 2008

Table 9.3 Section 106 financial contributions by type and by borough

Local authority	Education (£)	Employment (£)	Environment (£)	Highways (£)	Open/Amenity/Playspace (£)	Other (£)	Public art (£)	Health (£)	Transport (£)	Total (£)
Barking & Dagenham	0	0	550,000	0	0	50,000	0	0	10,800,000	11,400,000
Barnet	475,514	490,000	0	143,000	376,800	5000	0	0	0	1,490,314
Bexley	0	200,000	50,000	46,000	7290	25,000	0	0	35,500	363,790
Brent	2,748,483	0	284,000	13,000	10,000	475,000	0	133,500	3,284,450	6,948,433
Bromley	2,627,396	0	50,000	500,000	0	0	230,000	26,496	450,000	3,883,892
Camden	2,525,796	2,813,000	860,000	4,272,870	2,412,505	439,500	1,830,000	672,000	10,167,000	25,992,671
City of London	0	0	0	0	0	0	0	0	0	0
Croydon	252,813	0	421,750	35,000	825,896	158,176	62,000	217,265	592,763	2,565,663
Ealing	359,391	100,000	476,200	125,000	356,000	20,000	50,000	0	28,000	1,514,591
Enfield	189,556	0	50,000	0	0	0	0	0	0	239,556
Greenwich	10,381,796	2,133,715	185,000	38,000	1,369,910	1,655,000	85,000	517,050	3,722,500	20,087,971
Hackney	2,861,262	643,200	97,910	412,200	20,117	31,500	0	0	25,300	4,091,489
Hammersmith & Fulham	450,000	0	100,000	0	800,000	0	0	0	100,000	1,450,000
Haringey	95,000	0	0	0	0	0	0	0	0	95,000
Harrow	750,000	0	250,000	85,000	20,000	0	0	0	423,000	1,528,000
Havering	683,763	0	167,702	72,000	0	90,000	0	0	805,732	1,819,197
Hillingdon	2,299,415	0	47,989	15,000	358,049	194,800	0	134,291	233,700	3,283,244

Hounslow	84,954	0	132,800	0	10,000	0	0	190,000	417,754
Islington	0	0	3,343,250	667,888	834,500	400,000	80,000	26,240	9,797,888
Kensington & Chelsea	0	15,000	2500	0	31,500	100,000	0	0	163,000
Kingston upon Thames	92,500	0	0	11,000	50,000	0	0	0	153,500
Lambeth	2,455,310	25,000	48,000	836,354	659,023	638,909	30,000	85,500	4,778,096
Lewisham	0	50,000	10,000	555,661	0	680,000	50,000	168,510	1,514,171
Merton	199,481	0	5000	255,000	691,174	90,000	20,000	204,000	1,464,655
Newham	763,000	5700	135,000	894,210	87,500	17,225	0	40,000	1,942,635
Redbridge	879,300	50,000	0	0	0	51,600	188,000	209,250	1,491,752
Richmond upon Thames	119,086	0	0	0	10,225	0	3497	24,058	156,866
Southwark	515,814	193,466	585,529	4,030,000	904,510	3,489,051	152,290	486,266	10,356,926
Sutton	115,253	0	49,000	30,000	132,550	130,744	0	122,000	604,547
Tower Hamlets	1,705,899	245,000	638,000	314,120	12,722,000	2,773,000	4,988,345	18,872,459	42,807,823
Waltham Forest	180,466	0	33,850	58,617	51,160	4125	0	35,000	363,218
Wandsworth	0	0	0	536,000	103,000	50,000	0	1,091,450	1,780,450
Westminster	1,549,230	50,000	509,500	206,000	425,225	270,000	452,500	165,000	3,627,455
Totals	35,360,477	7,014,081	9,082,980	14,151,920	23,251,43	15,816,14	3,997,102	7,112,73	52,387,678	168,174,54

Source: MoliorLondon Database, 2008

Government reforms

Like its predecessors, the Labour government has been convinced by its own rhetoric for some time, namely, if only we can identify a suitable method for collecting *betterment*, then millions and millions of land value uplift, as a result of planning permission and/or developer profit, can be collected to fund strategic and local community infrastructure projects, at little or no cost to the Exchequer. While there has been some theoretical basis for this position, two strands of government departmental approach have emerged. The first, driven by the Office of the Deputy Prime Minister (ODPM), has been more concerned with improving the established Section 106 regime to make it more productive via the planning system. The second, reflecting the Treasury's aspirations, simply has seen developers as an easy financial target (not for the first time) and thus a relatively non-contentious potential contributor to taxation shortfalls.

Circular 05/2005, *Planning Obligations*

Circular 05/2005, entitled *Planning Obligations*, emerged from the ODPM and contained several clarifications and limited reforms, including:

- Para. B4, which provided a confirmation that minimum development size thresholds were not necessary. In contrast to affordable housing, there had in fact never been any requirement for thresholds below which planning obligations were not sought, but most authorities, for administrative and legal reasons, did not seek obligations on small schemes. This inevitably prompted accusations of 'threshold abuse' (correctly), that is, large numbers of applications that deliberately sought to avoid contributions by limiting their scale. Indeed, the cumulative impact of numerous small schemes on local infrastructure was often as great as one major development.
- Para. B9 notes that planning obligations should not be used *solely* to resolve existing infrastructure deficiencies, but there may be circumstances where such shortages can be addressed.
- It may be appropriate for the developer to make provision for subsequent maintenance, clearly addressing the long-standing question of revenue funding as well as capital contributions. Para. B18 also noted that while this would normally be short term until traditional funding sources took over, in some circumstances such provision may be required in perpetuity (which prompted a sharp intake of breath from the development industry!).
- Spare capacity in existing infrastructure provision also appeared to be addressed in para. B22, which advised: 'should not be credited to the earlier developer'. While this shift effectively supports pooling of contributions and a strategic approach to contributions that would suit the

Mayor of London, for example, most planning authorities continue to take account of spare capacity.

- In contrast to previous guidance (Circular 1/97) but very much in line with local authority practice, formulae have become much more common. Para. B33 encourages councils to employ formulae and standard charges where appropriate.

- Para. B10 drew attention to those planning applications, especially in regeneration areas, which on viability grounds could not meet their infrastructure requirements but which nevertheless had significant attributes, not least, for example, by encouraging much-needed inward investment. The planning authorities were often left in the dilemma of accepting such schemes but failing to provide infrastructure. In such circumstances, para. B10 underlined the need to seek 'the balance of contributions' from other public sector infrastructure providers rather than compromise policies. This provides the opportunity for setting different levels of charge in different parts of the borough, based on the ability of the development to make a contribution or based upon the priority of policy objectives for specific areas.

While Circular 05/05 restates the traditional 'necessity tests', namely that local planning authorities should require/seek obligations that are essentially fair, open and reasonably related in scale and kind to the development in question, in practice some councils have gone beyond the advice and developed new formulae for additional areas of infrastructure and extended these arrangements, such as Milton Keynes' so-called (roof tax) (albeit in that case only really workable with a small number of landowners, and English Partnerships – now the Housing and Communities Agency – acting as 'banker'), or 'full and discounted standard charges' (e.g. London Thames Gateway and West Northamptonshire Development Corporations). Such an approach can be appealing and has been given some support through the Government's suggestion for a Community Infrastructure Levy (CIL) (described below).

Overall, the circular was not radical but was an important development in obligations practice, and many local authorities have, as a result, produced revised supplementary planning documents which not only embrace the content of the circular, but have also improved and updated their obligations methodology and expectations. Clearly, where this has occurred, councils will have a stronger basis on which to achieve social sustainable policy objectives (at least in theory) and often an improved track record as a result.

Community Infrastructure Levy

Possible changes to the current system for planning obligations are envisaged through the Government's proposed introduction of a CIL. The purpose of a

CIL is to 'ensure that costs incurred in providing infrastructure to support the development of an area can be funded (wholly or partly) by owners or developers of land'.

Part 11 (Clauses 205–225) of the Planning Act 2008 enables the Secretary of State to issue Regulations to deal with all aspects of the operation of a CIL, including:

- Which local authorities are empowered to charge a CIL, which can be any local planning authority or principal council. It is not clear whether more than one authority in the same area will be a charging authority. However, it is clear that Urban Development Corporations such as the London Thames Gateway Development Corporation are not to be CIL-charging authorities, because they do not have plan-making powers.
- Defining who among owners and developers is liable to pay a CIL. (A CIL will still be payable whether or not the land increases in value as a result of the development.)
- Arrangements for deciding the amount of CIL locally, including having regard to the actual or expected costs of infrastructure.
- Setting out the basis on which a CIL is or can be levied (e.g. per dwelling, per unit of floorspace).
- Ensuring that a CIL collected is applied to funding infrastructure.
- Requiring charging authorities to prepare and publish a list of projects that are to be funded, wholly or partly by a CIL.
- Arrangements for applying a CIL, collecting and enforcing its collection.

Clause 216(2) in the Act includes a definition of infrastructure types to which a CIL may apply. (The regulations may identify additions to that list and/or exclusions.) Currently the list notes roads and other transport facilities, flood defences, schools and other educational facilities, medical facilities, sporting and recreational facilities, open spaces and affordable housing.

The content of the final 'list' is clearly important in the pursuit of social sustainability and, when compared with Table 9.1 above, may exclude some of the items that have been included in Section 106 agreements previously.

While planning authorities will be given a power rather than the duty to implement a CIL (at least for the moment), it is also apparent that the Government intends to rein in the scope of Section 106, effectively forcing planning authorities to implement a CIL if they wish to seek a contribution from development towards CIL-identified infrastructure. It is important to emphasize that Section 106 agreements would still operate, but only focus on on-site provisions that include affordable housing.

The Department for Communities and Local Government (DCLG) briefing papers on a CIL, issued in January and August 2008, indicate the extent to which the Government has still to resolve various practical and technical issues in implementing a CIL, although the Government has made it clear that, in the interim, local planning authorities should continue to develop standard charges, 'reflecting current law and policy'.

At the time of writing, the regulations have not been published, and so for the moment the 2008 Act and the briefing papers are the only formal documents that can be assessed.

Department for Communities and Local Government Community Infrastructure Levy Briefing Paper, August 2008

This paper delivers little advice about the key issues that were not covered in the earlier January 2008 DCLG briefing. In fact, the latest paper seems quite deliberately to have been drafted in a simplistic, rather naive way to hide the fact that the Department has little idea how to solve the difficult technical issues around setting a CIL.

It does, however, represent a potential threat to those LPAs (and Development Corporations) that have pioneered the use of formulae and standard charge arrangements.

It is quite clear in the paper and the Act that only plan-making authorities (excluding county councils) can be charging authorities. Indeed, to date, DCLG has appeared obsessed with the need for a CIL to be tied into the statutory development plan and that only those authorities who have an up-to-date development plan will be able to implement a CIL. In particular, the requirements for evidence and independent examination will limit a CIL to those authorities who have an up-to-date core strategy.

The failure to address the key issues of viability of development in any meaningful way means that the DCLG position is much as it was when consulting on their previous proposal for reform, namely Planning Gain Supplement. A CIL should be set at such a low level that there is little risk of harming viability or deterring development and, in consequence, there will only be 'exceptional cases' where a CIL has to be reduced or waived to allow development to happen. Based on our own consultancy work (Christopher Marsh & Co. Ltd) for numerous local authorities and the London Thames Gateway Development Corporation, the West Northamptonshire Development Corporation and currently the Thurrock Thames Gateway Development Corporation, even before the recent property crisis, this would mean that, across large parts of the country, a CIL for residential development will have to be set, at best, at very low rates. As a result, rather than collecting 'millions and millions' of additional funding for infrastructure, those planning authorities with well-organized systems of planning obligations may well yield less.

The briefing paper contemplates LPAs setting two or three different rates of CIL for different parts of their area; this accords with DCLG's desire that there should be substantial 'headroom' between levels of CIL and net development values. In reality, there are widespread differences across short distances in net development values, while existing use values, which are also crucial, vary almost on a site-by-site basis. Paras 4.18 and 4.19 of the August paper bear little relation to the real world.

The briefing paper generally ignores the reality of what it calls, in para. 4.40 onwards, 'payment in-kind', although it touches on the question of 'free' land for community facilities in para. 5.9. In order to deliver properly sustainable developments, with facilities to serve them, planning authorities must be able to continue to require sites to be made available by developers for open space, utilities and community infrastructure. The valuation of 'offsets' including land is technically complex, but it must be resolved if a CIL is not to significantly distort developer behaviour (including forcing local authorities to compulsorily purchase land for these facilities).

The commentary on affordable housing is also remarkably naive. On the one hand, it exhorts LPAs to take a much more sophisticated and transparent approach to setting their affordable housing policies (taking account, for example, of the availability of Social Housing Grants). On the other, it claims that there is no obvious link between development viability and the proportions or mix of affordable housing being required. This is itself inconsistent with DCLG's support for the use of various development appraisal 'tool kits', all of which explicitly model the relationship between the affordable and market development on each site and show exactly how development values alter as affordable housing proportions and tenure change.

Overall, it remains unclear why, in what is a discretionary system, most local authorities with well-established approaches to planning obligations would contemplate the CIL route. It will be protracted and resource intensive and is unlikely (despite the DCLG assertion) to yield 'millions' of additional revenue towards infrastructure provision. In January 2009, DCLG announced that CIL regulations will not be finalized until the autumn of 2009 at the earliest, noting that, because of the economic climate, it wants more time to consult and consider secondary legislation.

Planning obligations and the economic downturn

After a prolonged period of positive economic conditions, the planning and development system has been conditioned to coping with growth. Increasing housing projections and restricted supply have contributed to spiralling house prices, and the increasing need for affordable housing and new and updated infrastructure. In an era of sharply rising land values in many parts of the country, providing affordable housing and an expanding list of planning obligations was often deliverable by viable development proposals. Even where viability was more marginal, some compromise in planning requirements might well be sufficient to ensure implementation.

The nature and intensity of the economic downturn has presented a very different scenario, and the effect on planning obligations and the delivery of social sustainability via planning agreements is now heavily dependent on the length and severity of the economic recession. Pundits have mixed views, optimists suggesting some improvement by the end of 2009, but most expecting further falls in house prices this year and no recovery until 2010 at the earliest. The market characteristics and implications for the planning and development process can be summarized as follows:

- Sharp falls in residential and commercial property values.
- Corresponding falls in existing use values.
- Build cost inflation declining and tender prices beginning to fall.
- Banks refusing to lend to developers and/or insisting on much higher profit margins and equity inputs to cover greater risk.
- Land values falling quickly.

There is very little development activity; indeed, registered social landlords (housing associations) currently *are* the market, with many developers building out affordable housing units where funding is in place, while 'mothballing' open-market dwellings.

As a result, many development proposals are simply not viable in the current market or can only be made viable where planning policy requirements are relaxed or deferred. Some developers and, for that matter, planning authorities will simply wait for recovery. Where delivery is more urgent, innovative approaches may be necessary, including planning obligations contained in flexible planning agreements. On larger phased schemes, planning obligations are invariably delivered at particular 'trigger points' when they become necessary. Where possible, viability can be enhanced by deferring triggers and thus improving cash flow. More radical methods include sales value-related clawbacks.

This approach, either separately or in concert with other mechanisms, is the most common to date. It is founded on an agreed base sales value and a proportion of required contributions paid for on commencement, which is then indexed and, if sales over an agreed period/phase exceed the benchmark, then additional contributions are made. While the main advantage is its simplicity and the ability to monitor sales prices via the Land Registry, the details require care and, of course, if values do not rise sufficiently, then planning obligations will not be paid. Overall, there is no doubt that in the current economic climate there is increased pressure on planning authorities to agree planning agreements that fall short of the council's normal requirements, a process that inevitably focuses on prioritizing absolute infrastructure requirements and possibly compromising other obligations. The potential impact on achieving broader social sustainability is clear.

Conclusions and likely futures

No matter which definition of social sustainability is adopted, there is little doubt that, for many LPAs (especially in the south of England), planning obligations secured usually through Section 106 planning agreements have been a significant if not key contributor to the delivery of local (and occasionally) strategic community infrastructure. The range of legitimate obligations has evolved and widened to include an extensive range of physical, social and environmental contributions, albeit subject to considerable local variation. In 'normal' property-market conditions, and whether subject to reform in the form of a CIL or not, there is nothing to suggest that developer contributions would diminish in significance. While the development industry will always argue about the detail of planning agreements, there is a widespread acceptance that impacts on infrastructure should be mitigated and that it is equitable that developers meet their responsibilities. That process is complicated by various factors, including the provision of affordable housing and the increased requirements (and costs) associated with meeting the Code for Sustainable Homes standards.

The current economic climate, however, is far from 'normal' and 'likely futures' are heavily dependent on the nature and timing of economic recovery. In many cases, developments will simply be put on hold, but where development proposals are pursued there will be increased pressure to either reduce or at least defer the cost of planning obligations. That will inevitably focus attention on those key aspects of consequential infrastructure that are absolute, non-negotiable requirements, without which planning applications would be refused, as against meeting those community needs that are desirable but not essential. The pursuit of the wider social sustainable agenda via planning obligations is likely to be adversely affected until the economic climate improves.

References

Department of Communities and Local Government (2008) *Community Infrastructure Levy Briefing Paper*, HMSO, London
Department of the Environment (1981) *Planning Gain: A Report by the Property Advisory Group*, HMSO, London

Department of the Environment (1983) 'Circular 22/1983', *Planning Gain*, HMSO, London

Department of the Environment (1991) 'Circular 16/1991', *Planning Obligations*, HMSO, London

Department of the Environment (1997) 'Circular 1/1997', *Planning Obligations*, HMSO, London

Fordham, R. (1989) 'Planning Gain: Towards Its Codification', *Journal of Planning and Environmental Law*, pp577–584

HMSO (1980) 'Highways Act 1980' (Chapter 66), HMSO, London

HMSO (c1990) 'Town and Country Planning Act 1990' (Chapter 8), HMSO, London

Jowell, J. (1977) 'Bargaining in Development Control', *Journal of Planning and Environmental Law*, pp414–433

Marsh, C. (2003) *Planning Gain 2003*, Estates Gazette Research

MoliorLondon Database, MoliorLondon, http://moliorlondon.com/molior-about/, accessed 4 January 2009

Office of the Deputy Prime Minister (2005) 'Circular 05/2005', *Planning Obligations*, HMSO, London

10

The Urban Renaissance and the Night-Time Economy: Who Belongs in the City at Night?

Adam Eldridge

Introduction

In the later part of the 20th century, city centres increasingly came to be modelled around entertainment, leisure and recreation. The manner in which people have come to spend their non-working lives has subsequently become an area of policy and planning intervention. The growth of the night-time economy has, in particular, attracted a great deal of attention, with various tiers of government seeking to better manage and shape late-night behaviours, venues and locations. The introduction of special policy areas that limit the opening of new licensed venues, the use of street wardens, campaigns to tackle binge drinking and the establishment of groups such as Pubwatch, where licensees work with the police to better manage alcohol-related problems, are designed to minimize antisocial disorder and manage the effects of an alcohol-centred night-time economy.

These provisions and strategies have occurred with varying degrees of success, however. Concerns about 'binge Britain' (Plant and Plant, 2006), alcohol-related violence (Richardson et al, 2003; Winlow and Hall, 2006) and public drunkenness contribute to a highly negative, albeit distorted, view of British cities after dark.

There is an alternative narrative about British cities, which sits alongside the night-time economy in complex and often problematic ways. Far from the image of a drunken youth lying in a gutter, the 'urban renaissance' re-imagines city centres as desirable places to live, work and play. The mixed-use, mixed-tenure communities envisaged by the proponents of the urban renaissance are marked by a sense of social diversity, narrative sociality, inclusiveness and, ultimately, economic and social sustainability. In this example, city centres are dynamic, safe and typically aspirational communities.

There is a clear tension between these two visions (ODPM, 2003a). Rather than experiencing the urban renaissance as imagined by glossy brochures and marketers, some city-centre residents have had to watch as their local neighbourhoods have been transformed into hubs of late-night leisure geared towards a single market sector: generally, young people attending noisy and crowded chain bars. The ensuing conflict has been well documented by academics (Roberts, 2006; Roberts et al, 2006), as well as charitable agencies (Davies and Mummery, 2006) and resident groups (Open All Hours? Campaign, 2002).

This chapter subsequently explores how the night-time economy has functioned alongside and in relation to the urban renaissance. Rather than simply reciting the problems that have occurred between residents and late-night operators or proposing blanket solutions, the discussion is framed by a larger question about inclusiveness and belonging in the city at night. To explore this, I draw upon a series of projects investigating the night-time economy, conducted between 2004 and 2007 (Roberts and Eldridge, 2007; Eldridge and Roberts, 2008). In one particular project, we examined why some people avoided venturing out after dark. As well as concerns about violence, lack of transport and suitable places to go, a number of respondents spoke of feeling excluded from their local town and city centre (Eldridge and Roberts, 2008). In the light of attempts to create sustainable communities, of which a sense of belonging is a central component, this feeling that the city at night was 'not for me' was troubling. Of course, belonging is a vexed issue (Probyn, 1996; Bell, 1999) and is as relevant to studies of the daytime as the night. That is, debates about immigration, the so-called breakdown of communities and questions about cultural and national identity emerge from comparable anxieties about who is and who is not included within local and national communities. The well-cited Cantle report, conducted in response to riots in Bradford, Oldham and Bromley, points to the intricate nature of belonging in today's multi-cultural and post-industrial communities (Cantle, 2001).

Debates about belonging to the city at night are often framed in far cruder terms, however. In this instance, the issue is less about religion or race, though these are indeed important (Talbot, 2004), but instead questions about age, class and 'cultural capital' (Bourdieu, 1992). As rendered by the popular press, the city at night has simply become a space that is monocultural, homogenous and frequented by a minority of users. The discussion that follows subsequently explores some key questions and debates about how the night-time economy fits within the notion of a socially and economically sustainable community.

Cities as sites of leisure

The demise of traditional forms of manufacturing, trade and industry over the latter part of the 20th century resulted in a long period of city-centre decline. This period, termed post-industrialization or post-Fordism, has been extensively documented (Zukin, 1989; Sassen, 1991), and though its effects upon city centres are not equal or consistent, key identifying features can be summarized. In simple terms, the manufacturing and industrial sectors on which many city's economies were based were replaced from the 1970s onwards by the financial, service and tourism sectors. As manufacturing jobs moved out and typically moved overseas, employment opportunities in cities became focused around the service sector, entertainment, information and, increasingly, culture (McRobbie, 2002). This process was not uniform and many British cities today continue to reel from the closure of former industrial and manufacturing businesses.

Britain's night-time economy, in its current form at least, emerged in the late 1980s on the back of these broad economic changes. Town and city centres have always had late-night culture in some form, be that cinemas, theatres and dance halls to everyday pubs, restaurants and nightclubs (Schlör, 1998). Over the past two decades, however, the night-time economy has filled the vacuum left by the deserting industrial and manufacturing sectors (Hobbs, 2003; Hobbs et al, 2003; Talbot, 2004; Roberts and Turner, 2005). As leisure opportunities have expanded to include women, students, lesbian, gay and new counter-cultures, and become increasingly focused around the consumption of food and alcohol, city centres at night have become important leisure and entertainment hubs (Chatterton and Hollands, 2003).

The numbers of people who now venture out into city centres at night is significant. In 1997 the capacity of licensed venues in the city of Nottingham was 61,000. Within seven years that number had nearly doubled to 108,000. Over a similar period, Manchester city centre's bars and clubs grew to accommodate 250,000 people (Hobbs, 2005, p25). By 2007, according to the Department for Culture, Media and Sport:

> 177,200 licences and certificates were in force in England and Wales ... 162,100 were premises licences and 15,200 were club premises certificates. (Antoniades et al, 2007)

The night-time economy now represents a significant economic industry. As Hobbs argues:

> The pub and club industry employs approximately 500,000 people at the point of service delivery and turns over £22 billion, equal to 3 per cent of the UK Gross Domestic Product. (Hobbs, 2003, p4)

It should be kept in mind, as Jayne (2005) notes, that the relationship between cities and consumer practices are mediated via an array of macro and micro processes (p18). That is, the night-time economy needs to be considered as more than just a response to the decline of the manufacturing sector – and in more than just economic and quantitative terms. Instead, it has emerged in the context of planning, policy and international business strategies, as well as individual consumer desires and lifestyle. The shifting nature of subcultures or 'tribes' plays an equally important role, which are all then further 'constrained and enabled' (Jayne, 2006, p19) in relation to larger questions about race, age, class, sexuality and gender. As Chatterton and Hollands (2003) suggest, Britain's current night-time economy occurred in relation to a series of inter-related factors such as the greater participation of women in the workforce, new bars and clubs aimed at women and gay men, the expansion of higher education and a subsequent rise in student numbers, the corporatization of the pub sector and a later age in marriage (2003).

No less important is what Wittel (2001) refers to as 'network sociality'. 'Narrative sociality' is marked by employment, family and geographic stability. Traditionally, communities emerge as a result of long-standing social, economic and familial histories and networks. Network sociality, in contrast, is identifiable by a new and typically young demographic working in the creative and cultural sector. This highly individualized and nomadic population develop short and often transient relationships to each other, their jobs, education establishments and local areas (see also Sennett, 1998). In terms of the night-time economy, bars and cafes no longer function solely as sites of a shared rhetoric and familiarity, but instead as spaces to network with clients and colleagues. In short, the traditional 'boozer' is replaced by venues where people do not necessarily have a long-term sense of history or community. What this means for the goal of creating socially sustainable communities is unclear and is examined in more depth later. In summary, important economic, social and cultural shifts have impacted upon the ways that cities function – in both the day and night-time. Policy has also played a key role, with the championing of city-centre living being a crucial component of this discussion.

The urban renaissance

The call to revitalize city centres at night was spearheaded by Comedia, a group of researchers committed to the idea of developing creative and vibrant town centres. Their influential report, *Out of Hours* (Comedia, 1991), explicitly advocated inner-city living alongside promoting the evening and night-time economy. Rather than the traditional nine-to-five city centre, Comedia encouraged councils to develop their neighbourhoods as '18 hour a day, seven days a week, regional economic, social and cultural centre[s]' (1991, p44). Better lighting schemes, greater intelligibility, improved transport and building flats above shops were some of their proposals.

In hindsight, *Out of Hours* may be considered naive in that it failed to predict the massive growth of the night-time economy as based upon youth-orientated bars and clubs, and not family-friendly cafes and lively street fairs as they had envisaged. The report did, nonetheless, explicitly discuss the urban renaissance in relation to the night-time economy, unlike the later report 'Towards an Urban Renaissance' (Urban Task Force, 1999), which instead focused primarily on urban living and the regeneration of town and city centres.

There is increasing evidence to support the idea that the urban renaissance is taking hold. 'Towards a Strong Urban Renaissance' (Urban Task Force, 2005) the follow-up report published six years after the original, claims that the Government has addressed many of their original 105 recommendations (Bennett, 2005, p2). Though discussion of the night-time economy is again absent, the follow-up report does note some success stories in terms of re-populating city centres. Leeds, Birmingham and Sheffield have, in particular, all increased their city-centre populations.

At the forefront of the urban renaissance is Manchester. According to the Institute for Public Policy Research (IPPR), 'by 2001, about 10,000 people were living in the city centre, a rise of nearly 300 per cent [since 1991]. Population growth continued after 2001, and the City Council's best estimate for 2005 is about 15,000' (Nathan and Urwin, 2005, p2). Residential developments are not the only expression of a renewed faith in city centres. Extensive regeneration projects around docklands, malls and high streets typify the new market confidence in city centres and formerly run-down neighbourhoods. Hoskins and Tallon refer to this as the production of a new 'urban idyll', whereby tropes commonly associated with the rural have been appropriated in terms of city living; community, green spaces and nature; and the production of the city as a place of history and heritage (Hoskins and Tallon, 2004, pp26–30).

The figures regarding the expansion of city-centre residents are impressive but they have not been entirely celebrated. In Manchester, for example, 62 per cent of city-centre residents are aged between 18 and 34 and, as a percentage of the adult population, 75 per cent are single (Nathan and Urwin, 2006, p3). Moreover, 69 per cent of city-centre residents are in rental accommodation. Across the UK, 69 per cent of adults are home owners, suggesting that Manchester city centre is in direct contrast to the national average. Also, according to Urwin, 'in 2001 about 30 per cent of residents in Liverpool and Manchester city centres had moved in during the previous 12 months. A slightly smaller number of people left during the same period' (Urwin, 2005, p5). As Colomb (2007) notes, the Government may wish for new urban developments to be mixed socially. These figures, however, do not suggest these areas are socially diverse or long-term communities.

As Suzy Nelson has noted in Chapter 6, in her discussion of intensification and social infrastructure, the Sustainable Communities Plan defines sustainable communities as 'places where people will want to live and will continue to want to live' (ODPM, 2003b, p5). When such a large proportion of city-centre residents are transient and possibly intend to leave once they have children (Nathan and Urwin, 2006, p4), the urban renaissance of Manchester does not appear to be related to the creation of places where people live and want to live in the future.

Moreover, it is still not clear where the night-time economy fits within this debate. The aforementioned figures demonstrating the expansion of Britain's night-time leisure sector may appear impressive in economic terms, but problems with the night-time economy have been extensively discussed and extend beyond the well-cited rise of binge drinking (Plant and Plant, 2006). Given recent evidence that problematic drinking is as likely to occur in the home as in public (Holloway et al, 2008), it is important to acknowledge that while the night-time economy typically centres around alcohol-related venues, problems late at night would not necessarily be solved by simple prohibitions on alcohol. A lack of transport or quiet sit-down venues, for example, have been demonstrated to be as much of a deterrent to going out at night as the prevalence of intoxicated youth (Eldridge and Roberts, 2008).

Nonetheless, in recent years Britain's night-time economy has rarely been out of the mainstream press. The issue of public drunkenness, violence and anti-social behaviour have become almost interchangeable with the very idea of the night-time city. Though images of drunken youth obscure a great deal more that is productive, creative and vibrant about late-night cultures, it would be easy to assume that cities at night have become no-go areas for anyone wanting a 'civilized' night out.

Research conducted by Bromley et al (2000, 2003) has found this to be the case, while Pain (2001) has pointed to the high levels of fear women experience venturing out after dark. Though these fears may not always be grounded in personal experience, the perception of threat and danger is very real in the mind of some individuals (Watson, 2006). This fear is not alleviated by the pejorative and often inflammatory ways the city at night is represented: a drunken, violent and dangerous place, dominated by anonymous bars selling cheap liquor to uncivil people, or, as Judge Charles Harris, QC, once remarked, 'urban savages' (Britten, 2005).

Despite these comments, the regeneration of Britain's city centres, the rise in city-centre populations and the economic success of the late-night leisure sector are notable. Nonetheless, the corresponding picture of British cities at night stands in stark opposition to the goal of creating vibrant, diverse and socially inclusive cities. It is difficult to reconcile the goal of a mixed-use, socially sustainable urban renaissance with the corresponding, albeit often inflated, notion of an economy based upon chain-bars, short-term service sector employment and venues that people over a particular age may avoid. Important questions consequently emerge here about how the night-time economy can exist alongside and in support of the urban renaissance.

A clash of uses and users

Debates about who is moving into city centres, and why they are leaving, are examined elsewhere in this book, notably by Nelson. For my purposes, there is an equally important question here about the existing conflict between residents and the night-time economy and the ways in which current night-time uses may be deterring more socially mixed communities from developing. As early as 2003, the ODPM noted a potential problem for the urban renaissance agenda – not with the type of residents moving in to town centres, but with the existing way that towns and cities had developed as hubs for youth-focused leisure activities:

> Most European cities have a very inclusive evening economy where people of all ages participate in a range of activities. In contrast the evening activities of British cities are not so compatible with the inclusive ideals of the urban renaissance. They centre around young people and alcohol, leading to associated problems of crime and disorder, noise and nuisance. (ODPM, 2003a, p3)

Why the tension between the night-time economy and the urban renaissance has occurred is complex. Alcohol undoubtedly plays a role in late-night disorder, and data from Richardson et al (2003), Hobbs (2005a), or Plant and Plant (2006) reveal the extent to which alcohol is implicated in late-night skirmishes and antisocial behaviours.

Rather than covering well-worn ground, other contributing factors that have impeded a better understanding and mediation of the problems that exist between residents, visitors and late-night operators will be outlined. These problems include the belief that by adding the 'right type' of culture the problem will be resolved; a lack of foresight by planners about the likely impact of concentrating bars and clubs near residential uses, and the perception that city-centre residents are willing participants in all aspects of late-night culture. These points are discussed in turn, leading then to a concluding discussion about belonging within the city at night.

First, there is the view that, by adding the right type of late-night culture, current problems after dark will be resolved. Richard Florida's (2005) thesis that, by adding creative people to the mix along with a sizeable lesbian and gay population, a city will automatically become 'cool' and more economically viable has been rightfully questioned. It has not been entirely abandoned, however. Solving problems at night, in this case, is less about reducing alcohol-related venues than adding what is perceived to be the right type of culture; in this case, culture that fits within the notion of the urban renaissance idyll. Late-opening museums, galleries, cafes and libraries will allegedly attract a much more aspirational visitor which, in turn, will result in a more sedate night-time economy. Little evidence suggests this is what patrons actually want on a night out (Roberts and Eldridge, 2007), but the view remains.

Second, I am interested in what has ultimately been a failure to manage and plan for the night-time economy in relation to the urban renaissance. This failure has taken the form of allowing for unbridled entrepreneurialism, ignoring the needs of residents and presuming that only willing participants live in town and city centres. Across Britain, councils, licensees, security personnel and others are actively finding solutions to the negative aspects of the night-time economy. Many councils are involved in public–private partnerships with licensees and residents that seek to resolve potential conflicts. However, a corresponding lack of foresight and management has also been noted in research conducted by the author. The belief that the night-time economy 'was here first', or that the city in question had always been a leisure destination, has been expressed by a number of respondents, in both government as well as among late-night operators:

> Frankly we say to them, 'Well you have chosen to live in this very vibrant community, if you want to live in a quiet street, then there are [other] places where you can do that, for the same cost as well.' A friend of mine has got a penthouse flat. I've talked to her about this; I said, 'Don't you get a lot of noise from [the venue below]?' She said, 'Well yes but I don't have to live here, I can afford to live wherever I want. I chose to live here.' (Interview with council officer)

The officer concerned was highly competent and a rightfully respected member of the community. Nonetheless, framing clashes between residents and late-night operators in terms of 'choice' is not altogether helpful. Again, it should be noted that the majority of licensees and council officers spoken to were actively seeking out solutions to late-night problems and clashes with residents. Nonetheless, among a proportion of key players, there was little acknowledgement that developing the night-time economy, as centred around closely packed bars and clubs with late hours, was not always compatible with their corresponding attempts to attract a broader demographic into their town centre, as either residents or visitors.

In regards to the council officer's comments, there is an underlying assumption that living in the city, near to bars and other leisure outlets, is simply a matter of choice. This mantra of choice is a common feature of marketing brochures for new developments, where city-centre living is elided with a particular type of tele-visual lifestyle along the lines of *Sex and the City* or *Queer as Folk*. However, people live in the city for a variety of reasons and framing those reasons through such terms as choice and lifestyle can render them as far less serious than the presumably more substantial reasons people move to suburbia such as child rearing (Silverman et al, 2005). That is, when the decision to move into an urban area is conceived purely as about 'choice', we lose sight of the other factors that make city-centre living an option for some people: convenience, employment, family commitments, lack of transport, access to essential services, to be close to particular communities, finding the right sort of accommodation and the like. That is, we ignore that people live in the city for reasons that are no less or no more important than the reasons for moving into any other area.

The ongoing mantra of choice and lifestyle further obscures the number of people living in council or social housing alongside late-night hotspots. Hoxton, in London's inner east, is one such example where, despite its reputation for a vibrant night-time economy, there are a large number of local authority tenants who perhaps did not move to the area simply to take advantage of the lifestyle choices on offer. Figures from the area demonstrate that, as of 2001, and of a total of 86,040 dwellings, 30.7 per cent of dwellings in Hackney were rented from the council, with a further 20 per cent rented from a social landlord. A further 1.5 per cent was shared ownership (Hackney Council, 2006, p80). Across London in contrast, social or council tenants occupy 26.2 per cent of all dwellings, which is half that of Hoxton (Hackney Council, 2006). More specifically, the ward with the greatest proportion of socially rented accommodation in Hackney is Hoxton, at approximately 65 per cent.

In the early part of the 2000s, posters and graffiti stating that Hoxton was a late-night area became a regular site around the neighbourhood. These served as a reminder to prospective buyers that the area had a vibrant night-time economy and purchasers should be prepared to encounter a degree of late-night noise and disorder. While this reminder to prospective residents was not entirely misplaced, the perception that the night-time economy pre-dated residents was incorrect. In Shoreditch, 41.7 per cent of residents have lived in their home for between five and 20 years, with 20.2 per cent having lived there for longer than 20 years (Hackney Council, 2006, p91). This is considerably longer than the current night-time economy in Shoreditch, which only began to fully develop in the past decade. A similar example can be seen in Soho where, as Roberts and Turner (2005) argue, residents living alongside bars open until 11.00 p.m. are now living alongside venues open much later.

> In 1999, 149 premises held music and dance licences, an increase of almost 70 per cent since 1995. This has trebled capacity from 33,418 to 127,860, which is 73 per cent of the total capacity for the City of Westminster as a whole. (Roberts and Turner, 2005, p180)

In summary, there are well-publicized problems with the current night-time economy, relating to excessive drinking, the over-concentration of bars and clubs and mono-cultural leisure options (Hobbs, 2005; Hobbs et al, 2005). From a different perspective, there are *attitudinal* problems that do not help to alleviate conflict between residents and late-night revellers. The notion of choice assumes residents are willing participants in the night-time economy and obscures the reasons why people move to inner-city areas. There is also a call to simply add a more aspirational type of culture to the urban mix, in the hope it will lead to a more family-friendly and inclusive night-time economy. This not only ignores evidence that consumers enjoy a variety of leisure options, including some activities that may be seen as antisocial, such as binge drinking, it raises the final question explored in this chapter: Who exactly is the city at night for?

Socially sustainable? For whom?

For Loretta Lees, calls to re-inhabit city centres is further evidence of gentrification (Lees, 2003, p61). Lees argues that terms such as 'urban renaissance', 'urban regeneration' and 'urban sustainability' 'politely avoid the class constitution of the processes involved' (Lees, 2003, p61). There is a clear line of association here between how Lees figures the urban renaissance agenda and related attempts to 'civilize' late-night cities through adding aspirational forms of culture such as museums and galleries. Indeed, in terms of how the urban renaissance is typically imagined as an inclusive and diverse space, it has met a formidable hurdle in the way that late-night culture has actually developed. At present, late-night cities are far from reflecting only the tastes or aspirations of the urban renaissance champions. Instead, a moralizing rhetoric about patrons drinking the 'wrong' type of alcohol (alcopops), attending the 'wrong' types of venues (anonymous chain bars) or engaging in the 'wrong' form of behaviour (standing to drink, rather than enjoying quiet outdoor cafes) dominates mainstream representations of the city after dark. Following Lees' critique of the urban renaissance agenda, the question that emerges from this is how is it possible to create a truly diverse and sustainable city that functions as well during the day as at night?

Cities are always spaces where people connect and disconnect, but it would be incorrect to assume mixing everyone together will result in a happy hybridity. Cities are sites where difference rubs against difference, and recent studies by Latham (2003) or Watson (2006) are important in highlighting the potential for heterogeneity and cosmopolitanism in public life. And yet, as Amin and Thrift (2002) note, it would be naive to think we all mingle and intermingle with strangers without predetermined attitudes and expectations of 'others'. There are limits, in other words, to what we can expect cities to actually do and achieve. If the night-time economy is expected to act as a dynamic place where different ages, cultures, sexualities and genders interact and commingle, we need to be aware of the power structures that continue to challenge the socially sustainable and inclusive community model.

One such challenge is thinking through the ambiguous position of youth and young people in the urban renaissance and night-time economy rhetoric. On the one hand, young people are at the heart of late-night culture and, at least in the case of Manchester, also appear to be playing an important role in the city's urban renaissance. On the other hand, as noted by Raco (2007), the sustainable communities agenda involves a great deal of pathologizing of the 'wrong' type of tenant. Much the same could be said for the right and wrong type of late-night consumer and the role of young people in shaping both urban renaissance policy, and the night-time economy is not entirely clear.

The Government's view on how the night-time economy should operate favours public–private partnerships, such as Pubwatch, and bottom-up methods whereby residents are encouraged to participate in local issues such as licensing. Pubwatch meetings, consultation on licensing decisions and instigating other forms of entertainment at night, such as fairs and festivals; these are all important steps in involving the local community. However, it is already well-documented that not all people do get involved in actual local decision-making, especially young people, who may in fact be positively excluded (Rogers and Coafee, 2005). As Helms et al suggest, 'when the meanings associated with New Labour's various invocations of "community" are closely scrutinized, again we find that young people are rarely part of that community (Helms et al, 2007, p271). Moreover, as Raco (2007) also argues, many young people are further excluded from the urban renaissance due to prohibitive house prices, as well as the lack of alternative models to be part of the local community. In short, in the case of Manchester, young people are embracing the call to repopulate town centres, but it is not clear the extent to which they are similarly engaged in bottom-up community endeavours or participating in the local night-time economy, beyond acting principally as consumers or short-term workers.

Thinking through the position of young people in both the night-time economy and urban renaissance is, therefore, difficult. The problems associated with creating a true sense of inclusion and belonging at night, which should be at the heart of the social sustainability model, is compounded when a proportion of younger residents only intend to remain in their area for a short period of time. The question here should not necessarily be that young people do not live in the neighbourhood long enough to feel a sense of belonging, however. What it actually means to belong, and the means through which sustainable communities are formed, should not be reduced to simply a question of how long someone has lived or intends to live in an area. Belonging, when conceived more in these terms of *how* rather than *how long* (Bell, 1999), raises the question as to how people are invited to participate in their community. Through what rituals, practices, behaviours or activities do residents come to feel a sense of inclusion or exclusion? In these terms, fostering socially sustainable communities needs to recognize the means through which people are invited to form attachments –

during the day as much as the night. Rather than presuming students, short-term residents and those enacting a networked form of sociality do not form communities simply because they are not in place long enough or only attend impersonal chain venues, we may instead question the mechanisms available to engage with one's neighbourhood in the first place. As noted by Roberts (2006):

> Particular stress is placed on the need for a 'soft infrastructure' of innovative institutional supports and networks. These human connections and practices are nurtured and supported through the provision of a well-cared for public realm in city centres and semi-public spaces where people can meet. These are described as a multiplicity of places and temporary events, such as debating clubs and salons as well as bars and restaurants. Consumption is a backdrop to these 'deeply embedded' infrastructures and not their primary purpose. (p337)

At present, beyond bars and clubs, there is not a great deal of opportunity to be involved in the ongoing production and management of city centres after dark. In Scotland, under the new Licensing (Scotland) Act (2005), a young person (16–25) or young persons' representative is required to sit on the newly formed Licensing Boards. Each local authority has its own board, meaning in each area a young person is actively involved in shaping the future of their night-time economy. This type of strategy is important for several reasons. Not only does it bring young people into the decision-making process, the board will need to replace and 'update' young members when they reach a certain age. In this case, 'how long' they have lived or intend to live in the area is secondary to the fact that there is a means to be involved in the local decision-making process.

Following this point, Raco (2007) suggests that our definition of 'antisocial behaviour' could be rethought. Violence, causing disturbance to other members of the public, littering or public urination are all well-documented examples of antisocial behaviour at night. However, our understanding of this term could be extended to include actions that create the conditions of possibility for antisocial behaviour to occur. Limiting happy hours and discount pricing is one example. Local councils allowing for the privatization of public space, closing leisure facilities for young people and privileging the market over the needs of residents may also be defined as creating an antisocial city. The idea is provocative, but it highlights the need to think critically about what a socially sustainable, mixed and vibrant community should be. As well as bars, cafes and clubs, communities also need other spaces, rituals and opportunities through which to perform a sense of belonging.

The social sustainability model, predicated on the notion of people wanting to live and remain living in one area, may not adequately reflect the lifestyles and aspirations of more transient and mobile residents. We know, from places such as Hoxton and Shoreditch, as discussed earlier, that long-term residents do live alongside burgeoning late-night areas. But this is not necessarily the case in other areas such as Manchester or Leeds. Either way, the situation at present, whereby older residents are deterred from venturing out and young residents are routinely pathologized and absent from local decision-making, is far from the ideal model of an inclusive urban renaissance. A model that recognizes both short-term and long-term residents (who live in the city centre for a variety of reasons), whilst encouraging different participatory forms, will be far more conducive to fostering a better-aligned night-time economy and urban renaissance.

Conclusions

In conclusion, this discussion has not sought to recite well-known conflicts between the night-time economy and city-centre residents. I have also avoided proposing blanket proposals for better managing these conflicts. In one sense, it is not possible to apply the same policies to all areas. The situation in Manchester, where young people are a key part of the urban renaissance and night-time economy, is quite different to Hoxton, where residents tend to be older and based in social and council housing. This situation is different again to Soho, which not only has an entirely different morphology but a higher concentration of creative workers that may reflect the new 'network sociality'. Each area therefore requires different strategies to manage resident/visitor needs.

In a related sense, the reconciliation of the night-time economy with the urban renaissance needs to be examined, shaped and managed as a locally specific and ongoing process. In these terms, the failure to create vibrant and socially diverse late-night cities is not a responsibility that can be 'owned' solely by individuals. When state structures have failed in their role, by limiting opportunities for inclusive public engagement, then responsibility for late-night disorder and disenfranchisement from local communities needs to be shared. To reduce the discussion simply to the wrong types of bars or reductive discussions about lifestyle and choice is not always productive. When the means do not exist for more active involvement in one's locality, be that through gainful employment, democratic institutions and other soft infrastructure, then it should not be surprising that residents and visitors will treat city centres as highly individualized spaces based on a model of consumption over participation.

References

Antoniades, P., Maggi, P. and Pickering, E. (2007) *DCMS Statistical Bulletin: Alcohol, Entertainment and Late Night Refreshment Licensing*, Department for Culture, Media and Sport Evidence and Analysis Unit, London

Amin, A. and Thrift, N. (2002) *Cities: Reimagining the Urban*, Polity Press, Cambridge

Bell, V. (1999) 'Performativity and Belonging: An Introduction', *Theory, Culture & Society*, vol 16, no 2, pp1–10

Bennett, J. (ed.) (2005) *Towards a Strong Urban Renaissance: An Independent Report by Members of the Urban Task Force*, Urban Task Force, London

Bourdieu, P. (1992) *Distinction: A Social Critique of the Judgement of Taste*, translated by Richard Nice, Routledge and Keegan Paul, London

Britten, N. (2005) 'Judge says 24-hour drinking will create urban savages', *Telegraph*, 11 January, www.telegraph.co.uk/news/uknews/1480882/Judge-says-24-hour-drinking-will-create-urban-savages.html, accessed 26 June 2006

Bromley, R., Thomas, C. and Millie, A. (2000) 'Exploring Safety Concerns in the Night-time City', *TPR*, vol 74, no 1, pp71–96

Bromley, R., Tallon, A. and Thomas, C. (2003) 'Disaggregating the space-time layers of city centre activities and their users', *Environment and Planning A*, no 35, pp1831–1851

Cantle, T. (2001) *Community Cohesion - A Report of the Independent Review Team*, London: Home Office

Chatterton, P. and Hollands, R. (2003) *Urban Nightscapes: Youth Cultures, Pleasure Spaces and Corporate Power*, Routledge, London

Colomb, C. (2007) 'Unpacking New Labour's "Urban Renaissance" Agenda: Towards a Socially Sustainable Reurbanization of British Cities?', *Planning Practice and Research*, vol 22, no 1, pp1–24

Comedia/Calouste Gulbenkian Foundation (1991) *Out of Hours: A Study of Economic, Social and Cultural Life in 12 Town Centres across the UK*, Comedia, London

Davies, P. and Mummery, H. (2006) *NightVision: Town Centres for All*, The Civic Trust, London

Eldridge, A. and Roberts, M. (2008) 'A Comfortable Night Out?: Alcohol, Drunkenness and Inclusive Town Centres', *Area*, vol 40, no 3, pp365–374

Florida, R. (2005) *Cities and the Creative Class*, Routledge, London

Hackney Council (2006) *Housing in Hackney: Hackney Borough Profile*, Hackney Council, London

Helms, G., Atkinson, R. and MacLeod, G. (2007) 'Editorial: Securing the City: Urban Renaissance, Policing and Social Regulation', *European Urban and Regional Studies*, vol 14, no 4, pp267–276

Hobbs, R. (2003) *The Night-time Economy*, Alcohol Concern Research Forum Papers, www.alcoholconcern.org.uk/files/20031016_111354_Research per cent20forum per cent20Hobbs.pdf, accessed 1 July 2008

Hobbs, R. (2005) 'Gluttony: "Binge Drinking and the Binge Economy"', in Stewart, I. and Vaitilingam, R. (eds) *Seven Deadly Sins: A New Look at Society Through an Old Lens*, Economic and Social Research Council, Swindon

Hobbs, R., Hadfield, P., Lister, S. and Winlow, S. (2003) *Bouncers: Violence and Governance in the Night Time Economy*, Oxford University Press, Oxford, UK

Holloway, S., Jayne, M. and Valentine, G. (2008) ' "Sainsbury's Is My Local": English Alcohol Policy, Domestic Drinking Practices and the Meaning of Home', *Transactions of the Institute of British Geographers*, vol 33, no 4, pp532–547

Hoskins, G. and Tallon, A. (2004) 'Promoting the Urban Idyll: Policies for City Centre Living', in Johnstone, C. and Whitehead, M. (eds) *New Horizons in British Urban Policy: Perspectives on New Labour's Urban Renaissance*, Ashgate, Aldershot, England

Jayne, M. (2005) *Cities and Consumption*, Routledge, London

Latham, A. R. (2003) 'Urbanity, Lifestyle and Making Sense of the New Urban Cultural Economy: Notes from Auckland, New Zealand', *Urban Studies*, vol 40, no 9, pp1699–1724

Lees, L. (2003) 'Visions of "Urban Renaissance": The Urban Task Force Report and the Urban White Paper', in Imrie, R. and Raco, M. (eds) *Urban Renaissance? New Labour, Community and Urban Policy*, Policy Press, Bristol, pp61–82

McRobbie, A. (2002) 'Club to Companies: Notes on the Decline of Political Culture in Speeded Up Creative Worlds', *Cultural Studies*, vol 16, no 4, pp516–531

Nathan, M. and Urwin, C. (2006) *City People: City Centre Living in the UK: Manchester Briefing*, IPPR Centre for Cities, http://www.ippr.org/uploadedFiles/cfc/research/projects/centre_for_cities/Manchester_briefing.pdf, accessed 1 July 2008

Office of the Deputy Prime Minister (2003a) *The Evening Economy and Urban Renaissance*, ODPM, London

Office of the Deputy Prime Minister (2003b) *Sustainable Communities: Building for the Future*, ODPM, London

Open All Hours? Campaign (2002) *Open All Hours? A Report on Licensing Deregulation*, London, The Civic Trust and the Institute of Alcohol Studies

Pain, R. (2001) 'Gender, Race, Age and Fear in the City', *Urban Studies*, vol 38, nos 5–6, pp899–913

Plant, M. and Plant, M. (2006) *Binge Britain: Alcohol and the National Response*, Oxford University Press, Oxford

Probyn, E. (1996) *Outside Belongings*, Routledge, London

Raco, M. (2007) 'Securing Sustainable Communities: Citizenship, Safety and Sustainability in the New Urban Planning', *European Urban and Regional Studies*, vol 14, no 4, pp305–320

Richardson, A., Budd, T., Engineer, R., Phillips, A., Thompson, J. and Nichols, J. (2003) 'Drinking, Crime and Disorder', *Findings 185*, Home Office, London

Roberts, M. (2006) 'From "Creative City" To "No-Go Areas": The Expansion Of The Night-Time Economy in British Town and City Centres', *Cities*, vol 23, no 5, pp331–338

Roberts, M. and Eldridge, A. (2007) 'Quieter, Safer, Cheaper: Planning for a More Inclusive Evening and Night-time Economy', *Planning Practice and Research*, vol 22, no 2, pp253–266

Roberts, M. and Turner, C. (2005) 'Conflicts of Livability in the 24-Hour City: Learning from 48 Hours in the Life of London's Soho', *Journal of Urban Design*, vol 10, no 2, pp171–193

Roberts, M., Turner, C., Greenfield, S. and Osborn, G. (2006) 'A Continental Ambience? Lessons in Managing Alcohol Related Evening and Night-time Entertainment from Four European Capitals', *Urban Studies*, vol 43, no 7, pp1105–1125

Rogers, P. and Coafee, J. (2005) 'Moral panics and urban renaissance: Policy, tactics and youth in public space', *City*, vol 9, no 3, pp321-340

Sassen, S. (1991) *The Global City: New York, London, Tokyo,* Princeton University Press, Princeton

Schlör, J. (1998) *Nights in the Big City: Paris, Berlin and London 1840–1930*, Reaktion Books, London

Sennett, R. (1998) *The Corrosion of Character: The Personal Consequences of Work in the New Capitalism*, W.W. Norton and Co, London

Silverman, E., Lupton, R. and Fenton, A. (2005) *A Good Place for Children? Attracting and Retaining Families in Inner Urban Mixed Income Communities*, Joseph Rowntree Foundation, York

Talbot, D. (2004) 'Regulation and Racial Differentiation in the Construction of the Night-time Economies: A London Case Study', *Urban Studies*, vol 41, no 4, pp887–901

Urban Task Force (1999) *Towards an Urban Renaissance*, Department of the Environment, Transport and the Regions, London

Urban Task Force (2005) *Towards a Strong Urban Renaissance*, Department of the Environment, Transport and the Regions, London

Urwin, C. (2005) 'Faulty Towers? City Centre Housing Markets in the UK', *Centre for Cities Discussion Paper 3*, London, Institute of Public Policy Research

Watson, S. (2006) *City Publics: The (Dis)enchantments of Urban Encounters*, Routledge, London

Winlow, S. and Hall, S. (2006) *Violent Night: Urban Leisure and Contemporary Culture*, Berg, Oxford

Wittel, A. (2001) 'Toward a Network Sociality', *Theory, Culture & Society*, vol 18, no 6, pp51–76

Zukin, S. (1989) *Loft Living: Culture and Capital in Urban Change,* Rutgers University Press, New Brunswick, New Jersey

11

The Relationship Between Major Events, the Urban Fabric and Social Sustainability

Andrew Smith

Introduction

Major events have become a key aspect of urban policy in the UK and abroad, seemingly promoted from ephemeral attractions to vehicles for marketing and structuring whole cities. Obvious examples are the Olympics Games and other international sport events, but World Expos (Carricere and Demaziere, 2002), cultural festivals (Gold and Gold, 2005), even housing fairs (Jansson, 2005), have also been used as cornerstones of urban policy. Bidding for and staging these events is part of the shift towards entrepreneurial urbanism, and is often equated by authors such as Harvey (1989) and Hall (2006) with the values of neo-liberal regimes.

In the 21st century, urban governments are being encouraged to reconcile an entrepreneurial imperative with growing demands for sustainability. This is more straightforward with reference to events that need little investment in new venues and associated infrastructure, and/or where the events can be linked to sustainable themes. For example, London was able to justify its role as host of the opening stages of the 2007 Tour de France by emphasizing its role in promoting cycling in the capital (Smith, 2009). However, large-scale exhibitions and 'mega' sporting events are generally viewed by relevant non-governmental organizations (NGOs) as the antithesis of sustainability. Intense consumption and travel mean they are environmentally unsustainable at a global level. However, the prevalent use of events as part of efforts to rehabilitate urban areas can actually contribute to environmental improvement at the city and neighbourhood scales.

It is within this context that cities of various sizes (e.g. London, Sydney, Manchester, Hannover) have justified event developments via rhetoric associated with 'sustainable development'. The long-term economic and environmental effects of this type of development have been explored (Collins et al, 2007; Hagn and Maennig, 2008), but there has been insufficient attention to the social sustainability of events strategies. The aim of this chapter is to assess the relationship between major events, the urban fabric and social sustainability. The intention is to identify whether and how events could be used to achieve social sustainability, as well as to analyse the reality of the social outcomes resulting from previous event initiatives.

Social sustainability

In general texts on sustainable development, social needs are usually discussed in terms of equity, ethics and human rights. In the urban literature, the emphasis tends to be more on the qualities of the physical environment, rather than on the rights of urban dwellers. For example, some commentators see sustainable communities as those that exhibit a spatially compact form; high density, a balance of land use; and a settlement pattern that integrates with existing communities (Deakin, 2003). One of the key questions posed in this chapter is: Can major events help to deliver these qualities?

The policy literature exhibits a slightly broader vision of sustainable communities. UK policy conceives them as areas with jobs, leaders, community involvement, safe/green spaces, high density, good transport, varied housing types, public services, cultural provision, integration and strong sense of place (ODPM, 2003). But within this policy framework the rhetoric of citizens' own responsibilities is emphasized, rather than risk raising expectancy about 'rights'. Alongside basic rights defined by international agreements, the rights of urban dwellers are usually conceived within policy-making as a function of the right to participate in decision-making. Therefore, a sustainable urban community is one where people play a key role in its planning, design and stewardship (Raco, 2005). Initiatives to empower local people can be interpreted as ethical, democratic and therefore socially sustainable, but more cynical observers such as Raco see them in conjunction with the objectives of neo-liberal governments – that want communities to sustain themselves so they are not a burden. This is evident in the UK Government's Plan (ODPM, 2003), which aims to create communities that are sustainable by being self-sustaining; meaning they can adapt to the changing demands of modern life.

The aim of this chapter is to explore the relationship between major events, the urban fabric and social sustainability. Major events usually involve huge budgets, spent in a very short period of time in concentrated urban spaces. Therefore, these events inevitably highlight issues of social and spatial equity (Broudehoux, 2007). As well as the social/spatial distribution of event costs and benefits, this chapter is also interested in temporal distribution of event outcomes; as it may be difficult to reconcile short-lived events with the long-term sustainability of urban communities.

Events can be analysed in themselves, but also as vehicles to understand the city more generally. Major events can have a dramatic impact on the long-term structuring of a city (Batty, 2002). They can also provide concentrated and insightful examples of urban development processes. There is also a more abstract justification for a focus on events. Cities as a whole are conceptualized by some commentators as 'events', an interpretation that has become more prominent in recent years due to the 'festivalization' of urban space that has accompanied the new 'place making' agenda. Writers such as Broudehoux (2007, p383) consider that 'the city itself has been transformed into a space of performance'. Others see cities as collections of events. Indeed, Batty thinks it is possible to conceive of cities as being 'clusters of spatial events' (Batty, 2002, p1) and advocates associated analyses. In these examples, events act as metaphors for the city as a whole or accelerated examples of general urban processes. Therefore, analysing major events not only helps us to understand these events and their effects, but allows us to understand urban areas – and their social sustainability – more generally.

In subsequent sections, the relationship between events and social sustainability is conceptualized as comprising four key elements, listed below:

1   Events and the social sustainability of existing communities.
2   Event sites as models of (new) socially sustainable communities.
3   Events as vehicles for branding/funding socially sustainable communities.
4   Events as key services for socially sustainable communities.

This varied analysis aims to promote further understanding of major events, but also aims to contribute to debates about the social sustainability of cities. A more practical objective is to generate ideas and recommendations for those involved in event planning, a practice deemed to comprise both venue planning and legacy planning. These elements differ according to their temporal and spatial scope: venue planning is temporally constrained and focused at the neighbourhood level, whereas legacy planning usually aims to extend the temporal and spatial effects of events.

Events and the social sustainability of existing communities

Perhaps the most controversial dimension of the relationship between major events and social sustainability is the effects of events on existing communities. Major events have tended to privilege new people and new businesses, at the expense of resident communities. As Olds (1998) states, mega-events aim to attract new people, new facilities and new money to cities at rapid pace. In this section, two different perspectives on this issue will be forwarded. The first is a positive (and normative) assessment, identifying how events could be used to enhance the social sustainability of existing urban communities. A detailed case study (Manchester, 2002) is included to demonstrate that such initiatives can work. The second part will balance the discussion by reviewing many critiques where events are accused of compromising urban social sustainability.

Positive social effects

In recent years the value of events as levers for positive social change has been increasingly recognized. This applies to both mega-events and more modest examples: Waitt's (2003) evaluation of the 2000 Olympic Games indicates that community/national spirit was a powerful psychological reward for many residents of Sydney; and research in neighbouring New Zealand found that the major impact of a rugby event in New Plymouth was the increase in community spirit and morale (Garnham, 1996). For this to happen, Misener and Mason (2006) argue that the event itself must embrace the core values of residents, community groups and neighbourhood associations. Accordingly, communities should be consulted about the event and, subsequently, be actively involved in its staging. Involvement such as this creates institutionalized and non-institutionalized networks between community members and between members and other stakeholders. The latter may allow positive change to accrue through building 'bridges' between community members and elite decision-makers. These networks are seen as examples of the way major events can generate social capital.

On an individual level, events may also encourage feelings of citizenship and belonging among local people, particularly if they are actively involved as participants, spectators or volunteers. Some critical authors, such as Gotham (2005), see this as part of the events 'spectacle' – making people think they are valued, when they remain powerless. Others see the 'identity making' role of events as one which is more related to consumption – with the commercial imperative and associated sponsorship encouraging people to see themselves as consumers or aligned to a certain brand. Coalter (1998) answers these criticisms by arguing that even if events are commercially orientated, they can still provide satisfying forms of social membership and identity. Individual and collective identity can also be established/reinforced/expressed through the provision of changes to the fabric of urban areas that host events.

Although the 'iconic' developments often associated with events are sometimes dismissed as political monuments, or for the attention of outsiders, this is not necessarily the case. Events can bequeath public spaces in which communities literally come together. For example, the Olympic Plaza in Calgary, the place where medals were distributed at the 1988 Winter Olympic Games, has become a key location for community celebrations (Hiller, 2006). Events can also provide an incentive and platform to encourage dialogue between stakeholders about an area's future. Thus, the actual *process* of event planning can contribute to social sustainability by creating opportunities and mechanisms for community consultation, with residual effects on community cohesion and civic pride. The value of the process of event planning is emphasized by the productive outcomes from event bids – even those which ultimately fail (e.g. see Cochrane et al, 1996).

Case study: The 2002 Commonwealth Games Legacy Programme

As Misener and Mason (2006) argue, more research is needed to understand the relationship between events and social/community development. Accordingly, primary research was undertaken to explore the legacy planning associated with the 2002 Commonwealth Games in Manchester. A summary of this research is provided here, but for a fuller version please consult Smith and Fox (2007). The Legacy Programme adopted by organizers was noteworthy as it aimed to achieve 'bottom-up' social regeneration, rather than assuming that the benefits would 'trickle down' to the most needy. A range of social and economic projects were undertaken that were loosely linked to the Games. This 'event-themed' approach had several benefits: it encouraged more dispersed effects and encouraged more diverse impacts, as educational, health, cultural and skills projects were pursued alongside those directly associated with sport.

The seven projects incorporated into this £17.7 million programme are detailed below. Several can be seen as attempts to address the social sustainability of urban communities. For example, the PVP project aimed to provide useful experiences of work for disadvantaged individuals; Passport 2K was designed to increase confidence, engagement and integration among young people; and Let's Celebrate was intended as a way of increasing participation in cultural festivals (see Box 11.1).

Box 11.1 *The seven projects that formed the Legacy Programme for the 2002 Commonwealth Games*

Commonwealth Curriculum Pack – A programme which used interest in the Commonwealth Games to motivate children and teachers at school to enhance their information and communications technology skills. This was encouraged through the development of new curriculum materials and a website. These new learning resources also aimed to stimulate learning about the Games, and Commonwealth countries in general.

Games Xchange – This project provided the opportunity to promote and market Manchester and the North West (NW) region. This was achieved by providing information about the city/region to local people and visitors through a range of accessible, informative and innovative methods. An event information centre set up as part of this project aimed to train and give employment experience to disadvantaged individuals.

Pre-volunteer Programme (PVP) – An opportunity for people from specific disadvantaged groups throughout the NW to undertake accredited training and to gain experience through volunteering at the Commonwealth Games. This training was in addition to the instruction given to conventional volunteers. Those involved were not guaranteed roles at the Games, but the aim was to encourage PVP graduates to apply for positions and, if successful, to give them extra support and guidance if they experienced difficulties fulfilling their roles.

Healthier Communities – Provided healthier living initiatives throughout the region before, during and after the Commonwealth Games. The project provided assistance to health services in disadvantaged communities, primarily through providing community representatives with new skills, contacts and opportunities to gain further funds. It also aimed to develop more coherent links between sport and health initiatives. More specifically, the project was intended to provide support for the elderly and those with learning difficulties, and to encourage young people to make healthy lifestyle choices.

Prosperity – This project aimed to ensure businesses in the region benefited from the Commonwealth Games by forming strategic alliances between regional and Commonwealth organizations. It provided opportunities for local businesses to create sustainable trade links with Commonwealth countries. More specifically, the project aimed to identify, and disseminate information about, business opportunities relating to the Games. A business club was established and administered in the run-up to the Games to assist this endeavour.

Passport 2K – Provided out-of-school activities for young people aged 11–18 across the NW, who took part in a range of outdoors activities incorporating sport and the arts. The project combined a series of local activity programmes, with a number of regional events. The latter aimed to enable young people from a range of backgrounds and locations to meet up and participate in activities on a regional basis.

Let's Celebrate – Used celebratory arts, including carnivals and mela, to build the capacity of South Asian, African and African Caribbean communities and representative organizations in the NW. The idea was to award franchises of varying lengths to new and existing groups who had aspirations to develop their own events. The overarching aim was to promote long-term social cohesion, cultural diversity, local employment and the development of community-led cultural infrastructure.

One of the Legacy Programme's most notable achievements was its success in engaging and benefiting individuals from disadvantaged groups. This was largely due to the 'hook' of the Commonwealth Games. The PVP, for example, was highly successful in engaging 16- to 19-year-olds, ethnic minorities, people with special needs and the retired. While this may have helped to address social equity issues, the focus on disadvantaged parts of the region contributed to greater spatial equity. Another positive outcome was the provision of new opportunities for gaining qualifications and employment. The training provided as part of the PVP enabled 2134 individuals to gain one of the two qualifications offered as part of the project. Other 'human impacts' were also noted. A range of feedback from participants, youth workers and activity coordinators suggests that the Passport 2K project raised the confidence and self-esteem of participants.

In addition to helping disadvantaged individuals, the Legacy Programme seemed to provide social assistance for targeted communities. The Passport 2K project helped to achieve reductions in youth nuisance, greater access to sports/arts activities and the recruitment of volunteer mentors to support the young people participating. Let's Celebrate was important in establishing more representative and more effective community-based leadership of cultural festivals. The Healthier Communities project helped to establish a number of Healthy Living Centres (HLCs). These centres now compliment existing health provision and aim to reduce health inequalities in deprived areas. Although these HLCs (and other Legacy Programme initiatives) were only loosely linked to the Commonwealth Games, the associated funding, theming and backing was crucial to their implementation.

Social sustainability is a long-term objective, and it can only be advanced if projects have long-term effects. One possible danger of using events as a lever is their temporal nature, which may result in merely short-term benefits. Encouragingly, four of the seven projects that were supported by the Legacy Programme still continue to deliver, even though their funding has ceased. For example, Healthier Communities part-funded an HLC coordinator to support the creation and development of other HLCs. More HLCs consequently met and passed the UK government's 'New Opportunities Fund' criteria, and are now providing services to communities as a result. Healthier Communities also established regional sport partnership of health, sport and learning representatives, and this continues to operate successfully. The Healthier Communities project also set up a regional forum for local groups concerned with provision for the elderly, which still exists to enable local offices to work together on a regional basis.

Despite this apparent success, the Legacy Programme also exhibited some less sustainable characteristics. There was a conspicuous failure to involve local communities in the planning and implementation of projects associated with the Legacy Programme. This was partly as a result of the tight deadlines and competing priorities associated with event planning. There were other problems caused by having an event as the cornerstone of the regeneration scheme. Despite the programme's life officially running from 1999 to 2004, many interviewees doubted whether enough emphasis was placed on project activity and spend after the Commonwealth Games took place (in 2002). The perception was that much of the effort and project delivery was undertaken *before* the Games, with levels of interest and impact consequently dropping off soon after the event had finished. The majority of positive effects occurred prior to the Games and this has negative implications for the long-term impact of the Legacy Programme. There is also evidence that the post-event period was neglected at institutional level. The frequency of and attendance at board meetings dwindled after the Games. This, plus the premature departure of many staff (including the Legacy Programme's coordinator), meant that the programme underperformed during its post-event life (2002–04). A final problem was the lack of links between the physical interventions made for the event and the innovative parallel social projects pursued. This led to some accusations that the latter were merely tokenistic gestures used by event organizers to fend off criticisms of the £320 million spent on event venues.

Overall, the Manchester case is now commonly cited as an exemplar of good practice with respect to social and economic legacy planning. In terms of the intangible characteristics of sustainable communities as defined by ODPM (those with jobs, leaders, community involvement, cultural provision, integration and a strong sense of place), the Legacy Programme associated with the 2002 Commonwealth Games performs well. However, it should be remembered that these outcomes were not derived from the Games itself, but were mainly the product of more general social policy that was aligned to the Games to lever funding, participation and support. Ultimately, the event acted as a potent theme for social initiatives, rather than an active agent of social change (Smith and Fox, 2007).

The negative social effects of events

The lack of consultation in the Manchester case is illustrative of a wider problem with the use of events in social policy. Most advocates of urban social sustainability want to see more consultation, or ideally genuine collaboration, between planners and local people. Unfortunately, event planning usually involves less consultation and public accountability than would normally be the case. Indeed, Chalkley and Essex (1999, p391) feel that a major event 'sits outside the existing categories of planning'. This seems to be mainly a function of time pressures. As Carricere and Demaziere (2002, p78) point out in their analysis of Lisbon's 1998 World Expo, 'the urban development operation was faced with tight time constraints relating to the opening of the exhibition, leaving few opportunities for consultation with the local population'. But it is not always clear whether time pressures do genuinely hamper event-led developments, or whether such pressures provide a convenient excuse to fast-track developments that would have caused inconvenient opposition. Events frequently involve a

form of temporary authoritarian governance that sits awkwardly with the concept of social sustainability. For example, the organizing body of Vancouver's 1986 Expo was given the right to 'raise and disperse its own funds, the power of expropriation and authority to override all city by-laws, zoning regulation and planning policy' (Ley and Olds, 1992, p230).

Alongside dubious planning processes, there are other reasons why many are sceptical about the social sustainability of major events. Olds (1998, p5) sees events as agents of long-term redevelopment planning, with existing communities paying the costs in terms of 'displacement, negative health effects, the breaking of social networks and the loss of affordable housing'. Perhaps the most dramatic effects have occurred in conjunction with Asian Olympic Games of the past and present. A total of 750,000 people were forcibly relocated due to the requirements of the 1988 Seoul Olympics (Olds, 1998) and, by 2004, 300,000 Beijing citizens had already been uprooted as part of the preparations for the 2008 Games (Wan, 2004). As social sustainability involves building networks, attachment to place and a commitment to ethics and human rights, it is hard to imagine initiatives as socially unsustainable.

As previous chapters have highlighted, some regard the social sustainability 'project' as an attempt to ensure social disadvantage is not a direct function of place of residence. Contradicting this principle, it has been noted that the most disadvantaged people usually bear the punitive costs of major events (Newman, 1999; Waitt, 2003; Broudehoux, 2007). Thus, event planning is sometimes implicated in the revanchist city – playing a crucial role in the control of marginalized groups (Tufts, 2004). This may involve punitive measures for those seen as 'undesirable' (Atkinson and Laurier, 1998) or merely the conspicuous failure to mitigate against unevenly distributed negative effects. Major events can provide convenient excuses to force major changes upon urban residents, with opponents derided as conservative, myopic or even unpatriotic. Newman's (1999) research into Atlanta's Olympic Games provides justification for concerns about the effects of events on vulnerable residents. He found that low-income residents (most of whom were black) largely regarded the Games as another excuse for business leaders to reshape the city. These were the citizens most disrupted by venue planning and, rather than enhanced social sustainability, the outcome was a 'legacy of distrust'.

Even when marginalized groups are not further disadvantaged by events directly, there remains the possibility that an event will distract attention from their plight. In this manner, events can act as 'smokescreens' or 'carnival masks' (Harvey, 1989), behind which the inherent social unsustainability of some urban communities can be hidden. This is usually the position of those who theorize events as 'spectacles'. Gotham (2005) expresses concern that festivals, parades, carnivals and other events amount to instruments of hegemonic power that shift attention away from everyday social problems. Gotham, and others

inspired by the work of Debord (1994), dismiss the coalescing effect that events can have on communities as merely pacification and depoliticization. Although events may create and sustain a local and/or national collective identity, this may be part of a deliberate attempt to undermine existing identities, particularly those that threaten the interests of political and business elites (Waitt, 2003). Accordingly, Olds (1998) sees the social unity created by events as artificial, especially as it is used to push through urban redevelopment which would not normally be accepted.

Awareness of the negative effects of venue planning seems to be increasing, which may help prevent future malpractice. Canadian campaigners have been particularly vocal, perhaps because of the negative financial legacy of the 1976 Montreal Olympics. Fearing negative consequences if Toronto's bid for the 2008 Games was successful, local labour organizations insisted on guarantees of affordable housing provision, protection against eviction and the guarantee of civil rights for the poor and homeless, before any support was given (Tufts, 2004).

Event sites as models of socially sustainable communities

A more abstract dimension of the relationship between events and social sustainability is the noted historical tendency for events to promote experimental models of urbanism. This is particularly relevant to World Expos, which have often involved the production of innovative urban models at different spatial scales. At a basic level, innovative architectural models and prototype urban designs have been displayed at these events: 'Democracity' at the 1939 New York World's Fair is perhaps the most notable example. Other Expo sites were arranged as models of 'a city of tomorrow', which would encourage different social relations between its inhabitants.

For example, Montreal's Expo (1967) exhibited Habitat 67, a form of innovative housing linked to the supposed value of 'mega-structures' as an idealized urban form (Gold and Gold, 2005). This highlights the normative function of Expos and similar events. Rather than simply being events that reflected societies, Expos were always intended as ways of shaping those societies (Roche, 2000). The sites provided a vision of what cities *could* do to house growing urban populations and enhance social relations. Unfortunately, it was not easy to convert the sites into 'real' urban areas. This remains a problem with more recent World Expo sites, which are now designed as permanent urban extensions, rather than merely models, but which suffer from what Monclus (2006) terms 'investment overdose'. This is defined as 'the excessive concentration of resources in a limited space with the physical risk of the formation of enclaves or precincts poorly integrated to the urban structure or at the danger of an

excessive standardization, theming or banalization of the project spaces' (Monclus, 2006, p238).

Since its reintroduction in 1896, the Olympic Games has also provided cities with an opportunity to establish prototype communities. This trend can be traced back to Pierre de Coubertin's (the founder of the modern Games) desire to create a modern version of Olympia in which to host the event. He stated that he wanted a modern Olympia to be a grandiose and dignified ensemble; which was designed in relation to its role; which fitted in with the surrounding area; and which was neither too concentrated nor too diffuse (Liao and Pitts, 2006). These criteria seemingly influenced the design of subsequent Olympic sites, some of which now remain as successful residential areas (e.g. in Moscow, Munich, Helsinki). Liao and Pitts (2006) feel that de Coubertin's urban agenda had parallels with other proposals for urban utopias, including Fourier's phalanstère: a cluster of buildings in which people work together for mutual benefit. This suggests that there may be some links between Olympic areas and urban areas with socially sustainable credentials.

In Raco's (2005) critique of the UK government's Sustainable Communities Plan, he gives credit for the plan's reluctance to treat rural and urban areas as separate entities. This is also something de Coubertin would have supported, as he had a strong preference for Olympic areas that boasted urban and rural characteristics. Accordingly, Helsinki's 1952 Games involved the construction of a pastoral Olympic Park, harmonizing buildings and nature. These Games were also the first time an Olympic Village left a long-term legacy of municipal housing. Twenty years later, the Munich Games also involved a site that embraced green spaces, while providing social housing. Munich's Olympic Park – designed by Günther Grzimek – was a green space that was integrated into the cityscape without trying to encourage the feeling that users were escaping from urbanity. The ensemble was meant to promote personal fulfilment and quality of life, as well as inclusivity and democracy. This tendency to use Olympic sites as exemplars of innovative sustainable design continues to the present. For example, the Olympic Village built for the 2000 Sydney Games was designed as a prototype 'eco-town'.

The main site of the Sydney Games was Homebush Bay, a 760-hectare tract of land, 14 kilometres from the centre. Unfortunately, event organizers did not really have a clear idea about a role for this site once the Games were over. The original proposal envisaged it as a leisure and cultural 'destination' containing the main sports venues, alongside new museums and educational centres. A subsequent Masterplan (2001) proposed a 'significant metropolitan area not envisaged at the time of Sydney's Olympic bid' (Searle, 2002, p857), with a precinct structure organized around a new town centre and adjacent parklands. There is some evidence to suggest that, following upgrading and new building, part of this site (Newington, the aforementioned prototype eco-town) is emerging as a viable urban community. But on a wider scale, Homebush Bay's poor links to existing areas and an over-emphasis on commercial potential damages its credentials as a socially sustainable community. This new district could have assisted Sydney's pressing need to decentralize some functions and contain urban sprawl, while avoiding the dislocation of work and community (Costley, 2006). But despite a second period of building (2006–08), Homebush Bay has not yet demonstrated these characteristics. There is also a danger that housing provision here will follow the example of other Australian 'master planned communities' (MPCs), which seem to attract people who want to put distance between themselves and the urban poor (Costley, 2006). Reflecting wider apprehension about the rise of gated communities (Vesselinov and Cazessus, 2007), there is concern in Australia that MPCs are quietly eroding the possibilities for social and spatial equity.

Events as vehicles for branding/funding new socially sustainable communities

Event connections are useful for place-making because they provide recognizable, meaningful and historically significant identities for new sites. Event 'branding' is one of the key reasons that Olympic Villages such as Newington have become attractive places to live. As Costley (2006, p165) argues, 'people choose to move to communities because they recognize something in the marketing, covenants and neighbourhood design that appeals to them and how they want to live their lives'. The frequent involvement of high-profile 'starchitects' in events projects provides an extra incentive for high-income groups to inhabit these sites. Accordingly, the lack of social diversity is a serious challenge to the sustainability of these new communities. Barcelona's Olympic Village provides an interesting case. Here, renowned architects built good-quality, five-storey apartment blocks on a 47-ha site between the city's main park and the beachfront. Originally the plan was to use this as social housing, but the escalating costs of staging the Games meant private sale proved too tempting for municipal authorities. This introduces a key problem with event-inspired communities: the social objectives of event planning are often compromised because of the need to offset wider event costs.

Both Hemphill et al (2004) and Valera and Guardia (2002) have attempted to assess the sustainability of Barcelona's Olympic Village development. Although these analyses purport to measure its sustainable credentials generally, both pay commendable attention to the social dimension. After its completion, this area was officially named Nova Icaria, after an ideal 'workers community of the future' conceived in the 19th century (Hughes, 1999), or a nod to the name of the local area (Poblenou) during the

Table 11.1 *The sustainable urban regeneration performance of Barcelona's Vila Olímpica*

		Score/10
Economy and work scoring performance	Percentage of new enterprises still operating after three years	10
	Net jobs created	8
	Partnership structure performance	8
	Effectiveness of exit strategy	8
	End-user scheme satisfaction	8
	Quality of jobs created	6
	Performance of incentive mechanisms	6
	Incorporation of training programmes	6
	Number of jobs created per 1000 square metres	4
	Leverage ratios	2
Buildings and land-use scoring performance	Ratio of open space: built form	10
	Reclamation of contaminated land	10
	Office rental versus CBD rents	10
	Design quality	9
	Density levels in relation to plot size	8
	Balance of uses	8
	Quality of final product	8
	Quality of public space	8
	Usage of public space	8
	Quality of private space	7
	Occupancy levels	6
	Ratio of converted buildings: new build	2
Transport and mobility scoring performance	Leisure travelling habits	10
	Public transport links	10
	Land devoted to pedestrians	8
	Car-parking provision – residential	8
	Road improvements	7
	Integration of land use and public transport	7
	Land devoted to roads	6
	Work travelling habits	6
	Car-parking provision – commercial	4
Community benefits scoring performance	Access to open space	10
	Access to leisure facilities	10
	Access to medical facilities	10
	Access to entertainment facilities	8
	Local Agenda 21 effectiveness	8

Table 11.1 *Continued*

		Score/10
Community benefits scoring performance (*continued*)	Access to housing	7
	Access to educational needs	6
	On-site retail facilities	5
	Community ownership	5
	Access to retail facilities	4
	Access to cultural facilities	4
	Community group involvement	2

Source: Criteria and ratings extracted from Hemphill et al, 2004

socialist republican era (Rowe, 2006). Neither derivation is congruous with the affluent community that now lives there. Accordingly, 87.5 per cent of its residents instead call the area Vila Olimpica (Valera and Guardia, 2002). This is perhaps symbolic, not only of the rejection of the area's original social ambitions, but also of the importance attached to the event that inspired its construction.

Consensus on an area's name is also an indicator of the cohesiveness of a newly formed neighbourhood. Valera and Guardia concluded that the neighbourhood has gained a distinctive image amongst its residents and that this was derived from the (event-related) publicity used to promote it as a residential area. Thus, the area fulfils one criteria of social sustainability: it has a strong sense of place. This highlights a key advantage of events communities – it may be easier to forge a temporal/historical identity for new developments, enhancing their social sustainability.

Vila Olimpica was planned to encourage socializing: it was organized in blocks, with inner courtyards and communal gardens for public use. But the onerous work commitments of affluent residents have contributed to somewhat distant relations between neighbours (Valera and Guardia, 2002). Although the community may not be cohesive or diverse, the opportunities, facilities and services provided for residents contribute to Hemphill et al's (2004, p770) conclusion that Vila Olimpica 'displays a high degree of adherence to sustainability principles'. Their assessment used a series of weighted indicators to measure 'sustainable urban regeneration performance' (see Table 11.1). Of six developments analysed (in Belfast, Dublin and Barcelona), Vila Olimpica scored highest, with the authors surmising that it was a notable example of good practice. One key factor that differentiated it from projects deemed less successful was the significant presence of education and medical facilities. According to

Hemphill et al (2004), Vila Olimpica's only failings seem to be a poor new jobs to space ratio, low levels of economic leverage, the lack of converted buildings, the lack of car-parking provision, poor access to retail/cultural facilities and the low levels of community ownership and involvement (also see Table 11.1). These limitations may explain Valera and Guardia's worries about the lack of a cohesive community.

Event initiatives not only brand new urban developments, they can be used to fund them and drive them to fruition. A good example is South Hammarby in Stockholm – designated as the 'Olympic Village' in Stockholm's unsuccessful bid for the 2004 Olympics (Khakee, 2007). The development went ahead anyway, emphasizing how important events can be in levering the plans, funding and partnerships required to deliver innovative urban development schemes. Although this area has impressive ecological credentials, its social sustainability is hampered by the lack of certain services (e.g. childcare) and the exorbitant price of accommodation. A privileged and socially homogenous community is the inevitable outcome.

This lack of mixed-income groups seems to be one of the most common failings of event projects with respect to their social sustainability. One of Stockholm's rivals for the 2004 Olympic Games was Cape Town, South Africa. Although Cape Town's bid included a commendable social orientation, the city soon realized that delivering a sustainable housing legacy would be very difficult. High standards required by the International Olympic Committee meant that construction costs would have made the new housing more costly than needy residents could afford (Hiller, 2000). The need to satisfy an external stakeholder, plus the related motivation to use events as urban prototypes, often produces 'high-spec' – and thus high-priced – residences. This limitation is supplemented by other reasons why event planning often fails to deliver a sustainable mix of different housing. For example, the requirement in many event budgets for the sale of redeveloped land to help pay for expensive events means there is a disincentive to use such initiatives to provide low-income housing or mixed-income developments.

Events as services for socially sustainable communities

Costley (2006) sees sustainable communities as those with convenient centres that provide jobs, shopping, services and entertainment. Accordingly, if major event venues are used regularly, they can provide important services, in the form of leisure provision, for communities. The venues in which they are staged can host important community facilities and their symbolic potency means they can also offer salient vehicles around which citizenship can coalesce (Misener and Mason, 2006).

One new community that has emerged with an event venue at its heart is the 'Millennium Village', on the Greenwich Peninsula, London (Figure 11.1). The Homes and Communities Agency (formerly English Partnerships) have invested more than £225 million in regenerating this area. This project was instigated by the selection of the Peninsula as the site for the controversial Millennium Festival. The event left a legacy of improved transport links via the extension of the London Underground network. This is a common outcome of events, with Greek events such as Thessaloniki's role as Capital of Culture and the Olympic Games in Athens noted for their transport legacies. Events can also leave a more intangible transport legacy, with spectators who never use trains and buses often required to use public transport, which may then instigate new behaviours.

For several years it seems that transport access would be one of the few positive legacies of the Millennium Festival. The main venue – the Millennium Dome – was empty from 2001 to 2007 and had acquired a troubled reputation as an archetypal white elephant. But in 2007, the Dome reopened as The O$_2$,

Source: Author's photograph

Figure 11.1 *Greenwich Millennium Village: green spaces, high density, education/health provision, good transport links ... and a 23,000-capacity events arena*

with a 23,000-capacity events arena at its heart. So, while an event initially helped to fund and brand this site, an events venue is once more at the heart of the fledgling community that now inhabits it. In addition to the venue itself, a range of entertainment venues have opened within the Dome and new public space has been developed outside. Thus, it is envisaged that The O_2 will become the anchor, fulcrum and key service area for a sustainable Peninsula community.

The O_2 venue has a dedicated sustainability strategy, with one of its four key objectives being 'community engagement' (AEG, 2007). The owners claim to have undertaken community consultation during the (re)construction phase and promise to maintain communication with, and direct benefits for, local residents. The latter mainly take the form of special events and free tickets, which act as inducements or compensation for sceptical members of the local community. The venue is large enough to provide 2000 operational jobs, which due to good transport links are accessible to millions of Londoners. Nevertheless, the aim is that 40 per cent of operational jobs will go to Greenwich residents (it is currently 43 per cent; AEG, 2007). But the proportion of staff that actually lives on the Peninsula in the newly-constructed Millennium Village nearby is likely to be low. Nearly 1000 homes within this village are now occupied, with more units under construction. It is designed and promoted as an environmentally sustainable 'eco-village', with energy conservation measures incorporated throughout. The presence of a health centre and primary school suggest it could become a multi-dimensional place, rather than merely a housing development. Event connections may help to make this project a commercial success. But whether a sustainable community will emerge as a result is questionable. Mathiason (2008) is certainly sceptical: 'How many people fancy living next to a 20,000-seat rock venue?'

The idea of new communities centred around an events venue is something that has also been attempted in Manchester. A site branded 'SportCity' in East Manchester forms the main physical legacy of the 2002 Commonwealth Games. However, Mace et al (2007) question whether these areas should aspire to social sustainability principles. The presence of new sports facilities and large-scale services means that this area is most likely to succeed as a 'destination', rather than as a socially sustainable community (Mace et al, 2007). This rather pessimistic assertion is based on the increasing distances people are prepared to travel for work and leisure. It means that SportCity may serve the whole region as a themed destination, rather than an integrated urban area designed for local people. Furthermore, Mace et al (2007) suggest that high-density development (usually seen as a key feature of sustainable communities) is inappropriate for this area due to the large amount of available space. As Mace et al point out, event sites are often land-hungry, low-density developments that do not match a standardized view of a sustainable community. For peripheral urban areas with events venues at their heart, the most appropriate direction may be development as a destination, rather than a fully functioning urban community. This not only questions the value of events venues as services for socially sustainable communities, but challenges accepted notions of what form socially sustainable urban areas should take.

Conclusions

In the introduction to this chapter, sustainable communities were identified as those with jobs, leaders, community involvement, safe/green spaces, mixed uses, a compact form, high density, good transport, varied housing types, public services, cultural provision, integration and strong sense of place (Deakin, 2003; ODPM, 2003). The discussion here has suggested that major event projects have implications for all these dimensions. The Manchester 2002 example showed that volunteer programmes and other themed interventions can help deliver employment skills, social integration and cultural provision. Other projects, particularly Olympic Villages, showed that events can help to give new communities a strong sense of place and access to open spaces. Transport initiatives are often a key outcome of events projects and regular events can also be seen as valuable public services/forms of cultural provision.

The biggest challenges to the social sustainability of events projects are perhaps the poor record of delivering mixed-income housing, the low levels of community involvement and the poor physical integration that results from 'investment overdose'. Event spaces are often the antithesis of dense/compact urbanism and there remains some doubt as to whether they should be converted into conventional urban districts or developed as specialist destinations. As each destination and each event has it own priorities and characteristics, it is difficult to make generic recommendations. Nevertheless, the value of events as tools for social sustainability seems to lie more in their role as levers of social policy in existing neighbourhoods, rather than as ways of delivering new communities.

Among the array of ideas and examples discussed above, one recurring theme is the importance of temporal considerations. For example, the discussion has indicated that event planning needs to commence early and deliver long-lasting effects; that venue planning introduces specific time pressures that can compromise social procedures and outcomes; and that legacy planning needs to maintain momentum in key time periods (e.g. just after an event ends). The discussion has also highlighted that events are seen as ways of levering political consensus and funds, and therefore ways of delivering change/new communities quickly. Vila Olimpica, Greenwich Village and SportCity have also showed that events can give new communities an instantaneous 'history'. There are also more subtle reasons why temporal considerations are key to event planning. Major events can provide the right 'moment' to make certain interventions. In this sense, events involve temporally constrained 'windows of opportunity', during which support and funding can be secured to enhance the social sustainability of urban areas.

Major events are not only events in themselves, but markers of other key moments in the lifecycle of a city. Jansson (2005), drawing on the work of Goffman (1967), uses the concept of 'fatefulness' to represent the process through which events are often used in conjunction with new urban directions. This highlights a further significant dimension of major events: they can force certain actions and issues into the public sphere, producing 'fateful' moments from which there is no turning back. Discussions of time are particularly pertinent when you consider that one of the (paradoxical) challenges of delivering sustainable communities is doing it quickly. The UK agenda is heavily influenced by the shortage of housing in some areas, and therefore an ambitious building programme is under way. One way that events can help us understand more about these emerging communities is by illustrating issues concerning the establishment of new urban communities within a short and inflexible timeframe.

Major events should not necessarily be considered as unique and extraordinary; instead, they tend to represent accelerated and exaggerated versions of urban development. This is highlighted by the prior discussion in which the analysis of major events has raised issues that have implications for urban social sustainability more generally. These include the importance of socially stratified communities; the difficulties establishing social bonds between residents of new neighbourhoods; the challenges of combining urban entrepreneurialism with social sustainability; whether mixed uses are required for a community to be sustainable; and the use of populist hooks to access socially excluded groups. Many of the examples discussed emphasize that good event initiatives and good public policy are often one and the same thing. It is hoped that this conclusion, and the wider discussion presented here, highlights the value of understanding major events not merely as one dimension of cities, but as lenses through which the contemporary city can be understood.

References

AEG (2007) *Sustainability Statement for 'The O₂'*, AEG Europe

Atkinson, D. and Laurier, E. (1998) 'Sanitised City? Social Exclusion at Bristol's 1996 International Festival of the Sea', *Geoforum*, vol 29, no 2, pp199–206

Batty, M. (2002) 'Editorial: Thinking about Cities as Spatial Events', *Environment and Planning B: Planning and Design*, vol 29, pp1–2

Broudehoux, A. (2007) 'Spectacular Beijing: The Conspicuous Construction of an Olympic Metropolis', *Journal of Urban Affairs*, vol 9, no 4, pp383–399

Carricere, J. and Demaziere, C. (2002) 'Urban Planning and Flagship Development Projects: Lessons from Expo 98, Lisbon', *Planning Practice and Research*, vol 17, no 1, pp69–79

Chalkley, B. and Essex, S. (1999) 'Urban Development Through Hosting International Events: A History of the Olympic Games', *Planning Perspectives*, vol 14, pp369–394

Coalter, F. (1998) 'Leisure Studies, Leisure Policy and Social Citizenship: The Failure of Welfare or the Limits of Welfare?', *Leisure Studies*, vol 17, no 1, pp21–36

Cochrane, A., Peck, J. and Tickell, A. (1996) 'Manchester Plays Games: Exploring the Local Politics of Globalization', *Urban Studies*, vol 33, no 8, pp1319–1336

Collins, A., Flynn, A., Munday, M. and Roberts, A. (2007) 'Assessing the Environmental Consequences of Major Sporting Events: The 2003/04 FA Cup Final', *Urban Studies*, vol 44, pp457–476

Costley, D. (2006) 'Master Planned Communities: Do They Offer a Solution to Urban Sprawl or a Vehicle for Seclusion of the More Affluent Consumers in Australia?', *Housing, Theory and Society*, vol 23, no 3, pp156–175

Deakin, M. (2003) 'Developing Sustainable Communities: The Settlement Model, Design Solution and Matter of Environmental Assessment', *Journal of Environmental Assessment Policy and Management*, vol 5, no 4, pp551–573

Debord, G. (1994) *The Society of the Spectacle*, Zone, New York

Garnham, B. (1996) 'Ranfurly Shield Rugby: An Investigation into the Impacts of a Sporting Event on a Provincial City: The Case of New Plymouth', *Festival Management and Event Tourism*, vol 4, pp145–249

Goffman, E. (1967) *Interaction Ritual: Essays on Face-to-Face Behaviour*, Allen Lane, Penguin Press, London

Gold, J. and Gold, M. (2005) *Cities of Culture: Staging International Festivals and the Urban Agenda, 1851–2000*, Ashgate, Aldershot

Gotham, K. F. (2005) 'Theorising Urban Spectacles: Festivals, Tourism and the Transformation of Urban Space', *City*, vol 9, no 2, pp225–246

Hagn, F. and Maennig, W. (2008) 'Employment Effects of the Football World Cup 1974 in Germany', *Labour Economics*, vol 15, no 5, pp1062–1075

Hall, C. M. (2006) 'Urban Entrepreneurship, Corporate Interests and Sports Mega-events: The Thin Policies of Competitiveness Within the Hard Outcomes of Neoliberalism', *The Sociological Review*, vol 54, no 2, pp59–70

Harvey, D. (1989) *The Condition of Postmodernity*, Blackwell, Oxford

Hemphill, L., McGreal, S. and Berry, J. (2004) 'An Indicator-Based Approach for Evaluating Sustainable Urban Regeneration Performance: Part 2, Empirical Evaluation and Case-Study Analysis', *Urban Studies*, vol 41, no 4, pp757–772

Hiller, H. (2000) 'Mega-events, Urban Boosterism and Growth Strategies: An Analysis of the Objectives and Legitimations of the Cape Town 2004 Olympic Bid', *International Journal of Urban and Regional Research*, vol 24, pp439–458

Hiller, H. (2006) 'Post-event Outcomes and the Post-modern Turn: The Olympics and Urban Transformations', *European Sport Management Quarterly*, vol 6, no 4, pp317–332

Hughes, R. (1999) *Barcelona*, Verso, London

Jansson, A. (2005) 'Re-encoding the Spectacle: Urban Fatefulness and Mediated Stigmatisation in the "City of Tomorrow"', *Urban Studies*, vol 42, no 10, pp1671–1691

Khakee, A. (2007) 'From Olympic Village to Middle-Class Waterfront Housing Project: Ethics in Stockholm's Development Planning', *Planning Practice and Research*, vol 22, no 2, pp235–251

Ley, D. and Olds, K. (1992) 'World's Fairs and the Culture of Consumption in the Contemporary City', in Anderson, K. and Gale, F. (eds) *Inventing Places*, Longman, Cheshire, pp178–193

Liao, H. and Pitts, A. (2006) 'A Brief Historical Review of Olympic Urbanism', *The International Journal of the History of Sport*, vol 23, no 7, pp1232–1252

Mace, A., Hall, P. and Gallent, N. (2007) 'New East Manchester: Urban Renaissance or Urban Opportunism?', *European Planning Studies*, vol 15, no 1, pp51–65

Mathiason, N. (2008) 'Ghost of the Dome returns as clouds gather over Greenwich Peninsula', *The Observer*, 30 March

Misener, L. and Mason, D. (2006) 'Creating Community Networks. Can Sporting Events Offer Meaningful Sources of Social Capital?', *Managing Leisure*, vol 11, no 1, pp39–56

Monclus, J. (2006) 'International Exhibitions and Planning. Hosting Large-Scale Events as Place Promotion and as Catalysts of Urban Regeneration', in Monclus, J. and Guardia, M. (eds) *Culture, Urbanism and Planning*, Aldershot, Ashgate, pp215–239

Newman, H. (1999) 'Neighborhood Impacts of Atlanta's Olympic Games', *Community Development Journal*, vol 34, pp151–159

Office of the Deputy Prime Minister (2003) *Sustainable Communities: Building for the Future*, ODPM, Wetherby, UK

Olds, K. (1998) 'Urban Mega-events, Eviction and Housing Rights: The Canadian Case', *Current Issues in Tourism*, vol 1, no 1, pp1–47

Raco, M. (2005) 'Sustainable Development, Rolled Out Neo-Liberalism and Sustainable Communities', *Antipode*, vol 37, no 2, pp324–347

Roche, M. (2000) *Mega Events and Modernity: Olympics and Expos in the Growth of Global Culture*, Routledge, London

Rowe, P. (2006) *Building Barcelona: A Second Renaixença*, Actar, Barcelona

Searle, G. (2002) 'Uncertain Legacy: Sydney's Olympic Stadium', *European Planning Studies*, vol 10, no 7, pp845–860

Smith, A. (2009) 'Spreading the Positive Effects of Major Events to Peripheral Areas', *Journal of Policy Research in Tourism, Leisure and Events*, vol 1, no 3, pp231–246

Smith, A. and Fox, T. (2007) 'From "Event-Led" to "Event-Themed" Regeneration: The 2002 Commonwealth Games Legacy Scheme', *Urban Studies*, vol 44, nos 5/6, pp1125–1143

Tufts, S. (2004) 'Building the "Competitive City": Labour and Toronto's Bid to Host the Olympic Games', *Geoforum*, vol 35, no 1, pp47–58

Valera, S. and Guardia, J. (2002) 'Urban Social Identity and Sustainability', *Environment and Behaviour*, vol 34, no 1, pp54–66

Vesselinov, E. and Cazessus, M. (2007) 'Gated Communities and Spatial Inequality', *Journal of Urban Affairs*, vol 29, no 2, pp109–127

Waitt, G. (2003) 'Social impacts of the Sydney Olympics', *Annals of Tourism Research*, vol 30, no 1, pp194–215

Wan, F. (2004) 'Rights Group Urges Eviction Safeguards', *South China Morning Post*, 25 March

12

Conclusions and Observations
for Future Practice

It is clear that the concept of social sustainability necessitates a complex set of processes, involving a multiplicity of actors and agencies, located at different levels of community, neighbourhood and city-wide governance. Moreover, the concept entails an attention to power relationships, considering issues of autonomy, independence and access to opportunities in urban policy.

In this book we have identified a number of discrete but inter-related areas for policy inquiry: from housing provision, social infrastructure and transport services to resource generation for community facilities and wider economic processes. In the first instance, we believe that a regard for social sustainability needs to be embedded within wider decisions about economic development, environmental protection, community involvement and service delivery at every level of society. We see social sustainability as an integral part of the move towards wider community well-being.

We have demonstrated that, like other aspects of sustainable development, social sustainability is a multi-dimensional and cross-cutting issue; it is relevant to a variety of public policy and decision-making spheres, including housing, health, education, social and community services, local and strategic land-use planning, public transport and communication technologies.

An understanding of the concept and its application to an urban context therefore requires nested, multi-layered institutional arrangements for decision-making that are consistent in intent, coherent in approach and collaborative in delivery. These arrangements need to be carefully planned, equitably provided and continually monitored at community, neighbourhood and city-wide levels. While our case studies show that none of this is easy to achieve in practice, they also demonstrate that social sustainability should not be an unattainable objective.

In Section 1, we primarily focus on the neighbourhood or community level, considering planning and delivery mechanisms, with a particular emphasis on promoting mixed communities, providing appropriate institutional structures for community ownership, and developing local social capital. The over-riding issue here for social sustainability is how to avoid multiple deprivation, social segregation and other adverse consequences of area or neighbourhood effects that have been an evident feature of many low-income communities in the Western world over the past 20 or more years. Arguably, these neighbourhood effects are compounded by the concentration of particular groups within social housing, and the main policy solution has therefore been to achieve a de-concentration of specific households (such as those affected by low income, unemployment, economic inactivity and vulnerability).

Manzi's case studies in Chapter 2 confront these arguments head-on; his finding is that for most residents the key determining factor is the level of economic activity within communities and an associated ability to support infrastructure and core services. The central problems here, he suggests, arise from a lack of skills and position within the local population as a whole, in the context of an increasingly competitive global labour market.

While economic regeneration is a necessary condition for the development of sustainable communities, simply moving higher-income residents into existing areas will not be enough. In addition, resources need to be devoted to developing the skills and abilities of existing residents, so that they might also have the ability to gain employment from the new opportunities that are being brought into their areas. He also finds that, while landlords may pay lip-service to the notion of resident empowerment, the evidence at ground level from practitioners is that other priorities are likely to take precedence. Although there may be rhetorical commitment to an agenda of community participation, there remain significant cultural barriers to devolving power and autonomy and encouraging truly collaborative working practices.

These issues of power and autonomy are further explored within the later chapters in the collection. Still on the subject of housing supply, in Chapter 3, Bailey has considered how to make housing provision more affordable for all income groups through the new financial model of Community Land Trusts (CLTs); thus addressing issues of both supply and affordability in meeting local needs. CLTs aim to create a virtuous circle by promoting community engagement, developing democratic systems of governance to manage resources, and providing affordable housing and related community services.

Based on his study of five early examples of CLTs in different parts of the UK, Bailey concludes that, while the potential benefits may be considerable, there are considerable barriers to their wider adoption that must first be overcome. Most importantly, communities need to be offered the opportunity to collaborate in determining their local housing needs in the context of the wider housing market; moreover, they need to be able to select appropriate legal and organizational models for delivery, as well as identifying appropriate 'nil cost' sites for development and enabling planning permission to be granted. These types of community arrangements may, in fact, become increasingly significant, given the problems associated with traditional models of housing delivery in the context of the post-2008 economic downturn.

Within a wider international context, Lloyd-Jones and Allen argue (in Chapter 4) that the skills, capacity and ability of communities to undertake participative activities to plan and self-manage their own neighbourhoods should not be underestimated. Fundamental in this respect is the degree of control over the use of the asset concerned. The authors advocate a model of 'community-asset management' (CAM) to assist communities (in both the developed and developing world) becoming more sustainable. 'CAM' is a term used to describe the management, life-time planning, construction and physical maintenance of common assets to be carried out by the user-communities themselves in partnership, where appropriate, with local government, local businesses, non-governmental organizations and government agencies.

Of particular relevance to CAM is the strand of development theory concerned with sustainable poverty reduction and 'asset-vulnerability frameworks'. This focuses on the assets available to poor households and communities within the context of their vulnerability to outside 'shocks and stresses', which can have an immense impact on the degree of impoverishment within which they live.

In their chapter, Lloyd-Jones and Allen identify a conceptual framework, intended as a diagnostic tool to help policymakers and practitioners identify those capabilities that need to be supported in order to facilitate CAM within neighbourhood-specific development contexts. The authors conclude that building a neighbourhood-based social capability for CAM is not a simple process of defining skills and supplying training. It depends on a conjunction of demographic, organizational and physical factors, all of which are constantly changing, and involving the production of 'social capital'. While the notion of social capital as a resource available to a community and an asset to be conserved and built upon is now commonplace in the 'sustainable communities' discourse, the authors demonstrate that it is a concept that needs further development in order to function as an effective tool in identifying social sustainability.

As a number of chapters in the first section of the book identify, the concept of social capital is associated with enhanced health and well-being, education and economic performance at a community level, and also has a role in enhancing governance at the local level. In the final chapter of this section, Gandelsonas demonstrates the gendered and kinship lines along which social networks tend to be structured through three case-study examples in Argentina, Pakistan and Spain. She has examined how social networks constructed on gender or kinship associations are crucial both in offering access to local knowledge, commitment and neighbourhood support, and in the transfer of knowledge. However, she has also found that informal social networks appear less reliable than more formal community partnerships in enabling the transfer of valuable social capital over time, because they lack permanence.

In common with a number of experts on this issue, Gandelsonas therefore recommends that, in order to remain effective over time and to achieve continuity, members of social networks need to be more directly aware of the need to constantly improve the way in which their partnership works and be willing to directly resolve conflicts between different members' interests. She also recommends that in order to ensure that social capital will be transferred by social networks and/or partnerships in a particular context, the various stakeholders involved should operate under an equitable set of governance arrangements; involving principles of fairness, decency, accountability, transparency, efficiency and the rule of law for all stakeholders involved.

Having considered processes of neighbourhood and community governance, Section 2 examines themes within the wider field of urban spatial planning. These chapters consider urban density and social infrastructure planning; the connectivity of communities; accessibility planning; public transport provision; and the role of information technologies in 'virtually' connecting people to places and place-making. In the first chapter of this section, Nelson identifies the considerable challenges facing local authorities in the south-east of England in meeting the housing and social infrastructure needs (based on predicted population growth) over the next 20–30 years. In examining how growth is being managed in two London boroughs, she has particularly considered whether adequate social infrastructure, in the form of schools, will be provided for enlarged populations, within the context of policies designed to increase neighbourhood densities.

Nelson's chapter concludes that, while there have been some moves within these boroughs towards a more integrated approach to planning social infrastructure, current practice clearly falls short of the integrated collaborative approach to spatial planning advocated by the Government. However, in her experience, this is not a universal situation, and some local authorities have adopted more proactive and robust approaches to the planning of social infrastructure. This suggests that challenges are not insurmountable and that the good-practice experiences of other local authorities could be better disseminated and more systematically adopted across the region.

In Chapter 7, Lucas et al have identified that, even at their best, social infrastructure plans tend not to consider the important issue of access to services and how this might be achieved in more environmentally sustainable ways, using non-car modes of transport. The authors argue that the issue of adequate transport provision, both within communities and at more strategic levels, is an important one in the social sustainability debate. Connectivity is needed in order to link neighbourhoods both to each other and to key activities such as employment, education, healthcare, shopping and leisure, and other social opportunities. Adequate transport provision is required, not only in the interest of social equity – because lower income communities tend to be negatively affected by the externalities of road traffic – but also because a disproportionate number of low-income households do not own cars and so rely on public transport to access life-chance opportunities such as employment, education, healthcare and access to healthy, affordable food. The authors recommend that a socially sustainable society needs to ensure that everyone is able to reach the places they need to go to, in order to service their daily lives (economically and socially) without adversely affecting the opportunities of others or the local and global environment.

Lucas et al promote accessibility planning as a method for ensuring that such considerations are included in the planning of new developments, as well as in the retro-fitting of transport provision in existing communities. On the evidence of their two case-study examples (and considerable experience with the method in practice), the authors conclude that, although accessibility planning is a necessary tool for identifying the overall transport connectivity of new as well as existing developments, it is not in itself a sufficient condition. For this reason, they recommend it is vital that a multi-agency approach is adopted at an early stage in the development or regeneration of communities. This should include the involvement of not only key professional stakeholders, but also communities themselves, as it is usually local people who are best placed to identify their own local accessibility needs.

Both of the chapters by Nelson and Lucas et al have identified that key issues for social infrastructure, accessibility and public transport planning include a robust analysis of present needs, as well as a methodology for forecasting population change over time. The age and income and skills profile, and the proportion of households with children, are all significant factors in determining the nature of demand. Careful monitoring will be needed: to assess the number and size of new homes; the proportion of affordable homes; the appropriate location for new activities, service-centres and facilities, as well as appropriate transport services (including local walking and cycling provision) for accessing these destinations. Implementation of plans for new social infrastructure will also need to be regularly evaluated.

In Chapter 8, White and his colleagues examined a surprisingly neglected aspect of the debate: the potential role of information technology in the promotion and prevention of social sustainability. In their case study of teleworking as a way of reducing commuting journeys in the London region, the authors argue that, theoretically, teleworking can contribute substantially to environmental sustainability. In particular, it can reduce the need to travel, with resultant savings in use of energy, emissions of pollutants and need for road space, and potentially improve quality of life for individuals and communities. However, they also recognize that the overall net reduction in travel is not necessarily a simple matter of eliminating home to work travel on certain days, since additional local trips can be substituted. The authors warn that agencies should consider not only the economic, but also the social, implications of teleworking. Having the workforce distributed between home and office may ultimately lead to a loss of teamwork, which may lead to a reduction in the skill level of employees and lower levels in quality of work (through preventing collaboration between people with different skills and aptitudes). A further implication for social sustainability is that teleworking tends to benefit higher-income individuals in higher-status jobs, whose working practices are best suited to flexible working.

In the final section of the book, we turned to the all-important question of how the move towards more socially sustainable (as well as economically stable and environmentally neutral) communities can be financially and institutionally resourced. In these three chapters, the authors have discussed different ways that this has been attempted in the past. In Chapter 9, Marsh considers the potential for and value of planning gains from private developers. This is an increasingly significant mechanism in present policy in the UK; local planning authorities can require developers to provide additional funding for community infrastructure (such as schools, recreational facilities or public transport services) as part of the planning agreement for a new housing development.

However, as Marsh identifies, significant planning gains can only be sought where a proven need for additionality arises directly from the development in question and where this is needed either to secure the implementation of local planning policies (e.g. affordable housing targets), or to offset any impact of the development on or loss of an existing amenity or resource. Another problem is that developers are limited in the amount of planning gain they will be prepared to make, and this will be further diminished in times of low profitability from housing sales, in areas where the private housing market is sluggish and/or the opportunities for housing development are plentiful. Marsh notes that the nature and intensity of the current economic downturn and its effect on planning obligations mean that many development proposals are simply not viable in the current market, or can only be made viable where planning policy requirements are relaxed or deferred. Finally, and perhaps more obviously, planning gain will anyway not be forthcoming unless significant new housing development is evident and thus is not appropriate in areas of economic decline. This leaves the problem of how to resource new community infrastructure projects in the context of existing deprived and economically struggling communities. Local planning authorities will therefore need to reconsider many of their regeneration strategies in the light of the problems facing private developers and the reliance on planning gain as the key mechanism to achieve strategic objectives is therefore under threat.

Chapter 10 considers another area that is often neglected in the literature on social sustainability, that of how local authorities (intentionally or by default) have aimed to address the problem of their run-down town centres through invigoration of the evening or night-time economy. Eldridge's research has found that strategies have met with varying degrees of success, with the media primarily focusing on negative images of youth, antisocial behaviour and violent crime; while in practice some city centres have experienced a complete restructuring as a result of their night-time economy (through what is sometimes described as an 'urban renaissance'). One of the main issues for social sustainability explored by his chapter is to consider degrees of inclusiveness and belonging in the city at night. For example, one case study identified how some residents of the renewed city centre felt excluded from their local town and city centres at night and avoid venturing out after dark. Eldridge found that in certain areas the city at night has become a mono-cultural and homogenous space in terms of what it offers and the types of people it attracts. Local authority policies therefore often fail to recognize, plan for or manage the very diverse needs of the people living and working in their areas. At the same time the research has also identified a number of constructive strategies that have been initiated for managing the city at night more effectively. Consequently, many councils across Britain are now actively involved in public–private partnerships with licensees and residents that seek to better resolve potential conflicts and to actively find solutions to the negative consequences of an alcohol-centred economy.

In Chapter 11 (the final part of this section), concerning the economics of social sustainability, Smith considers how social sustainability is affected by the negative and positive aspects of 'mega-events' such as the World Cup, Olympic Games or celebrations for the Millennium, which have been used all over the world by planners and policymakers to generate the necessary revenue for the longer-term regeneration of the local areas in which they take place. Providing the necessary infrastructure for such events generally raises important public concerns about the environmental impacts of their construction prior to, during the events and their eventual legacy, as well as considering the spatial and fiscal equity of their impact. Smith argues that, at the local scale, if venue planning is viewed as a process primarily aimed at providing services for local communities rather than venues for one-off events, it is more likely to have positive social effects.

He concludes that to ensure such positive outcomes there is an urgent need to integrate social considerations within the planning of physical interventions as a first general principle, to ensure their social sustainability over time and space. His chapter highlights the important observation that good event planning and good public policy is often one and the same thing. This insight could be adopted as a general guiding principle for all those wishing to promote the social sustainability of our towns and cities, now and in the future.

In this book, we have purposefully shied away from offering an authoritative definition of what precisely constitutes social sustainability in the urban planning context; this is largely because we believe that sustainability represents a shifting and relational concept rather than an end state. However, based on the limited documentary evidence relating to this subject and an overview of the case studies presented within this collection, we would suggest that urban planning policies that aim to promote the social (as well as economic and environmental) sustainability of communities should be based upon the following core principles:

1   Provide all sectors of the community with a reasonable quality of life and good life-chance opportunities for social well-being (e.g. employment, education, healthcare, leisure, social and cultural activities).

2   Reduce social exclusion, minimize concentrations of deprivation, protect vulnerable groups, offer opportunities for community integration and social cohesion and ensure equity of outcome, both now and in the future.

3   Provide communities with the opportunity and resources to own and manage their own assets.

4   Provide a proportionate level of social infrastructure for existing and future projected populations, based on robust modelling frameworks.

5   Provide effective access to essential goods and services, either within the local community or through good public transport to services in the wider area, based on robust accessibility criteria.

6   Reduce environmental inequalities and over-exposure to negative health impacts such as pollution, toxic waste and road traffic accidents.

7   Strengthen existing social capital by encouraging local participation in decision-making and by facilitating and supporting effective community governance arrangements.

8   Ensure that local economic development projects, regeneration initiatives and other revenue-raising interventions do not disproportionately negatively impact upon existing populations and communities and/or that these effects are adequately mitigated in consultation with these communities.

This list is not intended to be exhaustive, but rather is aimed at promoting debate around what constitutes social sustainability; it aims to encourage others in relevant urban planning and related disciplines to join the debate. Earthscan have published a number of excellent titles relevant to the subject of social sustainability, which we recommend as further reading.

Index